RanDumb-er

First published in 2012 by
RanDumb House

Imprint of T.M.I

http://trickaduu.com

First Edition: February 2012

ISBN: 978-0-6155701-50

A CIP record for this title is available from the British Library.

Cover design & Typeseting by Kiche Black | Diverzant.org
Set in Bookman Old Style

RanDumb-er

The Continued Adventures of an Irish Guy in L.A!

Mark Hayes

RAN DUMB HOUSE

To My Grandparents...

Eileen and Nick Hayes

Julia and John Ryan

Dance. On!

(I Hope to God I Spelt All the Names Right.)

"Is freedom anything else than the right to live as we wish? Nothing else." ~ Epictetus

"Pants off. Free. Dumb!" ~ Me

Contents

Introduction

When Murk asked me to write the introduction to his new book, I said... Mighty!

Then I asked Murk... Does it have to be long?

And I think he said... No.

Even *mightier*!

I do hope you enjoy *RanDumb-er.*

Read. On!

Robbie Williams
Los Angeles
2012

Chapter 1

Big Bag of Nuts!

It was the best of times, it was nuts at times.

Bright lights. Dim city. Big dreams. Harsh reality.

Extravagant. Intense. Insane.

Celebrities. Porn stars. Married women.

I'm back. I'm in L.A. And it's Halloween.

Little did I know how underprepared I was. Halloween in L.A might just be the most nuts time of all. Randumb. Bizarre. Mighty. Seeing little green and orange oompa loompas running around while your senses are being pummeled from all angles. Hot women seem to be everywhere. Half of them naked. The rest half naked. Almost all of them sporting the best bodies money can buy. Imagine all that, if you can.

OK.
So.
Past few days have been kind of like that. Except. Actually even harder to describe. Particularly as I'm now packing my bags again. As I think I'm off on a private jet to the Bahamas.

As.
You.
Do?
I'm getting ahead of myself...

Halloween night, land at LAX. Collect my bags. Nervously queue up for the visa inspection. Get through. Skip past customs. Delighted. No pat down. No cavity probing. And my visa is real? Mighty!

Turn back on my long-awaited American phone. Call my buddy Chowder, who kind of looks slightly like Jude Law. Or so he says. Maybe a rounder version, I might add. He's outside waiting with his girlfriend Charlotte, who Chowder also likes to describe as his Megan Fox lookalike (which in fairness is the more truthful of the two). Stroll out the sliding doors of LAX. Suck in a deep breath of warm L.A air. Ahhh. Fast food. Smog. Heat. Betsy (Mighty!). I'm back! Dancing!

> "Chowder - Hope you've been taking care of L.A for me. Charlotte - Long time no see!"

Throw my bags in the boot of Chowder's car. Jump in the back. Feel funking mighty. I think. I'm back! Drive on!

Weirdly enough L.A smells and looks like home. In the sense that my senses were instantly used to it again, even if it's been 3 months since I was here last. Body temperature readjusted. Air didn't look foreign. Smells didn't seem like I was in a foreign land. Felt good. Seeing all the McDonalds, Starbucks and Subway signs. Sucking in the fume-filled air. Basking in the warmth. Complete opposite to Ireland. But still. Duck to water.

Felt like Chowder and Charlotte's adopted child in the backseat. Both of them asking how I was, how was the flight, do I have my seatbelt on? This would be a reoccurring theme. Chowder turns around,

> "What time are you going to the Playboy mansion then?"

> "Hmm. Let me check. I'll make a quick call."

Phone. Dring dring.

> "Howdy lady! I made it back- It's Mark... MARK... MARRRRRRKKKK. (Accent issues? Not a-funking-gain!) Not Merrick. M-A-R-K. Irish. Irish Mark, that's the one! How are you? Where am- I'm on the way to West Hollywood! WeHoooo. Yeah, just got back. How are you? What's the jam with later tonight? The

> Mansion? What time- You which now? Seriously? Why would you do that? But I told you I was coming back... OK. Funk. Yeah, no. How much to pay? Ehh. Yeah. No. No worries. Ciao ciao..."

Balls. Ehh. So then. Hmm...,

> "Chowder. What are ye up to tonight?"
>
> "Big night planned. Charlotte's Dad is in town. Going to dinner first. Party in the Roosevelt afterwards. Halloween is nuts here. Should be fun. Pity you can't come mate!"
>
> "Yeah. Pity alright. Although, you know what, if the offer's still open, I will come! Ye've been kind enough to pick me up from the airport. The least I can do is come out to dinner with ye."
>
> "Are you sure? We are going to Chaya, really nice restaurant, food is amaaaazing."
>
> "Yeah. I'm sure."
>
> "Will the girl not mind you canceling on her? What's her name, Tammy?"
>
> "Kammy? Nah, she'll be cool. No worries."

(Particularly as she just informed me that she gave away my free VIP invite. Thought something had happened as I didn't phone earlier. Asked someone else to go with her instead. Tut. Ape. Say nothing.)

Half an hour in, my plan had already changed. Halloween party at the Playboy Mansion: Out. Dinner and see what happens afterwards: On.

Get to my new temporary abode in West Hollywood. Chowder's friend Tara has a spare room. Quick hello. Dinner in half an hour. Dump my bags. Two minute shower. Whip on my costume. Back out the door. Barely even time for a movement. Jump in a taxi. Hubbulla. Hub-bulla? Hubulla! Eventually he understands the name of the restaurant I'm saying. Arrive at Chaya. In I stumble.

Introduced to Charlotte's Dad, Perry, his girlfriend and glamorous side-kick, Jackie, along with two directors from his company. All over from London for a few days. Sit down. Beer already waiting for me. Take a swig. Realise they're all looking at me. Oddly. Charlotte asks,

"What are you meant to be?"

"Eh, a banshee."

Obviously.

"Banshee? What on earth is that?"

"You know: Red top hat. White shirt. White tie. Pair of jeans... Typical Irish banshee!"

"Oh right."

Cue laughter. Ice broken. Bluff on.

Smile and thank Perry for inviting me along, ask if they've already ordered? Cue a perplexed look. Repeat myself. Realise that even though they're all English, they don't understand my accent in the slightest. Maybe I was slurring my words from the jet lag.

"Not too sure what you just said but would you like something stronger than a beer, a gin perhaps?"

"Ehh. Yeah. Please. Make it a double!"

Two gins arrive in front of me. Sweet Jesus. Dumb last words. Dinner. Unreal. Chowder was right. Cheers to Perry, or as I started calling him: "The Man". Dessert. Coffee. Port. Mighty. (Although the port was an acquired taste. I required my mouth to enjoy it.)

"What's the plan?"

"Roosevelt Hotel. Hollywood strip. Massive Halloween party."

"Sounds good. What about tickets?"

"Taken care of."

"Are you sure?"

"Yes. Don't worry about it. Just have a good time."

"Well if you insist..."

Limo waiting for us outside the restaurant. (Ha, mighty to be back in L.A!) Drop The Man and company off at their hotel in West Hollywood. Not up for the crowds in Hollywood.

Three of us head down in the limo on our own. Buzzing now big time. Delighted to be back. Night is shaping up nicely- Until. We hit gridlock. Almost midnight. And the traffic is that bad? Wuu. Good old L.A.

Eventually we arrive at the Roosevelt. Massive crowd outside. Huge. Thankfully, Chowder knows a guy. Sorted out the tickets. Greets us. Skips us past the crowd, who give us the nicest of dirty looks. Who cares, we're in!

Just as we enter, a girl who looks like a mix between Lucy Liu and a Barbie doll tells us to follow her. OK? Charlotte's on crutches (trampoline accident, snap of the ankle) so safer to come this way, she informs us. Seems dodge until we find out that the girl appears to be running the VIP lounge upstairs. Takes us the back route, asking if we would like to go in to the VIP lounge? This is weird; no doubt we're getting stung somehow... Ah who cares, we're in!

Placed is packed. People everywhere. All dressed up. All in ridiculously good costumes. (It is Hollywood after all. Not your raggedy Ann outfits that most people plump for back in Ireland. Although my banshee outfit really was top notch). Hot-looking nurses. Cops. Avatars. Witches. Village People. Clowns. Cavemen. Star Wars. Playboy bunnies. Tarzan girls. Playboy girls. Hustler girls. Lingerie models. Girls wearing bits of string barely covering an inch of their body. Girls in body paints. Girls. Girls. GIRLS! Seriously: Unreal.

(Did I mention it's great to be back in L.A? In Cork you wouldn't really see girls in such outfits. And in most cases if you did, you probably wish you hadn't looked. My eyes!)

Roosevelt is big. Historic Spanish-style hotel in the middle of Hollywood, named after Theodore Roosevelt. Hotel lobby inside, DJ playing there. Next to that is "Teddy's" which is a dark, swanky club that almost feels like a wine cellar, filled with beautiful people. Another DJ in there. Big room off of that where I think the first

Academy Awards was held way back in 1929. Another DJ in there? Jesus, they're everywhere. Pool area outside called the Tropicana Bar with cabanas all round. And to cap it all off, there's another DJ on a little stage in the middle of the pool outside. Impressive work all round. (Apparently Marilyn Monroe stayed in one of these cabanas for a while, and now haunts it. Apparently.)

Anyway, amongst all of this we had somehow ended up at a private party in a VIP suite outside, overlooking the pool. Our new friend, Maggie Wong worked for a company who had rented out the suite. Only cost them $60,000 to rent it out. For one night. Great value! Unfortunately for Ms. Wong, hardly anyone from the company decided to show up. Which is why we had been invited along. Make up the numbers. Seat fillers. Works for me. Particularly as it was the only part of the hotel that had a free bar included. Betsy! Maggie Wong utters the magic words,

> "Help yourselves to any drinks you want."

And we're off! Myself and Chowder made a beeline for the six foot tall fridge full of vodka. Oh sweet Jesus. Booze. On,

> "Would anyone like a booze?"

Girls want some wine. No worries. Lots of expensive looking bottles in this fridge. Except. Balls. No corkscrew. Not to worry... Found a coat hanger! So now, like a banshee I'm ramming open $200 bottles of wine with my coat hanger corkscrew. Call me MacGyver! Oddly enough, my quick thinking has impressed Maggie Wong. Or maybe it's the banshee outfit,

> "Looooooooveee your red hat!
> Love it!!!"

Either way, she seems to have a soft spot. Myself and Chowder booze on. Guzzling down mango vodka. Doing a bit of mingling in the VIP suite. Big room inside. Leather couches. Plasma TVs. Chandeliers. All that lovely VIP gibber. Big bar on one side. Big balcony outside. Only twelve people in here. Meet the folk outside. Nice people. Doctor. Writer. Candlestick maker. Only now do I realise that the pool area below us is rocking! Way better than this suite. But. No free booze out there. Hmm.

Free booze or rocking party? Drink on or mingle? I know: Drink drink drink. Ahhh. Now. Let's go for a stroll and have a laugh!

Unfortunately Charlotte is ruled out for strolling around. On crutches and all. Meaning Chowder is staying put too. Tut. Time to go for a solo wander. Looks mighty, back in a few. Actually, seems Maggie Wong wants to come have a look around too. Come on Maggie, let's go on an adventure!

After the relative calmness upstairs, it feels like we're thrust into a zoo full of models down below. Beautiful people gone wild. Music, drink and whatever else, has them all pumped up to the max. Jumping. Dancing. Creeping. Rocking. Boozing. Spilling. Screaming. Hooting. Hollering. The dogs have been left out. Gridlock everywhere. No hope of getting inside to the hotel. So far this stroll has been ten feet. Maggie grabs me by the arm,

"Follow me."

Lead the way, Ms. Wong! Around by the far side of the pool we go. Mingling. Saluting. High fiving. Going well. Until. Hit another gridlock. Jesus, this place is packed. What should we do? Go back upstairs? Chill a minute? Maggie Wong says chill,

"Let's just hang here."

Cool. So we chill. I'm looking around. Gazing everywhere. Taking it all in. Where have all the green fields gone? Hang on... Realise someone's hand is rubbing my banshee pants. Maggie Wong? Hey hup. What's going on here? Look at Maggie. She smiles. Keeps rubbing. Tells me she likes my banshee costume. Loves my accent even more.

"Why thank you. It is my best asset, to be true."

Well besides my... location. Duu. While Maggie is rubbing my wong, she asks if the people are still on the balcony.

"Ehh, let me check... No don't think so. Why? Who are they actually?"

Hmmm. This feels nice...

"Oh, well, that's kind of my husband and a few of his friends- "

"Emmm what now?"

My wong wangs.

"As in your husband or just someone's husband?"

"Yeah, mine. Ha ha. Why, can he see us?"

"No he can't see us but I can feel his wife rubbing me!"

Wong looks at me.

"Should I stop? Do you not like it?"

"I do, Ms. Wong, but it's kind of wrong, so probably for the best. Call me when the divorce goes through."

Night ends with me back up in VIP. Wondering if the husband saw. Deflecting Maggie's eye daggers. Sipping on boozes. Dancing around the balcony. And repeatedly singing what appears to be the new anthem of the moment Empire State of Mind. Loving it! Even if it is a song all about New York and not L.A, it will have to do. Cheers-ing everyone with my bottle of mango vodka. Great to be back...,

"In New Yorrrrrrrrkk... there's nothing you can't do,
now you're in Newwww Yorrrrrrrkkkkkkk!!!"

Cheers everyone. Mighty VIP welcoming party for me. Banshee is back in town! Greatest return night ever!!!

Slug. Chug. Dumb. Done. Maggie whaaat?!

Chapter 2

Wait. What. I Forgot? My Scissors!

Next day.
Woke up.
Face in the pillow.
Drool everywhere.
Pants still on.
Red top hat next to my face. Sweating buckets from the heat. Eyes blurry. Slightly blinded. Where the funk am I?

Oh yeah.
OH YEAH!

I'm back in this beautiful land of WeHo!
Do the check:
Phone.
Wallet.
Passport.
iPod.

All good. All accounted for. Text on my phone:

> 'CHOWDER: Come up to the SkyBar pool at the Mondrian hotel. We're all laying out. Maybe have a booze?'

Taaaaxi! And we were off once again. Heard the Mondrian was a nice hotel. Not sure what to expect. Obviously some sort of a nice pool. Turns out to be savage. Looks like a pool the Greek Gods might've had. Or one you'd see in an American Gigolo remake. Marble. White. Trees. Loungers. Blondes. Brunettes. Meatheads.

Beautiful people town. Lifestyles of the rich and famous. Plus: me.

Spot the group. All panned out on a big white poof under a tree dripping with mini-chandeliers. Surrounded by food platters and drink buckets. Chicken. Shrimp. Lobster. Grapes. Strawberries. Berries. Orange juice. Dom Perignon. Gin. Oh Jesus. Chilled house music playing from hidden speakers. Perfect weather. Hot but not sweltering. Even the fact it was November and this hot was mighty. Far from the wet fields of Ireland now. Top off. Tan on. Betsy. This is the good life!

High fives all round. Recap the night. Struggle to make sense of it. Time for a Bloody Mary. Daytime boozing. Back up on the horse. According to a text in my phone, I'm also meant to have a date today. Met a girl in the taxi on the way home last night. Or so she told me. No recollection. Nobody had.

Told to invite her up to the pool. She's in, would love to come. So we all sat. Drank. And looked around. Mighty views from the pool overlooking L.A. Mightier views around the pool. Forgot how good-looking the women in L.A are. Not saying women in Ireland aren't, ahem. Just that here, they are tip-top of the pile. Mix of everything. All perfect looking (no wonder so many girls are beyond self-conscious here). Models. Dancers. Porn stars. All-American. Asian. Latin. Europeans. Russians. Australians. African. Every corner of the globe. Quality is ridiculous. Even better... The amount of good-looking women here. Everywhere you look. Or maybe it's just in this part of town. Either way: Unreal. Got me half pumped for my blind pool date. More the merrier!

Chowder had a flashback that it might've been a blonde girl. Good-looking, he thinks. Happy days! So we all kept an eye for a blonde girl. Kept seeing good-looking blonde girls. Distracted by all the good-looking blonde girls. So much so, none of us noticed the, eh, sound-looking brunette who appeared out of nowhere.

"Mark?"

"Ehh, yeah, why so?"

"It's me."

The non-blonde-sound-looking girl from last night.

"Oh yeah. So it is."

Balls.

"Do you not remember?"

No I do not.

"Oh yeah, I do..."

Dose. Turns out to be really sound (as in she had a very nice personality). Just slightly odd.

"Where do you live?"

"On the sea."

"Oh yeah, what beach?"

"No. On the sea. I live on a boat."

"You live on a boat?"

"I live on a boat."

Was not expecting that.

"Where's your home?"

"Well, I have no real home. I live on a boat. Just stayed in my friend's house by here last night. Didn't want to get a taxi all the way back to the boat."

Hmm. All I heard was: I have no real home. You might say: My pool date was with a homeless person? Or am I now just drunk? What's going on? Where am I? L.A?

I must text home to Ireland actually, tell my parents I'm alright. But am I alright? Yeah. Just have one more drink. You can decide what to do then. OK. Great plan. Hang on. Back at the poof. Girl has gone. Seems the mermaid had to go back to the sea. Short. Sweeeet. Date over. Night time on!

Again. Same enjoyable rigmarole, a routine I will never get bored of: Home. Shower. Put on my gladdest of rags. Get picked up a car service. (Pam the driver. Older lady. Jolly laugh. Mighty woman!) Chauffeured down to a restaurant called Koi. Again. Unreal food.

Ridiculously good. Healthy too. Giddy up. Japanese style this time. (French last night?)

The Man, Jackie and the rest of their crew are in great form. Fans of the mighty L.A lifestyle. Banter flowing at the table. Bottles of wine and champagne trying to keep up. English quip. Irish charm.

Dinner. Finished. Back to the SkyBar. Gallons more booze. At one point I'm behind the bar, showing the head barman how to make Baby Guinness, which is a shot consisting of Kahlua on bottom and Baileys on top. Looks and tastes mighty. Shots for everyone! Yay. Party on. Gets a bit blurry.

Last call. Chatting with two girls. Two sisters. Both blondes. But they kind of look like Kardashians, in a good way. (No one said they were natural blondes.) Dark. Dirty. Hot. New Yorkers. Staying in the hotel. Lights come on. Bouncers start barking at people. Herded out of the bar. Sisters invite me up to their room for a nightcap. Giddy up! Up we go. Penthouse? Penthouse! Jesus. This is unreal. Big huge living room in the middle of the suite. Couches to the right. Bedroom to the left. Glass windows and doors. Wrap around balcony. Big. Huge. Giant. Billionaire. Penthouse! Girls... What the funk do ye do??!

In we go. I've got my arm around one sister. She has her hand on my belt. The Other Sister goes to get drinks. I excuse myself. Bursting for the bathroom. Like a racehorse.

"Ahhhaa."

Knock on the door. Other Sister comes in. Bottle of vodka in her hand. Two glasses.

"How's it going? Can I come in?"

Obviously. Hands me a glass. Fills it up.

"Cheers."

"Cheers!"

Slurp.

"You know my sister's married, right?"

What the funk...,

"No. No I did not. Are you serious?! Does everyone here that's married have roaming hands?!"

"I'm not married..."

Cue embrace. By embrace I mean we kiss for a second, she opens my pants and drops to her knees. One fabulous swoop. Oh Jesus. Forgot how good American girls are at tooting on my ponder pipe. Slurping for dear life. (Me. Obviously. Drinking the vodka!) Slurping it down. Heaven. Drunk. But in heaven. Except. One problem...

Her giving me a toot feels unreal. So much so I'm closing my eyes, mmm'ing away. Unfortunately whenever I start doing this, I also begin to sway. And, as my eyes are closed, start to get the spins.

"Oh no. Jesus. Stop. No no, not you, Other Sister."

I'm talking to The Spins.

"Mmmm.

Ohhh."

Spinning.

"Mmmmmmm.

Oohhhh noooo."

Can't stop spinning. Funk. I'm drunk. Realise now I've been served straight vodka. One of my nemeses. Hits me hard. Suddenly I'm waaay too drunk. Survival mechanism kicks in. Get out of here. Must. Go. Home. Now!

"Schorry I'm reallee sohrry but slorry I musthh guh. Goosed. Too drunk. Noo.

Must.

Go."

Other Sister understands. I open the bathroom door. Scuttle out. See the first sister on the bed.

"Where have you been? What were you doing in there?"

She asks with a wink (or maybe I was just blinking really slowly and drunkenly at this point. Who knows?)

"Ahh shaba. I'm lorry. Musty eh goes."

Make a beeline for the door. Clip the couch on the way. Pan out face first onto the couch. One bounce up and down. Lie there for what feels like a deep sleep but really only ten seconds. The Spins. Back. Bad. Funk. Don't want to puke. My brains shouts at my dumb body: You know what to do: Get. Home. Now! Haul myself up. Scuttle off. Out the door. Down the elevator. Into a cab. Might have walked into a bush. (Walked. Fell. Tomato. Potato.) Either way. I'm home. Safe. And. Sound?

Woke up. Face down. Arms out. Legs together. Crucifixion style. Eyes look to the right. Quickly to the left. No one next to me. Mouth tastes dry. No puke at least. No wet on my bed. Tongue just feels like a carpet. Quick check: All allocated and accounted for. Look at my phone. Text:

'CHOWDER: Come up to the pool at the SkyBar. We're all laying out again. Maybe have a booze?'

Deja-funking-doodle-duu? What day is this? Did yesterday just happen? Where am I? Did I dream that? Run my hand through my hair. Confused. Lost. Although. Feel a few twigs in my hair. Maybe that did all happen. Only one way to find out... SkyBar on!

Again. Repeat. Pool. Poof. Sun. Music. Food. High life. And. Booze. Wash. Repeat.

Had to be done. Only way to avoid the inevitable down I was running from. Putting off jet lag. Now ducking and dodging a cruel hangover. Don't worry about that now! Just have one drink. Only cure. Just the one... OK! dumb part of my weak brain, you've sold me. Yeah, I'll have a mojito please! Again. Ended up all over the place. Daytime, poolside. Nightime, randumb. Dinner. Italian place this time, Cecconi's, which is apparently where all the stars come to hideout and eat pizza and meatballs. Needless to say, quite tasty. Greatest octopus I've ever had. Although have I had octopus before? Not too sure. Also discovered I am a fan of rosé. Like all real men. Obviously. After the dinner: Drunken Hollywood Haze. Very.

Very. Blurry.

This is how blurry. So after dinner, we went back to the Mondrian Hotel. The Man and The Jackie went to bed (early flight). Chowder fell asleep in the corridor. Leaving Charlotte and myself in the SkyBar, wondering where everyone else was and why the SkyBar was so dead. Where else should we go? Body Shop! Which is a place where girls dance on tables and the likes, you know, sans clothes. I think that's how we ended up in there so early anyway. In we go. Charlotte sits down. I go to the bathroom to relieve my tiny bladder (maybe I just fill it up a lot). Come back from the bathroom. And must be drunk. Seeing as I am strolling around, like I'm lost. So lost, I randomly sit down. Next minute, I see Charlotte,

> "Sharrrlot?? Is that you?? What are you doing here?"
>
> "You just came in with me. We came here together."
>
> "We did? As in, we did? Really? Jesus. Don't remember that. Where are we again?"

So it was time to go. Back to the SkyBar. By now I was feeling a bit ragged. Tired. Worse for wear. Charlotte made the smart choice. Went to bed. I made the ape choice. One last night cap.

Sitting at the bar. Up on a stool. Eddie Griffin (comedian, odd ball, angry man) to my left. Denis Rodman (former NBA player, odd ball, eccentric man) to my right. Some actress is talking to them/at me. Telling me she was a porn star. Not sure if I believed her. Not the brightest shining star I'd seen. She did look she was in porn though, I'll give her that. Enormous fake boobs. Big fake lips, like two little bananas. Tight silver dress that looked like it was painted on. Smart expression on her randumb face.

While she's talking to D Rod (as I call him, not sure if he liked it) Eddie Griffin is looking at me. Pretty sure it's the look of a man who doesn't like white Irish guys named Merrick. Jealous of my... I don't know. Maybe I'm paranoid. After a few jibs and jabbers about who I am, and what I'm doing here, Eddie tells me the world is about to end. Tonight.

> "Oh yeah?"
>
> "Yeah man! You don't believe me?"

> "No no, I do (not) believe you. Could you tell me why though?"

Eddie swivels on his chair. Points to the sky. From the SkyBar. I look up. Eddie tells me solemnly,

> "There's a ball of fire headed straight our way. All y'all motherfuckers better believe me. It's ending... TONIGHT!"

> "What now?"

Try to follow Eddie's finger. See a red light in the distance. Red light of a radio pole it looks like. Some sort of flashing red light in the distance. Not a fire ball. Not the impending end of the world. Merely the rambles of a drunk man.

> "Here, Eddie, that's just a red light..."

> "Hush your mouth, homeboy! You calling me a liar?"

> "No, Edward, I'm not. I'm merely saying that's a red light of some sort. Never said you're a liar. Just you're either drunk. Or a dope?"

Don't think he gets the meaning of dope. I do know he gets angry. Guzzles down a drink. Swivels his chair. And starts just eye-balling me for dear life. Sitting on the stool next to me. Giving me the dirtiest look. Infected stink eye. On cue, D Rod pops his head in,

> "Me and Molly here are going upstairs, finish this party off right. Come if you want."

I assume he's saying this to Eddie and his other friend, more so than me. Either way, I take this as my cue... to go upstairs to what seems like an orgy! Obviously!!! (I joke.) Three black men and an Irish baby, plus one dodgy lady? Nay for me.

Home. Collapse into bed. Dodge the dudes. Dodge the Molly. Fall asleep. Wondering if the world is really going to end. Or if the sick pain in my stomach is down to the fact I've yet to go to the bathroom since I've arrived back in LA. Still yet to have a movement. Delightful.

Groundhog. Woke up. Eyes bulging. Deep breath in my nose. Deep growl from my stomach. Heaved myself straight up onto my knees. Looked around. Realised where I was. Realised it was Monday. Realised I can't hack more drink. Wondered why the song It Was All a Dream! was singing in my head. Checked my phone. Text:

> 'THE MAN: Are you alive?'
>
> 'ME: I believe so?'

Another text:

> 'CHOWDER: Just checking to see if we can get you on board with us. Pack a bag and I'll let you know!'
>
> 'ME: On what board? Let me know who? Where am I? Why am I? What's going on?!'
>
> 'CHOWDER: We're going to Antigua. Seeing if you can come on the private jet with us! Do you not remember?!'
>
> 'ME: Eh. No. I knew ye were all going down with Charlotte's Dad for a week. Didn't realise I might be going too!'
>
> 'CHOWDER: Well, get ready. I'll let you know.'

Sitting on my bed. Boxers and socks. Shoulder slumped. Pretty goosed. Wondering: What's going on?! Who is: The Man? Am I going on a private jet? No way. Am I just dumbly drunk? Should I pack? Do I need to? Still haven't unpacked since I arrived. Haven't phoned home either. Must check my emails too. Oh God, my life is either all coming together or quickly falling apart.

Laptop. Online. Loads of emails:

> 'Are you in L.A? Did you leave already? Where are you?'

Oh yeah. Forgot to tell most people I was leaving.

> 'Ha ha, yeah, I'm gone. Back in L.A! Mighty!'

Copy. Paste. Send. Need to brush my teeth. Grab my wash bag. Must shave too. Look through my wash bag. Mind starts running circles. Past few days felt like an acid trip. Jolts. Bolts. Twitching. Brain struggling to make sense. Calm down. Calm down. It's OK, it'll all be OK... Oh. Dear. Jesus.

> "Where are my scissors?"

My scissors.

The little scissors that I've had since I was young. Went with me on that school trip to Germany. Journeyed to Hong Kong. All over Greece. Europe. The States. They've been everywhere with me! One of a kind. How could I not have brought them?! I always pack them. Must be a mistake. Please God, no!!!

For some weird reason, this causes my mind to fall apart. Seriously. Maybe the past few days and the gin monkeys were involved too. But the scissors triggered it all. Straight onto Skype. Phone home. No answer. Phone my brother. No answer. Sister, nothing. Where is everyone?! Go online. Facebook. Chat. Who can I get to check in my house for my scissors? Chatting with randumbers online:

> 'Hey, how are you? Ok, look, I need my scissors. Can you go to my house and check if it's there?'

People asking me:

> 'Who's this? Have we even met?'

ARRRRGHHHH!!! Useless! I need help. I just need someone to get me my scissors!!! Roommate overhears me. Pops her head in the door. Sees me sitting in a mostly naked slump. Deliriously look up at her. Like Gollum, but with wilder hair.

> "Do you need a scissors? You can borrow one of mine if you like? I have about five."

Twitches kick in,

> "Thanks for the offer. But they're not the same. You don't understand. This scissors is irreplaceable. One of a kind. I use it when I'm shaving. Trim my hair. All that stuff. Any other scissors can't do it like this one does it. YOU DON'T UNDERSTAND!!!"

Needless to say, she doesn't understand what's going on. Neither do I. Just asks me how I'm settling in. Hasn't seen me all weekend. I tell her I'm going home. I need to go home. Wasn't ready for all this. Not without my scissors at least.

"What? Are you OK?"

"Don't know."

All I know is that I'm now checking flights back to Ireland. How much? When is the quickest I can get back?! I'll just go back for a day. Just one day. Collect my scissors. Say goodbye to people like I should have. Prepare myself a bit more mentally for this trip. You know, moving halfway across the world on your own. And then I'll come back. Then everything will be fine. Then my mind won't feel like it's falling apart. Then I'll be ready. I just need my scissors. That's all! Roommate looks freaked out. Asks if I want a cup of tea -

"No thanks, just need my scissors, ha ha, ha ahaha."

That's all. Start to get frantic. Maybe it's in my bag. Maybe it fell out of my wash bag. Rip open my suitcase. Tear everything out in a wild rush.

"Isithereisitthereisithere?!"

Nothing. Balls. Suitcase two. Same drill. Throwing clothes, shoes, underwear, books and teabags all over the place. Nothing. Jesus Christ. I know where it is. Next to the TV in my room. I left it there so I wouldn't forget. HOW DID I FORGET!?!

"AND WHAT'S WRONG WITH MY BOWELS?!!!"

My stomach kicks me in the bowel region once more. Uggghhh. God. Goosed. My brain kicks me in the head. Oh Jesus. I'm funked. It Was All a Dream pipes up once again. What's going on?!

Turns out my phone is ringing. Somewhere on my bed. Underneath all my suitcase stuff. My life belongings. Separating me from my phone. Throw everything off the bed. See my phone on the pillow. Jump on it like a naked mad man in his boxers. Chowder's name flashing on the screen. Not now Chowder, not now! I need to sort my life out. Phone stops ringing. Rest for a second. Immediately starts again. And again. Until I realise:

Oh Jesus. I forgot.

Chowder!
Antigua!
Private jet?!

Or am I going home for my scissors?!

Press the answer button,

"Heh-Hello..."

Chapter 3

The Flying Gin Monkey

Woke up in a big huge bed, still drunk, I think, looked around and saw a tiny window next to me. Looked out and realised I was on an effing private jet! It was unreal! Amazing.

Walked through the double doors of the master bedroom, out into the main part and everyone else was dancing around to house music.

Jet was rocking!

Literally bouncing.

Up and

Down.

Stewardesses were stressed we were bouncing and dancing around too much but the pilots were cool, told us not to worry. They were loving the music! Ha-ha, it was amazing. Eight hour flight. Over waaay too soon...

Which is all that Chowder told me, in a voicemail, that I listened to when I woke up, in a bed, with no sheets, in a room, with yellowy white walls, and no A/C.

Beads of sweat all over me. Parched mouth. Furry tongue. Heavy head. Weak body. Wondering, yet again: Where the funk am I? Oh God, what am I doing? And (most importantly), have the gin monkeys left yet? Can't hack another day of them. Not without my aforementioned scissors by my side, at least.

So Saturday, Sunday, Monday: Unreal. Beyond mighty. Maybe the most fun three days I've at any point of ever being in L.A. Although it's tough to get three good days in a row most places. Back in Cork two out of three would be the tip. Maybe have an unexpected mighty Friday night. Chase that high Saturday. Fail. Brutal. Go again Sunday, almost out of disgust with the night before. Best one of the bunch. End up getting a mini-bus down to Kinsale for the day with group of buddies. Adventure on. Two out of three, ain't bad. Anyway, couldn't really have asked for more of a bang to come back with here. Well. Except maybe getting a bang, if you know what I mean boss. And I think you do. Duu! Ehh, yeah, great three days. Random. Dumb. Fun.

To balance that out, yesterday was absolutely, beyond belief, mind wobbling close to a meltdown, horrendous. Seriously. That bad. What goes up, must come down. And when gin is involved, that down was deeper than I've ever been. Debbie Downer was dragging me to the depths of downtown. All the way down. Dangerously to clown town.

At one point I did actually check for a flight back to Ireland. Escape the hangover. Just go for a week. Pick up my scissors. Recuperate. Come back again. This time, more prepared. Then I realised being stuck on a plane with such a bad hangover might make my brain explode out of my head. So that was canceled.

Just didn't want to be anywhere. Not here. Not up there. Just wanted a hole to go hide in. Couldn't even find that. Failed. Loser. Chump. So. Instead, like all good apes, I just freaked myself out as much as I conceivably could. Some ape. I blame the gin. Horrendous self-loathing. Covered in The Fear.

Woke up yesterday and decided I needed to get my life in order. So I did what anyone would do: I made out lists. Things I need to do. Really need to do. Kind of need to do. Long-term goals. Everything. Never ending list. Need to sort out a lot:

1. Social security.
2. Bank account.
3. Food shopping.
4. Gym joining.
5. DJ gigs.

6. Acting classes.
7. Stand-up venues.
8. Write new material.
9. Start writing my book (maybe this should be #1).
10. Get my camera fixed.
11. Get in touch with people here in L.A who I need to talk to.
12. Contact people at home in Ireland.
13. Tell some I'm OK.
14. Tell others I've left Ireland.
15. Retrieve my stuff from my old roommates.
16. Buy a new American phone as this one I have now is really horrific.
17. Try to make sense of all the stuff that just happened in the past three days.
18. Buy a desk and a chair for my room.
19. Get to know my new temporary roommate.
20. Microwave.
21. Sheets.
22. Buy a new or retrieve my old George Foreman.
23. Make out a weekly plan of what I need to do on a daily basis.
24. And, most importantly, buy a new scissors. Obviously.

Good old lists. Bring such tranquility and order. Except when they are never-ending rambles of gibberish. Reminding me that I am truly starting from scratch once again. Lots. Of. Lists. Too much to do. Oh Jesus. Where's the gin?

Writing all this down, while having a horrendous hangover; not helpful. At all. Freaked myself out like never before. Brain started spiraling. Muttering a new mantra to myself. Overwhelmed. Underprepared. Overwhelmed. Underprepared. Over. Under. Ovder. Oder. Oer. Or. Oh my sweet Jesus I'm going to lose my mind.

Realising I kind of left Ireland in a rush. Visa arrived. Wasn't that what I was waiting for? Holding me back?! Eh, yeah? So now, it's here, invite to Playboy Mansion too... Go, go, GO!

Go I went. Left Ireland quietly. Told a handful. Not really a fan of going-away parties. Particularly seeing as most these days are for folk who are going traveling for three months. And they're having a big going away party? I haven't seen him in about four months as it is! No thanks.

I'll just slip off. My going away party should be after I've left. People realise... He's gone, has he? Ah that's just great news! Wuu huu! Let's celebrate! We got rid of him, finally, funking ape. Party on!

So when I went online to try and talk to someone from back home, my conversations were a bit scattered. Gin monkeys. Surreal few days. Melting down over a scissors. Wondering if I'm going private jet flying to a Caribbean beach? No wonder I was having harebrained conversations with people.

Juggling all mediums. Facebook, Skype, Twitter, email. Making little to no sense of anything to any of the people I sparked up conversations with:

> 'Hiya boyo! Yeah, long time no talk. What's it been, four months? I'm good. Well, no. I'm bad. Can't find my scissors. I'm in L.A! For how long? Not sure. Might be leaving again today. No no, got here just three days ago. What's going on? No clue! Still there? No. Hello? No. Well funk you anyway! Your going away party was crap too! Oh, you're back. Just on the phone. Sorry about that. Ha-ha ha ha.'

Shut down my laptop. Went downstairs instead. Tried to talk to my roommate, Tara. Realised my voice was absolutely goosed from the past few days. Too much boozing. Shouting. Roaring. Laughing. Kind of had no voice left. Strained, husky mouse. Plus. No energy to string out a proper sentence. Just littering the air with random, pointless words,

> "Hi... High... Ha."

Laugh...

> "Cat... Life... Yeah."

Mumbling. Clearing my throat. Making Tara immediately regret letting me move in with her.

Around now is when I remembered the unimaginable: Left my scissors at home in Ireland! My scissors! The one I always use!!! The one that cuts in a certain way that no other scissors I have encountered cuts the same. How could I?!

Had to start taking deep breaths. Almost came close to making myself pass out over the thought of not having a scissors. (Out of all the home comforts, a scissors? Really?)

Cue Tara telling me she has plenty. All shapes and sizes. It was a nice gesture. But I didn't care. They weren't the same. They wouldn't do. I needed air. I had to get out of the house.

So, I decided to go take care of something really important of my never-ending list: Buy a new phone. I really needed a new phone. That would sort everything out. A phone. Even though I have two already. I needed a third. Right? Yeah.

Zombied my way up to the phone shop. Up to Sunset. Found a store. Guy behind the counter couldn't understand my accent. My slurs. Took a pamphlet from the shop. Went back outside to read it. The pamphlet would help. Tell me which phone I needed for everything to be OK again. First step in the right direction. Except it was a confusing pamphlet. Picked up the Spanish version. No help. Head got dizzy again. Needed assistance from someone working in there.

Walked back into the shop. Well, I walked into the clear glass door of the phone shop. Bumped face first off the door. Stumbled back a few feet. Stood there. Staring at the door. For longer than a few seconds. Decided I couldn't hack it. Defeated by a closed door. Wondering why it wouldn't open for me.

Feeling freaked that I couldn't even manage to buy a phone that I didn't even need. Took it as a sign. Just left instead of trying to open the door again. Guy behind the counter giving me strange looks. Not sure why.

On the way home I walked past the SkyBar. Decided to call in. See if anyone was by the pool that I might recognize. Maybe have a drink. Only thing that could cure me surely. Saw a few English girls we had been hanging around with one of the days. I could bounce my hungover buzz off them. They'd be in the same boat.

Big wave when they saw me. Felt at home. Sat down with them. Felt better. Until I realized they were in a different boat. Big boozing boat. Full of energy. Full of questions. I could barely grunt out a yes or no,

"Ugh. Yuh. Ugh."

Attempted to be normal by asking regular questions. That didn't really make sense...,

"Why are ye on holidays this time of year?"

(Why wouldn't they be? My mind still sometimes thinks that other people take holidays only during the summer holidays. These girls weren't teachers or students. Could holiday whenever they want. I knew all of this already!) Told me they wanted to go on a holiday. Decided to go at this time.

"Oh right.
Em."

Tried to explain my school holidays thinking process. In ughs and yuhs. Kind of threw me off. Told them I actually had to leave again. They all laughed,

"Sit down, chill out."

"How long have you been living in L.A?"

"About three days now."

They laughed,

"No, seriously..."

"About 72 hours or so. I think I must go home again though."

They laughed, although not as heartily this time. For some reason I said I really must go home. Almost close to tears at this stage (not sure why).

"Why are you leaving?"

"I have to buy a scissors."

They laughed. I left. Puzzled looks and shouts of,

"Come back."

"Sorry. I have to go. Must buy a scissors."

Which I did. Along with a George Foreman. And then I went home. Slightly less freaked. Jumped into bed. Found the hole I had been looking for all along. Lay there. Under the covers. Staring towards the ceiling. Wondering why I was close to tears.

Realising I was scared.

Surrounded by The Fear. Big move. Big step. Easy part was actually getting back here. Hard part has only just begun. How was I going to achieve all my lofty ambitious plans? I couldn't even buy a new phone! Oh Jesus. By now, almost hugging myself. Vulnerable ape. Overwhelmed. Underprepared. Fully freaked. So I just lay there. In the fetal position. Until I fell asleep. Wish I thought of doing that earlier. Dose. Live and learn. Sleep on!

On the plus side, woke up today, unpacked all my stuff, bought some chicken, went to the gym, bumped into a nutter there who stared at me like Herbert the Pervert from Family Guy, my voice came back, realised people are back to looking at me with confused expressions as they struggle to understand I too am speaking English, think I sorted out two DJ gigs, came home, cooked the chicken on the George Foreman and I was, eh, normal again. Back. Detoxed. Weird hangover, gone.

Finally ditched Owen, my own worst enemy. Goodbye, Owen!

Seeing as all of that has now happened, I can safely say that it is savage to be back in L.A. Pumped! Not that I was ever not. Although yesterday... More that I didn't really know what was going on. Overwhelmed. Underprepared. All on top of a gin hangover? Dodgy start. Got over it. Just been wined and dined for three days straight! Me whining about that was pretty pointless. Moan off. Own off. Baby steps on!

No more sitting and staring in despair at what I need to get done. Just. Go. Duu! Who cares if what I sorted out so far are more like baby feints in the right direction. My bigger goals should be right around the corner at this rate!

Sure.
Gymed.
Georged.
Settled.
Back in the bubble!
Now. Let the adventures begin...

Chapter 4

Forgot a Lot

Realised I've forgotten a lot of things about L.A.

Feels like I just woke up from a coma. All kinds of things. How people like to stare each other down here on the streets. Seriously. Stop and stare. Everyone constantly watching everybody else. Necks craning. Who's who. Everywhere. All the time. Judging. Hoping. Do they recognize this person? Are you famous? Can they go home and say they saw Joe D-List walking on the street?

And then you take off your sunglasses.
See the hope disappear from their faces.
Replaced with disappointment.
Realised you're a nobody to them.
Or at least you're nobody to the people they were going to tell.

In Cork people on the street really only stare at you for that long if they want to fight you. Slight chance if they want to hump you.

Here in L.A it's different.
Intense.
Weird.
Obsessed.
All the time.
Welcome back!

On the other hand, I did also forget how there are so many celebrities everywhere here. Hence all the eye-balling. Sitting at a bar. Hmmm, this girl next to me looks like Rihanna. Oh right. It is Rihanna.

Getting coffee. Ladies first... She looks a lot like Dita Von Teese - Oh, it is her.

Oh right. All over the shop. No longer that people kind of look like famous people. Now living day to day amongst the famous people. Although better off not knowing who anyone is. Can't mistakenly mistake them for being themselves then. If that makes sense? Moving on...

Forgot how there's always, always, always something going on in L.A too. Seriously. All the time. Everywhere. All sorts.
Gigs.
Clubs.
Openings.
Closings.
Premieres.
Galleries.
Launches.
Every. Single. Night.

Heaven.
Hell.

Heaven: Brilliant that there's so much going on. Particularly compared to Ireland where your options are usually:

1. Pub.
2. Watch TV.
3. Drink at home.
4. Cinema.
5. Read.
6. See a cover band you don't even like.
7. See a band you don't even know. Or really like.
8. Tommy Tank. (Which means... Hmm. Google it.)
9. Cry.
10. Sleep.

Not an abundance on offer, really. One, eight, nine and ten would be the most popular choices, I do believe, in that order. Hell: If you've got a rubber elbow. A need for adventure. And an inability to decline appealing offers. Offers which would seem like a competition prize back in Ireland,

> "Want to go V.I.P to an exclusive Crystal Castles gig held by Adidas with a free bar, gift bag included?"

"Eh, I was just going to chil- what am I on about, I'm in!"

Not that anyone is moaning about these daily offers. Always more fun to go with the flow. Especially when the invite mentions exclusive, V.I.P and free bar. Hard to say no. Even if twenty minutes earlier you swore you'd stay focused until you got your life in order a bit. Although when you have a rubber elbow, any invitation is pounced upon.

"Exclusive opening of an envelope filled with anthrax... Want to come?"

"Opening of what now? Actually, I don't care, will there be a free bar? Will I get a V.I.P sticker? Yes? I'm in!"

Gig turned out to be a good laugh. Free bar, not so much. Two barmen for 300 (select few?) people. In a hot, sweaty room. Clever sneaks whoever organised it. Took ages to get a drink.

Weird seeing so many people at a gig form such an orderly two person wide queue as well. Probably would've caused a riot back in Ireland. At least a scrum shaped formation heaving at the bar.

"GIVE US DRIIIINNNKKKK!"

Not here. Too many hipsters. Scenesters. All types of "sters". All looking cool. Funky as funk in fairness to them. Forgot people push the fashion limit. Full to the brim of every imaginable kind of hats, gloves, scarves, glasses, dicky bows, braces, feathers, peacocks, and the kitchen sink. Funky town.

Speaking of funky, the after-party after that first party was on in a place called Bardot. Cool bar full of ridiculously hot funky women. I remember my old roommates (ridiculously hot models) rarely bought anything themselves. Gifts coming in from all angles. Flowers, handbags, clothes, shoes. Even groceries. Men always paying for everything. Wined. Dined. Boozed. In return, they go places and look hot. Rich men. Hot women. Really hot.

Everywhere.

Wall to wall.

Good. Looking. Women.

Completely. Forgot. About. Them.

Calm down, I obviously mean that in quantity. Plenty of good-looking women in Ireland too. Just seeing as there are about 9 million people in L.A, and not as many people in the whole of Ireland, the difference is obviously going to be massive.

MASSIVE. Different levels everywhere. In quantity. Quantity. Quality. Tomato. Potato. Personality. Thankfully, I have a secret weapon. Which so far has been razor sharp!

My most talented instrument: My accent.

Having an Irish accent is like handing out little bags of gold to strangers. Amazed by it. I'm amazed at how they take everything at face value. Sometimes it's baffling. Other times it's too easy. Funny when things unintentionally get lost in translation.

Telling an American girl that the reason I'm not up for talking to her buddy anymore is because he keeps 'licking my hole'. In Ireland, this is a figure of speech when someone is just being a kiss-ass. Not an actual literal act. Hard to explain that in a crowded bar. And when the guy you're referring to is a highly homosexual man.

On the other side of this forgetful coin, I also forgot how you might oddly end up getting someone's number in very randumb scenarios.

In Ireland, I'm guessing at least 90% of numbers are exchanged in bars or nightclubs. Here, anywhere, everywhere. Out buying porridge in the shop,

> "How's it going…"
>
> "Oh my Gawd, where are you from? Take my number, call me!"

On the way to the gym. On the way to the bank. While on the phone outside your apartment. While buying a microwave from a girl whose ad you saw on Craigslist. Turns out she lives around the corner. And. She's a model. Ahem. With a weak spot for an accent,

> "Let's get drinks?"

Sure thing, microwave woman! Nuts. Random. Everywhere. In the coffee shop, girls just lash out numbers,

> "Call me. We'll do coffee."

Even though we're in a coffee shop right now, both holding coffee.

> "Yeah, let's set a date!"

> "Ehh. How about right now? I'm Irish. Raring to go!"

> "Ha-ha, you're funny, call me."

Now don't worry. I'm well aware that the majority of the numbers being handed out to me are pretty pointless to get. I did not forget what usually happens after a number is given. Send a text:

> 'ME: How's it going? We met in the coffee shop. You asked me out for coffee.'

> 'RANDUMB GIRL: Coffee?'

> 'ME: Coffee.'

> 'RANDUMB GIRL: I forget, who are you?'

Rinse. And. Repeat. Thank you. Seriously. Over and over. Slightly different to home. In Ireland numbers are kind of guarded. If they're exchanged, something's probably definitely going to happen between ye. Here, it's the second thing people say after telling you their name and most of the time counts for nothing.

> "Hi, I'm Amber, 310-310-3100, CALL ME!!!"

Two final things I kind of completely forgot amongst all of my moving motion.

Firstly, I must write a book.
My first book.
And secondly, I must find a job.
Quick.

DJ gigs.
Time to go hunting.

Although speaking of which, I did just get an offer. And the only, only, only reason I said I would go was purely as I thought it would be good for the book... Ah for book's sake! That might be used a lot from now on for any dubious offers. Plus I ehh, did think it was a wildlife convention. Something like 'Save the Lions!'

Except this one was for cougars.
Just not that kind.
The older type.
Invited to a Cougar's Convention. Where Ms. Cougar USA would be crowned.

Ha, go on the L.A!
Tough to say no. You know, for the book and all... Duu!

Chapter 5

Me Loose Ends

What a difference a day makes... A whole week or two can be huge! Not so long ago I was freaking out over a pair of scissors. Sweating the small stuff. Beyond belief. Still blame that gin. Now, slowly but surely, I'm over a hump. Dealt with the shock. Kind of slightly settled back in. Ish. Almost.

Loose ends have still not actually been tied up. For example, I've tried on a few separate occasions to meet up with my old roommates. Layla and Jess. The two models. Who also do other stuff. Not really sure what that actually ever was, to be true. Folk can be vague in L.A.

"What do you do?"

"Ah you know..."

"No, I don't. That's why I asked."

Nice girls. Well, until I tried to meet up and collect the rest of my stuff from them. Dodge. City. Only had a few letters and postcards belonging to me. Delivered after I left the last time. Birthday cards with a bit of money, and the likes. Not a whole bucket. But still.

For whatever reason, the girls dodged me. Tut. And to think, I thought our friendship was unbreakable. You know, like all good roommate friendships. Don't they last a lifetime?! Never realised the high fives and deep connection ended the minute one moves out. Live and learn. So that's the end of that. Back to my loose ends.

Next on my list: Must write my first book. Oh yeah. Publisher is on my back. Need to sort that out.

Google... "How do you write a book?"

Also on top of the list: Must get a job. Savings are in the bank. Book advance money. But still. Only so long all that can last. Rent monkeys will be on my back. Need to sort that out first actually. Well actually, what I'm going to do first today is write a few emails home.

OK. Done. Great job! Next... Write up a list of things to do this week? OK! Done. Wuu! Big pat on the back. Good man yourself. Don't forget, you also had breakfast earlier. And made a cup of coffee with your new coffee press. Wuu huu. Good for you! You're flying. What now? Oh yeah - Lunch!

Jesus, what an amazing day. Almost as good as the other night. Cougar Convention. When the dates got messed up, missed the convention and I just ended up going to Barney's Beanery for a pitcher or two. That was amazing work too! Really hit the ground running since you got back. Good work, Mark, you're a winner. High five. You clown.

One positive did come from those couple of pitchers. I think I might've got a DJ gig in Barney's again. Toni, the bar manager, still seems to like me. Gave her a bit of Irish gibber and it looks like I'm back dancing. Giddy up! Come on the money! Although yet to be fully confirmed. Keep the faith.

Also. Chowder and Charlotte are back in town from Antigua. Meeting up with Chowder was like talking with an old war veteran. As if we were both in Vietnam. Re-telling our versions of what really happened those first few days. Did I imagine it all?

Everyone else I spoke to tried to empathize with my spiraling mental state after the first few days. Getting blank looks of: OK, well done, get over it. Me pleadingly thinking: You weren't there maaan... You don't know what really happened!

Chowder was there though. He had signed me up for it all. He could relate to the madness that ensued. Filled in some of my blanks and vice versa. Dispel any grey areas of doubt where I might've convinced myself something bad happened. Turns out, in fact, it was the complete opposite. Banish The Fear for good! Mind can be put at ease now. Just bounced the funny stories off each other.

Told me about his little voyage to the Caribbean. Quite a trip. White beaches of Antigua. King-sized beds and leather couches on the private jet. Sounded unreal. Although I think my head might have imploded if I had woke up drunk on a king-sized bed on a private jet, so probably better off that I stayed in L.A for that reason alone. Baby steps and all. Gradually build up to that level of randumbness. Maybe I'll be ready for that next month.

Speaking of getting back to basics, I've been back playing soccer again up in Robert Williams' abode (or Robbie "sold over 70 million records worldwide" Williams, as the rest of the world might know him). Some pitch. Still the greatest 5-a-side in the world! Saw a lot of the lads from before as well. Jay Moe. Dave "No Longer the Angriest Man in the World But Now Just Kind of Funny" Jetski. Malcolm. Chris Dyson. Rob W. All as sound as ever.

Rob was pumped to see me back. Fan of my gibberish Irish slurs I think. Although he seemed slightly concerned my book wasn't finished yet,

> "Do you not get distracted in L.A?"
>
> "Eh, yeah. I do. A lot."
>
> "Well hurry up and finish it. Go find somewhere quiet."

This is true. Good point. Although I have already actually told myself no more distractions until the book is done and dumb. Seriously. And then I got a text after the game:

> 'JETSKI: Want to come out tonight for a while?'
>
> 'ME: No, cheers boss. New me...'
>
> 'ME: Pardon? You want to bring Jordan – the Page 3 glamour model – over to my house to go boozing?'
>
> 'ME: Wait. What? As in Jordan? With the really big giddy ups?! Emmm.'
>
> 'ME: OK so.'

'ME: For book's sake!'

Except it turned out not to be Jordan and her BFF coming over. Just Jordan's BF. Or boyfriend, as it's more commonly known. UFC fighter I think. Also a part-time cross-dresser, I was told. No Jordan either. Just him. And his manager, Jane. Who turned out to be kind of sleazy. Being weird towards me all night. Chatting me up. Not sure what they had been told, but at one point I overheard them whispering,

"Maybe he'll cast me in his sitcom?"

"Yeah, pitch him what you do - This could be a good move!"

Shaking my head. Fools. Trying to use me. If only ye knew the truth. Jane giving me the eye. Telling she was also a producer,

"I could scratch your back if you scratch or massage mine."

"Oh right. As in literally?"

I see what's going on: You're trying to sleep with me. Cop on now, no. Purely because you're not really my type. So please: Cop on. Trying to make me break my rule about not trying to sleep my way to the top. Integrity is key! (If I ever do get the chance to actually turn down that offer, I will make sure to let you know. As of yet, emm, no.) On the upside, I might've got another DJ gig lined up in a bar we went to, The Den. Might. Must wait and see. I did at least get some free whiskey shots,

"You're Irish? Here's a Jameson me old laddie!"

Free. Booze. On. And then I somehow ended up at a party in a mansion somewhere in L.A. Weird enough Persian party.

House reminded me of the one in Beverly Hills Cop II. With the shootout? You know the one. Although it did look like it was still in the 80's. Place was dripping in marble and gold. Leopard skin walls. Zebra rugs. Chandeliers swinging. Expensive 80's style.

No complaints. Savage bar outside. Looked more like a kitchen, if my memory serves me right. Stocked up with more drink than a small Irish pub. Brilliant. Blurry. Boozy. Trying to make cocktails.

Horrific concoctions. Shot-gunning cans instead. Classy. You can take the boy out of college but you can never rar diddy rar...

Stood by the pool. Overlooking L.A. Feels like I've been here before. Back again in the L.A! Dancing. Now... Where's the orgy room?

Alas. No orgy room this time. Got talking to a Persian girl instead, Minoo. I am a fan of the dark hotness they possess at times. This was her parent's house. And me chatting with her and her chatting back did not go down too well with her brother. Something about me not being Jewish? Don't hate me because I'm Catholic. Religionism! Won't stand for this!

"I'm leaving, who's with me?! Minoo, are you with me?!"

Meh. No. She was not. So I left. Alone.

Realised I had no clue where I was. So I went back to the bar outside by the pool. And ended up fooling around with one of Minoo's friends. On a sun bed. As us non-Jewish folk like to do. Yee huu!

Quite clearly the new me is doing well. Job hunting and book writing? Off to a flier!

A.
Wuu.
And.
A.
Duu!

Chapter 6

The Sexth Sense

"As I threw her to the ground her buxom bounced with delight, so I gently nudged her face with my foot, leaving her gasp for more..."

Opening line of my new romance novel. The one that I'm writing while procrastinating on writing the book I'm being paid to write. You know the one. Although maybe I should do the romance novel next, in order to tie over the folk who want to read more about...

Ahem.

Schex.

Shee shuu.

You know.

Duu!

Whatever it is that you may call it. Something which is distinctly lacking from most of my tales. The dirty details, at least. Innuendos might be bouncing off the walls. But details have been stripped bare. Stark. Naked. Teasing. All talk. Little action. Apparently that paragraph is some sort of an innuendo by my subconscious. Perhaps. If so, horrendous. Moving on...

Perhaps it's an Irish thing. Remember when you were young and watching a movie with your parents in the room and you suddenly got the feeling that Sylvester Stallone and Sharon Stone are going to be more than just acquaintances and then next minute they're in the shower... together... naked?!

Quietly panic. Don't know if you should stay in the room and pretend like you've not even been watching the movie all along? Or pretend to be asleep? Maybe get up and leave? I know - Just start fake-coughing, that will distract everyone's attention. Yeah. Fake cough on. And then that just makes everyone even more aware of the situation. One of the most awkward moments ever known to boykind.

Well, that buzz kind of stays throughout the ages I found. Meaning you don't openly ahump and talk about it in any way. Just how it's always been. So maybe that's why I write so little about it. Realising my parents, grandparents, younger cousins and friends of the family would start to read about my adventures - randumb and otherwise. (If I had it my way, I'd like them all to think I was a nun. Although that would be a bit weird: Nun Hayes.)

Or maybe it had nothing to do with any of them and was perhaps merely out of pure and utter respect for the other parties involved in the... you know... Dancing. Adventure. Duu. Ahum.

Perhaps all of the above! Perhaps. Who knows? Well. I do. But as I said... Moving on.

Actually – No. Staying put. Perhaps I should write about it more. Particularly when I now live in the
Sex
Town.
Everywhere. Anywhere. Wherever you look. Literally, at times.

Perhaps sex does sell. Perhaps I should write the rest of the romance novel, telling purely of those kinds of adventures in this world. Perhaps.

Especially as L.A seems to be the most sexed up place that has ever existed. Possesses the libido of an 18 year old dude mixed with a 30 year old lady. Finely tuned beast. Highly revved-up engine. Fully pumped at all times. Raring to go. If it were an animal, L.A would be a full-on horny rabbit. Call him Roger.

Not only all of this but I also think that I have an odd sense. Sense of something is about to happen. Or could happen. How do I describe it? Maybe I'm just a Roger myself? No. Too easy.

Ever read the book Blink? When you somehow just know something straight away but you're not sure how? But you know. Does that happen to you? No? Yes? Good. There's more of us out there. Kind of the exact same as that. But mine is purely related to... Duu.

Let's just call it: The Sexth Sense!

You know when you meet a girl and then you get the feeling they like you and perhaps would like to engage in a bit of dancing. Everyone knows this buzz. I hope.

Well. Some folk wait for weeks and months only to find out that they don't actually know after all. Or else they've ruined the buzz and the girl no longer wants to. Others do know this buzz but it might take a while to sink in. And a few others know this buzz almost instantly. Blink. Wham. Bang. Yes. That person wants to hook up. She is looking to cavort. Corrupt. Seduce. Abuse. Whichever way you want to look at it.

Usually when I walk into a room or a bar or a bedroom, this sense triggers off in some part of my head. The fun part. Jingles. Jiggles. Ooo me giblets! Common sense tries to interrupt my giblets' fun.

So I retort with: Not saying she wants to right now. But, Common Sense, I am saying that a glint just came out in her eye. Shone. Sparkled. Growled. And I'd now bet my house on it that I'm right.

Common Sense shrugs her head. Doesn't believe me. Right so, fecker. Here I go.

Well. Wait. Is she hot? Yes. Wuu.

Alright so. Here I go. Re de de...,

> "How's it going?
> Tip o' the...
> Top o' the...
> Just the tip o' the, I swear..."

And we're off!

See. Told you so! Not sure how. The Sex Sense.

My inner conversations are a good hoot at times. Until I absent-mindedly start saying them out loud. Particularly when I might be in the middle of the act...

> "Jesus, her boobs are disappointing, aren't they?
> Dangling like sandbags around her knees almost.
> Tut.
> Those cheating push-up bras...
> Why is she staring at me as if she's about to hurt me?
> Oh shi- "

Shut up Mouth, this is out loud!

And then I get punched. And then I run away naked, wearing only my socks. Carrying my pants. T-shirt. And one shoe. Tut. Dose.

So my point is: If you know, you know. And if you don't, dose. You're missing out.

Now right now I imagine you're probably screaming at the page, thinking,

> "That G$%@ S&^ F@#$%toe A*@#&#$* arrogant ape dope!!!"

Calm down. Not trying to say this is some sort of magical ability that means I can pick and choose when and with whom I want to cavort with. Well. Not fully. And I'm not saying it in an arrogant way. As in: I can have any woman in here! I know they all want this piece of this slab of Irish meat! Nay. Just that I usually know who does - and doesn't - want to dance with me.

Let's also not forget that in LA it could be anyone at all who may trigger this sense. Some are good. Wuu. Others dodge. Run! And more often than not: Dodge. A. Duu. To be true.

See, unfortunately gender or age doesn't dishearten some folk. Male. Female. Old. Young. Fetish. Normal. Cat lover. Leprechaun lover. Accent lover. Hair lover. All kinds of folk could be throwing you the glint. Triggering the "sex"th sense. Anyone. Or. Everyone. All depends really on what kind of orgy you're attending. Wa-wa-wahey boss! Oh Jesus.

Now I'm also not saying that this is some sort of super-human power I have either. No clue when it doesn't involve me. No clue if that girl behind the bar wants to sleep with you. However, from all the free booze she's horsing into me, I'm pretty sure she's up for an Irish gallop.

Also doesn't work as a way to warn me about potentially sticky sexual situations. Doesn't warn me not to walk into a public bathroom. Even if something bizarre and sex related was going on there. If only it was. Did. Had done. Like two days ago, when I went to buy some chicken in Pavilions. Walked in. Immediately get an urge to be bursting for the bathroom. Small bladder. Large consumptions of water. Making me spend far too much time in bathrooms.

Well. That and my mirror gazing. Hours on end. Just looking in the mirror. And crying at what I see. I joke. Gaze off. Shine on!

Bursting. Scuttling around the aisles. Balls. Quick. Close. Need the bathroom! Security guard points me to my destination. My ill-fated destiny. Down the corridor. Door at the end. Just about to push the door open and enter when something stopped me. A sense, you ask? Was it the sexth sense stopping you, saying hang on, something sup?! Nay. Door sign said: Pull. Me be: Push. Tut.

Pull I did. And in I went. Thankfully not one of those ridiculous public bathrooms that they sometimes have here. The ones which are really just a one person bathroom but with an added urinal on the wall. So some dude could be sitting on the toilet and leave the door open. Being kind to the next guy. As he can then use the urinal. While dude number one is sitting on the toilet. Doing a one plus one.

Thankfully, normal bathroom. Two urinals. One cubicle. Except: Both urinals taped off. Police cordoned-style.

Mighty.

Rush to the cubicle. Push the door. Into a Mexican guy who was just exiting the cubicle. Early 20's. Give him a Hows-it-going-why-am-I-giving-you-a-hows-it-going-nod-in-the-bathroom nod as he walks out.

I go to walk in. Stop. Some old dude? Huh? Also coming out of the same cubicle? Zipping up. Belting up. Pants were down. Just pulled them back up. While I did the math... Sweet holy Jesus. What is going on?! I just wanted to buy a chicken. Not walk in on this. Whatever this might be?!

Wonder if me nodding to the Mexican guy was some sort of 'Me next' kind of nod? Oh Jesus. Before I could ask him any of my long list of questions, he scuttles off. Old dude hobbles off out the door as well. Leaving me confused on the toilet. Tut. Stupid sex sense. Must've been turned off.

Quite the rambles. I was also going to include a story of how I think I mistakenly offered a short car ride to a prostitute as well. But that story was nipped before it could take off. Leaving the gym in Chowder's building. Girl who had parked her car a few down from mine looked lost. Asked if she was OK? Didn't hurt that she looked quite hot while looking lost. Teri Hatcher in Superman, style.

She didn't know the way out. Asks if she could jump in and maybe I could drop her off at the exit gate? No worries. Chowder lives in a classy building. My Serial Killer sense hadn't been triggered.

Unlock her door. Hops in. Small talk. Hup diddy ho,

"How's it going?"

"I'm going to the bar across the street."

"I know the Sunset Marquis well. Should be fun. Are you going meeting friends or what?"

"I'm workin'."

"You're working?
At this hour?
Oh. Right.
What is it that you do?"

"Personal stylist."

"Hmmm..."

Hello, sex sense.

"Personal stylist, you say?"

So I have a theory: There are so many personal stylists in L.A. Bizarre amount. Most of them are good-looking girls who seem to have wads of cash. All stylists. Not too many actually that stylish. Just dressed up well. But not looking cutting edge. If that makes sense? Made me dubious that they actually were stylists. Made me think something else. And then one day I find out a girl I suspected, was actually a whure. Sorry, a high class whure. Interesting, I thought. Theory: Proved!

After hearing about this girl, I obviously then got out my big brush and painted them all with the same stroke: UCLA is to strippers as personal stylist is to whures. Nice front to tell folk. Obviously not applicable to all but perhaps a large chunk. Just a theory. My theory. Hopefully one which will not get me lynched.

So. Pop goes that theory in my head. Good-looking girl. Well-dressed, yet not stylish. Just met in a car park. Vaguely telling me she's working now... As a personal stylist!?! Next minute her glint jumps out. Sex bells ringing. Oh Jesus. Get her out!

Not a fan of whures at all myself. Never saw their appeal. (Why pay?) Even more so, my brain has fully ran off. Particularly as Chowder lives on a street where his neighbour is Lindsay Lohan. Meaning on the way in, paparazzi were parked up outside her building. Looking for a photo. Looking for a story. Oh Jesus! Run imagination, run!

Pap smears outside on the street. Personal stylist/whure in my car. Oh dear God. Brain, run away! As fast and as dumb as you can! What happens if they snap a few photos? Didn't something like that happen to Hugh Grant?! Am I actually comparing myself to Hugh Grant?! Am I brain? Am I?! Stop the car,

"This is as far as I can bring you, sorry."

Gives me a puzzled look. Glint still shining.

"You should get out here if that's OK."

Glint, gone. Replaced with a,

"F**k you!"

Out she gets. Slams the door. Making me think she realised I was saying no to any potential money for cavorting ways. Making me think my sex sense was right: Whure.

Drove out the gate. Head down. Hood up. Just in case any of the pap smears were reading my mind and tried to Hugh Grant me. One guy either took a charity snap in case I might've have been someone of note. Or else his camera went off by mistake. Either way, I think I got away with it. Touch wood. Thank you, sex sense.

Some rambles. As I said, not a superhuman sense that warns like a Spiderman or Lassie sense. Only works for me. Although it does sometimes kind of work when I know the girl wants no action from any guy. Be it me or any other person within twenty feet of me. Then the sex sense does trigger. In the way an alarm bell rings to say get out of the building. When it's on, it's on. When it's fully off, it's kind of on too. If you get my rambling gist.

Bringing me all nicely to my point. I think. Let's hope. And it is: Sex. For. Pay. Apparently that's how the system works in L.A. You want to work here, you're going to have to sleep your way in. Or suckle the right... Yeah. Seriously, it's dodge. For all kinds of jobs too. Not just the ones where I hang around street corners and pimp myself out. Everyone is sex mad here. Everyone knows how desperate some people can get here. Mix the two: Sex. Mad. Campers!

Everyone just walks around here eye-funking each other to death. Spreading conjunctivitis as wide as they can. Do I recognize that person, is she checking me out? No. Don't be silly. She can't see that you've an accent! How about those sleazy, creepy dudes floating around all over WeHo? Forever prowling it seems. Prolonged stares. Weird eye-games. Staring competitions. Accidentally winking back. It's just all very confusing!

So far my job hunting has gone a bit like this,

> "Hi, are you looking for a DJ at all?"
>
> "Yes. Potentially. Sleep with me and you might have the job."
>
> "Hmmm..."

Called up to the gym where I used to DJ before, Crunch. My old buddy Jaymes (with a Jay). Or Jim, as I liked to call him. Flamboyant. Gay. Flailing. Funny. Big fan of Irish accents.

> "How's it going Jim, old buddy, old pal!
> Long time no see. Yeah I was away.
> Yeah, good few months. You didn't notice?
> Delightful.
> Anywho, how about I come back DJing here

again?
Once a week like before, see how it goes? Jim? JIM!?"

Jim had zoned out/started ignoring me. Instead telling a girl also working behind the counter of how I'm Irish and I have an accent and I play all of Jim's favourite songs.

"Ha ha, I sure do Jim, there's a reason for that. So...
When should I start?"

Jim replied with a cat-like clawing of the air. And a silent lion-like roar with his mouth. Rolling his head around. Biting at the air now. Asked,

"What are you going to do for me if I set it up? When are we going dancing?"

"Ehh, how about I'll make you dance around the gym if you hook it up?"

Jim starts playing with his chewing gum. Mentions,

"The main manager isn't here now. Call back again tomorrow."

"OK so."

While Jim starts to blow a bubble at me, I swiftly depart. Heard a POP and some growling as I scuttled out the door. It's been fun Jaymes!

Next day I just showed up with my DJ gear. Said nothing. Set-up. Plugged in. Pressed play. Saw the main manager pop her head out of her office. Look up at me confused. Gave her a wave hello. Uncertain wave back. Two thumbs up. Sealed the deal. Shook her head smiling. Back in, like a chancing Flynn!

One gig sorted. Time to get another old gig back. Barney's. Toni, the manager, is a big fan of Chowder and I. Well, more our accents. Either way, free food and booze on. Brought his English charm along. Great call by me. All going so well. Harmless flirting. Lining up the gig. Sorted. Good to go. Until Chowder jumps in. While I'm in the bathroom, he decides "to have a laugh". As you do do,

"Uh Toni, my friend Mark likes you. Why have you

> never gone on a date?"

Some. Funking. Clown.

> "He does?"

> "Yeah, you guys should date! He really likes you. Just thought you should know."

I return. Toni looks at me differently. Well this is awkward.

> "Chowder, what did you say? Oh mighty. You clown. This is going to ruin the whole system!"

Not that I don't think Toni isn't good-looking. More there's no sexual spark. Kind of looks like Michelle Rodriguez. Which I don't really find appealing. (It's all me Toni, all me!) Anyway, Toni's now blowing us off for the rest of the night. Charges us our full bill at the end of the night.

> "You're charging me for drink?! You were pouring it down my throat usually!"

Tut. Awful carry on! Toni tells me she now actually doesn't know yet about DJing (whereas two hours earlier I was back in).

> "I'll be in touch. I'll have to see."

Funk. Balls. Chowder! Head home. Bed. Sleep on. Phone buzzes at about four in the morn. Text from:

> 'TONI: Still awake Irish man? Come over to my house. We can talk about the DJ stuff. I have a bottle of Jack Daniels too.'

Too groggy to make sense of the text. Fall asleep while I'm trying to reply with a:

> 'ME: Pardon?'

Wake up the next day to another text:

> 'TONI: I have a DJ set for you tonight. My friend's party. Cabo, across from Barney's. Be there at eight.'

'ME: OK? Sounds good, cheers!'

Down I go. See the party all set-up. Mexican birthday. People wearing big huge dresses. Like wedding dresses, just different colours. Ask the barman where I should set-up my DJ stuff? Just looks at me oddly. Birthday girl comes over, Lana. Wearing a baby blue wedding dress. Enquires,

"Who are you?"

"Oh hi, I'm Mark, are you friends with Toni? She told me to come along to- "

Next minute I'm being hugged by a Big Bird. What the funk?

"Oh, Toni, that's you there in a big yellow wedding dress, what's going on? I was just talking to Lana. Where should I set up?"

Toni grabs my bag,

"Don't worry about that for a while. Here, have a drink. OK?"

"Although, just let me set up first, then I'll have a drink. The barman says the place closes at eleven, so let's get the music going!"

Toni tries to introduce me to her other multi-coloured-wedding-dress-wearing friends.

"Hi, hi, how are things? OK, I should set up, where do I go?"

Now Toni tells me again to stop worrying and to just chill out. Have a drink. I'm here now, might as well enjoy myself. Which is when I realized I had been set-up. There was no gig. This was some sort of weird date. Which Lana confirmed when she introduces me to her parents as,

"Toni's date - Merrick?"

"Yeah, Merrick, hi."

Five minutes later: Taxi. Home. Chumped. No pay. No gig. Just some sort of weird wedding birthday date. Text:

'TONI: Where are you? Why did you leave?'

No reply. Text:

'TONI: Call over to my house. We can talk about the DJ stuff. I have Jack.'

Sweet Jesus. No reply. Text:

'TONI: If you don't come over now, then... You should just come here now.'

No reply. Funk off. Ye sex-crazed town. Replied:

'ME: Sorry, I can't now but we can talk about the DJ stuff tomorrow day or I could start tomorrow night if that suits?'

No reply. And that was the end of that. Wuu. Woke up. Breakfast. Tara handed me a book she thought I'd like: Bright Shiny Morning. Book about L.A. Thank you. Told her about my dark dull night. She agreed,

"Definitely sex for pay situation,"

"Mighty."

I murmured, while flicking through the book. Land on a random page. As you do. Depressing landing point. First paragraph I read went something along the lines of...

"Brad. Actor. Moved at 20. Works as a bouncer. He is now 30.

Barry. Singer. Moved at 18. Works in the ticket window at the Wax Museum. He is now 31.

Katy. Actress. Left her husband and three children to become a star. Works at a grocery store. Cries herself to sleep every night.

Bert. Writer. Moved at 24. Bartender. He is now 50."

Nice. Depressing. Funk that. Won't be me! Oh Jesus, don't let that be me. Alright. Time to giddy up. Priorities swapped over.

First I'm writing the book. Then I'll find a job. Book first. Money second. Done. Dumb. Dancing! Mighty plan. I think. No more sex distractions. Focus on. I swear.

"She shivered with fear as I approached from the rear..."

Sorry. Second line of the romance novel. Shaping up nicely. Alright. No more distractions. Starting. Now...

Chapter 7

Howl at the Moon

Ah the chicken aisle. Where all the hot chicks hang out...

Over the past few days I've realised there are a bucket load of things I don't quite understand. Such as, why would you wear jeans in the gym. As in not to the gym, but actually in the gym. Working out. On a treadmill. Going all out. Hell for leather. Also wearing what can also only be described as a sports bra. Or else a very, very, very small and tight belly top. Didn't get it. Particularly as the person in question was a guy. Bizarre. Not a fan of using a treadmill as it was. This incident ensured that I won't be trying them out again too soon.

Another baffling point for me is the women in L.A: They. Are. Beyond. Amazing. Randumb tidbit: As the legend goes, when the mythical California was first discovered, people thought it was only an island, ruled by a Queen and populated only with female warriors who happened to brandish gold weapons.

Well, to me L.A is still an island just brimming with beautiful women. All shapes, sizes, nationalities, styles, looks, attitude. All sharing the same common trait: "Holy funk, she's hot." Seeing is believing. Quality matched with quantity. Some sight.

And another thing: I wonder what water they're all drinking. Seriously. Fountain o' youth. Older they get, the younger and hotter they become. Something's up. Not ordinary to look so young. I know, I know... Surgery. Still though, there's more to it. They look after themselves so well. Quite ridiculous.

Take the other day. Hanging out in Trader Joe's. Poultry section. Mulling over which piece of chicken to invest in. Sparked up a complete gibberish conversation with a girl next to me. Looks like Gina Gershon from Showgirls. (On a side note, she is ridiculously hot in my book. This one here. Google her.)

Anyway, told her that in Ireland, chickens are born without heads. Which is where the phrase came from. Funnily enough, she believed it. Asked me if,

> "You'd like to meet up sometime?"

Talk more about headless chickens.

> "Coffee?"

> "Sure! You're my type, as in I think you're hot, coffee on!"

So as I'm taking down her number, she starts saying,

> "I shouldn't really be doing this. You're young enough to be my son."

> "Your son? How old is he, 6 or something?!"

Didn't get it.

> "How old do you think I am?"

> "I don't know, mid 20s? Early 20s?"

> "Oh stop."

> "Stop what?"

> "Don't tell anyone... But I'm 41. Almost 42!"

> "Excuse me? No. Funking. Way."

> "Way."

I was wrong. Although I didn't actually believe her until she showed me her I.D. Week off being 42. What?! Fountain of youth!!! Swapped numbers. Bob's your Uncle. Fanny's your Aunt. Headed home. Thought that would be the end of that. Not because of her age. More because of the date aspect of it all. Even if it was just a coffee, in America-land, that's a date. Oh Jesus. The whole dating malarkey. Rules. Regulations. Games. Americans are kind of obsessed with the whole thing. People are going on dates every night of the week. All out there, looking for the one. Must be blind or something.

In Ireland, you don't really go on dates with people you don't know or haven't really met before. Not straight away anyway. Not the average punter. I'm estimating a lot of couples in Ireland met this way...

You go out with your buddies to a pub, or a club. You booze on. You get some Dutch courage. You spot a girl you like. You go drunkenly dance on the dance floor behind her. Move in. Hips gyrate. Belted away. Or else she gyrates along. If so, you're dancing. Surrounded by other drunken soon-to-be-lovers. Ye stumble home. Do your drunken thing. Wake up the next day. You're happy with the ending. She's probably *filled* with regret.

Then either that's it. Or. You might arrange to meet again. Some other pub. Some other time ye are both drunk and at your happiest. Only after a good few weeks of this carry-on, a sober trip to the cinema is suggested.

> "OK. Why not? I feel comfortable enough around you now to do that. What should we see?"

So off ye go. About one month after initially meeting. First official date. Cinema. Big smiles. Awkward coughs. Small talk about how,

> "We should've just went to the pub, huh?!"

And then you get married. And hate your life. Not all cases. But a few. And I digress. Back to L.A... People always seem to be trying to trick me into going on dates with them, in my experience, anyway. Take that DJ gig thing the other night. Bizarre. Masking them as something else. Fooling you. First dates made out to be formal kind of interview processes. So what do you do, how well do you do it, and how much do you make? Hmmm. Interesting. Sounds particularly horrendous if the date is boring. Tediously time consuming. Another night wasted getting coffee and having mundane sober talk. Whatever happened to just having a few boozes and seeing if ye get on with each other?! Tut.

So. I thought it would be no more. Until I spoke to my buddy Ronan "'Nancy" Noonan. Not sure where that nickname came from. Maybe I just like the way Nancy Noonan sounds in my head, suits him, so I call him Nancy. Anyway, Nancy had recently moved to Chicago on his own for work. Here for the long haul too. And since he arrived, Nancy has been all about the dates. Big fan.

"Great way to meet people."

He would say,

"And some of them are actually tolerable."

So, on the advice of a Nancy, I decided to give it a whirl. Now living in America. Time to give dates a chance. Never know, might be fun? Just depends on how long headless chicken banter can last perhaps. Few drinks and it could be a laugh. Time to embrace the date!

And embrace I did. Decided to leave my writing well earlier this evening. Hibernation Hayes (also known as Bear Boy) was left out of the cave. Wild eyed. Bushy haired. Threw on a nice T-shirt. Spray of cologne. Good to go. Date on!

Venue was the Coffee Bean at the top of my street. Tad nervous, to be true. What if she murders me? Or, worse still, what if she's loud and embarrassing? Crossing the road. Filled with regret. Dread. Shame. Jesus. Why am I going on a date? Coffee date? No booze?! Some clown. Although Kim did say she'd prefer coffee than a pub. Dose. Climb the steps up to Coffee Bean. What am I doing? Too late now. Although maybe she'll bail. No. There she is. And... She's looking pretty well. OK. Let's stay a minute.

Spot Kim in the corner. Sipping coffee. Wave a howdy with my head. Jumps up. Runs over. Hugs me. Awkward embrace, from me at least. In my head, everyone else in Coffee Bean is looking at us with pity. How embarrassing. They know this is a first date. All looking at us with such disgust. While an enthusiastic Kim is waiting for a response from me...,

"Eh, not too bad, how's it going with you?"

"Great! Want some cough-eeeee?"

"Yeah, sure!"

Balls. For some reason a dose of dread comes over me now as Kim breaks the embrace. This is not going to be amazing fun. I can feel the stiffness already. And. No booze about to loosen it off. Ugh (or Ughatha Christie as some of us prefer to say).

As we're going inside to order me a drink, Kim stops suddenly at a table full of people. Huge look of fake surprise on her face. These are people she knows! This is her group of friends actually. All here, at a table, right next to where she was sitting?! What are the chances?! All get up. All hug. All hello. Me standing next to her like a complete goober. Smirking smile. Wondering what's going on? Why didn't I just pre-booze? And why are all her friends here? Looks like I'm getting introduced...,

> "Mark this is my friend Tania, one of my best friends. And this is Amber. And Kerry. And Naomi. These are my best friends!"

Hmmm. Suspicious.

> "We actually were all at an amazing party last nigh- I mean. Yeah. So, girls, what on earth are you all doing here?!"

World's worst actress. Re de de. Turns out they're all brutal actresses. Quite clearly I've been sabotaged. Brought all her friends along. In case I was a rapist. Or a racist. You never do know, I suppose. Still, felt ambushed. Disliked the date even more then.

Fake greetings over. Inside. Coffee. Kim tells me what a surprise it is that all her friends are here. What a coincidence! Best friends, sitting in the table next to her. And she didn't even see them the whole time! Amazing! Spoof. Making matters worse, when we go back outside, her friend asks me if I'll pose for a photo. For funk's... Already feel like I've somehow been duped (not sure how) and now photos (for some reason I'm not a fan of posing. For photos. Day to day posing I seem to have no qualms about. Odd.) Fake. Smile. Forced. Just like this whole scenario so far. Uncomfortable buzz. Dislike of dates escalating. Plan my escape. Wishing I was back down the writing well, sitting around in my boxers, writing my book. Appears Kim has different plans,

> "Up for an adventure, Irish man?"

Away from here and your gaggle of photo-taking friends?

"Definitely. Must head home after that then though, deadlines and all."

Escape. On.

"No problem. Just a quick trip."

So we hop in Kim's SUV, soccer mom style. Ha. Go on the clichés! Drive off down Sunset. Down my street. Pass my abode. Wonder if I could jump out and roll to safety while the SUV was moving at this speed? Would I be hurt? How hurt? Too late now. Central locking I see. Tut. Keep on going south. Small talk flowing. Keeps explaining why her car is so dirty. Her son plays soccer. (Oh, maybe we could be friends, my age and all?)

"My daughter plays soccer too."

"Oh you've a daughter as well?"

"She's 22."

"Marvelous."

This is a full-on Ashton/Demi scenario in the making right here! Gibber turns to me. My accent. Ireland. My hair. My accent. My accent. And also one or two lines about my accent. I'm gathering Kim is a fan. Keeps laughing at anything I say. And I mean anything at all. So I decide to throw out of a few testers which make no sense whatsoever to see if she is merely fake listening/-laughing along,

"Kim, here's a good joke for you... What's the difference between a can of coke and a fork? One is a can!"

Kim replies with a,

"Oh my Gawd, hilarious! So funny!!!"

Every. Single. Time. Kim keeps giving me odd looks. Already confessing she has a soft spot for me. Asks me to,

"Stop being so cute."

Literally, I'm sitting in the passenger seat, planning my escape, mumbling answers out the window. Cute?

"So Irish man, do you like ice?"

Hmm. Is she on about drugs or what here? Play it cool. You're meant to be the hip young one,

"Ehh, no, although I wouldn't mind a booze."

Kim laughs. Then gets serious,

"I'm a recovering alcoholic."

No booze. But. She can bring me to some ice. Only now do I realise we've been driving down all back alleys. Odd.

"Where are we going?"

"It's a surprise. Get you some ice. Maybe some snow too if we're lucky."

Ice? Snow? What is she on about? Funking roasting outside. She's hardly trying to take me up the mountains, is she? No. That's just silly. What makes far more sense is what ice and snow might actually stand for...

Ice: Crystal meth.
Snow: Cocaine.

Oh Christ. Drug run with a druggie on my hands. No wonder we're going down all the back alleys! Funk balls. How did I get into this?! How do I get out of it? Who is this woman? Weirdo from the chicken aisle? Jesus! I don't want any of her ice or snow. This is dodge. Why am I on a date? Why am I on a date with a druggie?! Why am I... Oh. Turns out, I was just being a tad paranoid. Turns out, we were going somewhere far worse than a drug den.

We were going to: The Grove.

Most intense place in L.A. Pressure cooker of commercialism filled to the brim with human beings. Mini Disneyland in West Hollywood. Except there are no rides. Just shops. Restaurants. Shops. Cinema. Shops. Water fountain. Shops. And. More shops. Along with waaay too many people. Worst kind of people too: Slow walkers. Now I want some ice. Now I need some snow. Ughatha.

"How come we're going here?"

"You'll see."

Cackles a now deranged looking Kim. In we go. People bumping off me. My mind starting to have a wee little freak out. From isolation in the writing well for the past week to this. Cluster funk of madness. Packed to the brim too. Claustrophobia twinges. Intensified by sheets of people everywhere. Why is it so busy? And,

"Kim, why are we here?!"

"You'll see!"

She cackles once more. Drags me towards the water fountain. Hundreds gathered.

"Quick."

She screams,

"QUICK! Get to the middle of the crowd."

I hear a bell ringing somewhere. Someone starts mooing. Maybe it's a train noise. No clue. Freaking out. Feels like I'm on drugs. Head goes dizzy. Am I tripping out? What's happening? Look over at Kim. Giddy. Points at me...,

"Now, look up!"

Up my eyes go. And I see... Snow. Falling. Ice. Dripping. Down from the skies. In L.A?! Well, fake snow and fake ice falling from a pipe overhead. Crowd erupts! Yay. It's officially Christmas! Celebrate. Shop, shop, shop! Spend, spend, spend! Buy that happiness!!! Look over at Kim who is beyond delighted,

"Do you love the snow? Because you're Irish and all!"

"Yes. I do. Great hoot. Let it snow!"

Still feels like I'm on drugs. And the fact that it's snowing while I'm roasting feels bizarre. Maybe I've been too far down the well. But good plan coming here. Actually cool to see.

"Cheers Kim!"

Nice touch. Great time. Now then,

"Can we go?"

On the drive home, I make a joke that Kim was like a snow wildebeest. Cue an abundance of laughter the likes of which I've never heard before. Starts to make wildebeest noises at me. Howling,

"Owwooo. Arooo."

Like a demented wolf. Funny enough. The first four howls at least. After that, slightly odd. Anytime I said anything, all I heard was a howl. Only speaking normally to tell me,

"You are different from most first dates I've been on."

"Thank you? A... Duu?"

Cue more hysterics.

"Are you sure you're not on some sort of drugs- Hey hup, this is my stop. Well then. That was nice."

Cue awkward pause. Appears we have come to the end of the date. End scene. Hmmm. What happens now? So we're sitting in Kim's soccer mom SUV. Outside my house. I'm kind of looking out the front window. She's kind of just looking at me. Awful long time for such a stare.

"OK then, thanks for all that. Great time. Cheers."

Reach for the door. Locked. Ha. Of course. Wildebeest is still just sitting looking at me. Quietly (and I'm not making this up) starts howling at me,

"Awooo. Owwwoo."

Chuckle chuckle.

"Ha ha. You're funny, Kim."

Squirm squirm. Not sure how to end this. So I ask her,

"How do first dates usually end?"

"Owwwwoooo! Awooo Ooooooo!"

"Ha. No. Seriously. Fill me in. Because these doors are locked."

"Usually you just say goodbye. But I want to do more. Maybe."

"Oh yeah, like wha- "

Howl unlocks the doors. The click distracts me. Followed by a quick launch of her head towards me. Not passionately. More just ensuring it happens. Pucker up. Eyes closed. Might as well give it a whirl. And. Commence... You know what it felt like: A handshake kiss. Seriously. Boring enough. I imagine exactly like what a kiss in a movie scene must feel like. Let's get this out of the way, kind of a thing. Maybe mixed with a kiss an old woman gives you on the cheek for your First Holy Communion. My thoughts, anyway. Howl pulls away. Almost strikes an anguished pose from a romance cover.

"We must stop! I won't be able to control myself! Must stop. This is only the first date!"

"OK. Fair enough. I'll be off in home so..."

Open the door. Howl seems to be taken aback. Grabs me by the arm.

"Where are you going? Can I see what your place is like?"

Ehh. Emm. How do I say no to this? Balls...

"Yeah. Cool. Quickly though. I need to write. And your howling is odd."

Time for a quick tour. Through the little garden area of the apartment complex. In the door.

"Spanish style villa, as you can see. Two story. Here's the living room, dining room, opens into the kitchen."

"Owooo, arooo" softly heard behind me.

"Where's your room?"

"Upstairs. Two bedrooms are upstairs."

"Can I see it...?"

"I suppose. Yeah. Come on so."

Quick note. I'm sober. She's sober. Didn't actually cop on to what my intentions should've been, or what hers were, to be true. If I had been drunk, it would've been - Let's have a look at the springs on my bed, shall we?! Leave your pants at the door! Up we go. Bathroom. Bedroom. Howl doesn't want to step inside. Tells me,

"I'm afraid of what I'll do if I go in. I can't control myself. Owwwwlll owwwwhhhhh."

"O. K. Your howling is kind of weird. Let's go downstairs so?"

Head for the stairs. Howl first. Me a good few steps behind. Howl turns to me before the last step.

"I'm not having sex with you. Not on the first date. No matter how much I want to."

"Ehh, ha, OK. Control yourself so, lady."

Think this reaction surprises her. Looks perplexed. Next part was odd to me. Retorts with,

"If you want, you can have my sunglasses, they'd look good on you."

Quick look at her sunglasses.

"I'm OK."

By now I'm sitting midway on the stairs. Hoping this howling oddness will end.

"Are you sure you don't want them?"

"Yeah, thanks though. I must do some writing actually..."

"Well is there anything you do want?"

“What do you mean?”

“Anything I can do to you…?”

Now Howl is on her hands and knees. Quietly howling. Crawling up the stairs. Hey hup. I’m still close to bursting out laughing every time she howls (might’ve been half in fear) but I think I know where this is going… Crawl crawl. Howl howl. Starts unbuttoning my jeans. Rips them open. Pulls open her shirt. Whips out my ponder pipe with one hand. She seems pleased. Starts rubbing her beautiful breasts with her other hand. I am pleased. Jesus, this has taken a mighty turn. Now we’re howling! Hot body. Tanned. Toned. Sexy stomach. Big. Fake. Boobs. Glorious!

“You like these?”

“Very nice.”

I squeak. (Don’t really have fake boobs in Ireland. Mythical creatures. I remember years ago hearing about a girl in Cork who got a boob job. Never saw who she was but if she was out and someone saw her, it was reported like someone spotted a unicorn,

“I saw her!”

“Who?”

“Fake boobs!”

“No way. Spoof. Where?”

“She’s gone but she was over there.”

“Lies!”

Now don’t think I’m obsessed with them. Big fan of all shapes and sizes. If they look like they suit the body type to me, I’ll think they’re glorious! Just that I find fake boobs curious. Want to investigate them further. Make up my own mind if I like or dislike them. Before coming to America I’ve only ever seen one set of fake boobs. And they were bandaged up. And still tender. Too sore to touch. So that was lovely. And a very passionate night. So, yeah…) Kim starts rubbing my ponder pipe along her nipples. I’m sky rocketing at this stage. Full on dancing. Give out a soft,

“A-Duu!”

This pleases Kim, who in fairness, knows what's she's duu-ing. And is magnificent at it. Licks her lips. Looks at me. Opens her mouth. Howls. And gobbles up... Ahem. American women are amazing! Jingling my bells. Tooting on my ponder. Touching herself. Leaning back on the stairs. Thinking perhaps I've been a tad harsh on the whole dating scene. Perhaps I need to get out there more. Perhaps... Jesus, this is unreal. Where was I... Who cares... Howl on Kim... Oh yes. Now we are fully aruuing! This is too good. This is freedom!

Time seemed to freeze. Or else zip by. Who knows? It was savage.

Cherry on top. Howl sensed what was coming. Looked at me. Opened her mouth. And smiled while I dispersed my knowledge on her. Funk me. It was a delight.

And Nancy was right.

Date on!

Chapter 8

An Irish Gem!

Us Irish, we love our tea. At least five cups a day, plus just the "one more, why not" before bed. Tea, tea, tea for me. So there I was last night, doing my thing.
Filled the kettle.
Watched it.
It boiled. (The saying is false!)
Cup.
Tea bag.
Spoon.
All ready.
Picked up the kettle. Pour the water into the cup.
Last second, defaulted.
Change of heart. Changed my mind. Saved the tea bag.
Spilled water on the counter instead. Literally that last of a split-second change.

Reason being: Society. Telling me that I needed to sleep, not have a cup of tea. No such thing as a quick cup. Better off going to bed. Wrecked. Tea off. Sleep on. Hmmm. OK, society, if you insist?

Past week my night owl has been turning into an early bird. Late nights slipping in to early mornings. Writing finally in full flow. Thank funk. Publishers have politely asked for the first draft. Oh Lord! Head down. Write on.

Sunday was my record so far. Up until six in the morning, working away. Although that was also a hangover side effect I do believe. Body and mind can disagree at times. Body wants bed, goosed. Needs sleep. Brain wants to stay up, have fun. Race along. Tease me. Throwing me nuggets of good book stuff. Can't go to bed now, brain screams. You never know when I'll give you lines like this again! You better stay up and write this gold down! Funk you body. Dominating brain in full control. Mind standing over matter. Toying with it. Beating it down!

At least now I'm in the swing of things. Ploughing on. Which is good for the writing buzz. Just not good for society and her rules. All my life she has been trying to condition me for a 9 - 5. Dictating my day. Particularly my hour of rising. Doesn't care if I'm burnt out or work better at night. No, no, no. Just as long as I'm not a bum and don't stay in bed tomorrow. Can't waste a glorious day! Not in this society. Who cares if you're more productive at night and get more done? Vitally important you get up early. Just in case anyone asks "What time are you up since?" Trying to convince me that even if I get less done by being so tired, it's still better to be up early. Good work, society, thanks for that! Fairly dumb. Or is it me?

Either way: No more. Shunned. Hibernation time. Cram time. Head-down-until-the-book-is-done time. Now living in my own time zone. Particularly with deadline time running out. Obsession time. Gollum style. Until the book is finito, I shall be a possessed little writing Wally. Surfacing only for food. And the odd DJ gig, if and when I find them.

Also. Dates. May have to be culled. Starting with the Howler.

So, overall that night was adventurous. However, turns out Howler was a sixteen year-old girl in a forty year-old's body that looked like a twenty-two year-old's body. If that makes sense. Weird texts going on. Every second one was a howl. Seriously:

> 'HOWLER: Hi how are you?'
>
> 'ME: Not too bad, yourself?'
>
> 'HOWLER: Owoooo aroooo awwoooo!'
>
> 'ME: OK?'
>
> 'HOWLER: When are we meeting again? Last time was hot, right?'
>
> 'ME: Yeah, wasn't too bad at all. Stairs fun all the way!'

'HOWLER: Awoooo aroooo oooowowoooooo!!!'

Couldn't hack it. Particularly as she did like to constantly mention that her son and daughter were more my age. Which made me wonder how they'd feel about their Mum howling at me. Which in turn made me think of her just as someone's Mum (albeit with a hot body and a howling mind). Once that image came into my head, I felt that was that. Plus, there was no real spark. So I cut that to the friend pile. Too busy with the writing and all. Although, I did have another date last night.

Different style this time. Tatiana. 26. Looked like a mix of Pink and Angelina Jolie. Kind of. Small. Dancer. Feisty. Funky. Met her in the gym while I was DJigging. Fan of the remixes. Fan of her tattoos.

"We should go talk about music sometime."

"Sure thing. Do you booze?"

"Yes."

"Do you howl?"

"No?"

"OK. Let's go out!"

Went to a place in Hollywood called the Piano Bar. Cool little spot. Bar. Piano. Name tells it all really. Dodgy start. Tatiana opens up with,

"I don't like your jeans. I don't really like your style."

"Cheers."

"That's OK though, you're Irish."

"Oh cheers again."

In return, I decided to tell her what I wasn't a fan of,

"One drink in, you seem like a cranky person. Also, you can't hold a conversation when I stop talking. And. Despite the fact you're good-looking, you're coming across as a bit of a stuck-up ape. Still though, we're boozing, and, you're hot so I will survive for the time being."

Cue look of offence from Tats. Retorted with,

"Don't worry, in Ireland what I just said is actually a compliment. It's OK. I'm Irish. Remember?"

Cracked a smile. Followed by a death stare. Banter and gibber just about flowing. Not great. But the booze was helping. Tats was big into astrology. Or at least knew enough about it to kind of freak me out. Tried to guess my star sign. Not a hope,

"You can't psychoanalysis me; I'm Irish!"

Cue Tats rattling off,

"I bet you're a Gemini."

"What?"

How does she know? No way am I that easy to read!

"No I'm not. Although what made you say that?"

Next she described my way of thinking.

"Don't be preposterous. You've that all wrong."

Oh Jesus, how does she know?!

"And I bet you do this too..."

OK, enough is enough. Where was she getting all this information from?

"I just know a fellow Gemini when I meet one!"

She's one too. Interesting. What does this mean? Balls, she's at it again. Reading me like a book. Putting me in a box. Not a fan for some reason. Trying to sit on my hands or bite my tongue as I listen along. Shaking my head. That's not me, I don't do any of that. Ever. Stupid.

"Sorry. Your theory is invalid. No. Stop! OK!!!"

Cracking,

"I can't lie! How do you know? Freaking me out! I am a Gemini!"

Tats was proud of her work. Although little did she know she just gave me the perfect excuse to say or act however I wanted. Sorry, it's because I'm a Gemini. And I'm Irish. Can't help myself. An Irish gem: GeminIrish!

Speaking of Irish, all sorts of Emerald folk in the Piano Bar. Actual Irish and wannabe Irish. Dudes from Van Morrison's band. Playwrights. Musical randumbers. All of whom I realized are kind of like me. As in we all prefer to be the only Irish guy in the group. Like two awkward magnets pushing against each other when introduced,

"So you're actually Irish?"

"Oh yeah, I hear your accent."

"Well."

"That's great."

"Whereabouts you from?"

"Cork."

"I'm from Dublin."

"That's cool."

"Yeah."

"Ok."

"Cool."

"See ya later bud."

"Yeah, have a good one."

Mandatory conversation. Americans think that because we're both Irish we either:

a) Know each other. Or,
b) Will get on like a house on fire. As opposed to the reality,
c) Would prefer to have fun with the American folk who think our accent is the greatest thing since the George Foreman was invented.

Did also meet a lot of faux Irish folk. All of whom seemed to claim that whatever drink they were drinking was actually brewed in Cork. Lying to themselves to keep the 1/17th slice of Irishness in them happy,

"I'm drinking an Irish drink so I'm Irish!"

Buying me round after round to celebrate our Irish ancestors. Nodding along. Sipping their German ale (which they know for a fact is brewed in Cork, Ireland). Accepting their round of Scottish whiskey (that's apparently also brewed in Cork, Ireland). Turns out they've also been to Cork, as they mention to the barman. Although none of them can remember enough details to tell me anything about the place,

"North Ireland, by England, correct?"

"Ahem.
Spoofs."

"What?"

Now that I think about it, the pub was full of those folk. I had guys tell me they're delighted to meet an Irish guy over in L.A I ask,

"Why so?"

"Because my ex-girlfriend is from Scotland."

Oh right. For the sake of this conversation with you, my ex-girlfriend is from Canada. And you're American. So that's the same thing, right? Isn't that amazing?! No way, you visited Denmark before? That's more or less the same country as Ireland! Did I ever tell you I was in Mexico before. And you're from America. Identical! High five. Yes, this tequila was brewed in Ireland. Cork: The home of tequila! Good work buddy!!!

In fairness, good old laugh. Better than them all hating the Irish. Did leave the Piano Bar a tad drunk. Tatiana seemed to be enjoying herself. Or at least enjoying me and my gem ways. Took me around to a couple more of her local haunts. Dark, rocker bars in Hollywood. Everyone tattooed up. Pierced down. Extreme style. Kind of not my style. But I was accepted. Once they realised I was an Irish gem, of course.

Only on our pub crawl did I properly get some conversation from Tatiana. Found out she was a Suicide Girl. Which is kind of like a Playboy Bunny. Just with tattoos and funky hair. I think. Not too sure. Made sense at the time. Also made sense seeing as she was covered with tattoos herself. And. Seemed to be wearing soccer socks. And. A T-shirt. That's it. No wonder she didn't like my style! Still can't figure out whose is better or worse.

Anyway, bars shut. Good hoot of a night. Tatiana only had the one booze. Driving. Asks if she can drop me home? (And save me money getting a cab? Of course!) Scuttling along in her big, slick, red pick-up truck. Memories of The Bucket all flooding back (my former wretched, egg-white, bucket of manure, pick-up truck). Tried to explain my Bucket story. Didn't get it. Kept laughing though. So funny. For an Irishman. Cheers. Pull up outside my house. Which is when I realised once again: Oh no. Awkward end of date moment. What's the protocol again? Do we carry on boozing or which? Hang on, I'll ask her...,

"So eh, what do we do now?"

Oh right, handshake kiss. Here we go. Through the motions. Where's the passion!?! Tatiana tells me she wishes it wasn't the first date. Why so? Because she really wants to come in and spend the night. Oh right,

"So why don't you?"

"Because it's the first date. Can't do that on the first date."

But she would really like to. Really wants to. Indicated this by rubbing my ponder pipe.

"So you want to spend the night...
But you can't?
Are you not allowed?

I don't understand..."

In fairness, Tats explained it clearly,

> "I want to have sex with you tonight. But I'm not going to because it's the first date and I have my rules."

> "OK. Fair enough. Cheers for the fun night. We'll be in touch? Mighty. Good duckaduu!"

Hopped out of the car. Strolled in home. Made a cup of tea. And decided: No more dates. No more first dates at least. Actually, no more forced dates. Not because she didn't have sex with me. More because she did want to have sex with me but didn't do it because it was a first date and she has her rules. Which to me makes no sense. Throw that rule book out the window!

Ergo: Dates. Are. Done. No real spark yet again. They wanted to hear me speak. I wanted to see them dance. Once I looked past their looks, neither girl shone. If I stopped talking, not much zip would come back my way. Only requests for me to say more. Using me for my accent! Not that I'm pushed or anything. Just wanted to see what all the date fuss was about. So now I know.

And then I poured boiling water onto the counter instead of into the cup. Splashing scalding water onto my toe. Making me decide there and then: Society off. Dates off. Book on!

Chapter 9

Granny Smith

Harking back to Cork school days, I must admit I was a fan of the odd sick day now and again. (I'm also a fan of the fact I just opened with a hark, what a lark!) Who wasn't a fan of sick days in school though? One was good, two even better and if you were sick for three, might as well stay out for the full school week. Nice little holiday out with a crippling whooping cough. Come to think of it, I'm sure I missed thirteen weeks of school one year because of that cough. Maybe that's where my ability to catch up and cram like a mad woman developed. Great digression.

What I'm trying to say is that I broke my toe. Again.

Well, more that some big galoot of a Scottish man broke my toe the other day. Up playing soccer at Rob's. Not sure who this guy was. Didn't seem to like that I was Irish though.

"So you think you're a hard man, d'ya?"

As if I was trying to swoop his title. No, you plug. Didn't like that I put the ball through his legs either.

"So you're a fancy boy too, is it?!"

"Huh?"

Next time I'm through on goal, just as I shoot, Scottish Clown leads with the studs on to my foot. I shoot. I score. I whack his late arriving boot with the follow through.

"Owwwyouape!"

Straightaway I knew: Big toe. Broken. Again. Some clown!

Took it as a sign that maybe I should've been at home working. Not up gallivanting on the soccer pitch. Maybe I was just playing crap and God wanted me off the Field–of-Dreams. Not sure. I do know that my toe now looks like a baboon with a balloon. Big. Red. Swollen. Sometimes goes blue. Tremendous fun.

Now, I know what I'm meant to do. Elevate. Chill. Rest. Ice. Basically, take a few sick days for myself. Unfortunately, can't afford to do that at the moment. Dose. The procrastinator in me is gutted. Writing while lying down in bed usually leads to kipping. Naps. Lots of them. And also, I've unfortunately been booking more and more DJ sets. Jig on! (And by unfortunately I really mean thank the Jesus. Scraping by money-wise month to month is no hoot!)

For far too long I've been surviving on: Savings. Book advance. Odd few DJ sets. Selling a few mixes to weirdos in the gym. Now I call them weirdos only because they ask for my number to book me for a set in a bar or club or party and then just phone me to say,

> "Hey, you gave me your number in the gym, we should meet for drinks and dinner and discuss some work opportunities more."
>
> "Huh? Let's just discuss it now on the phone. What are you on about going for dinner?"

Clown. On the upside, these clowns are also buying my mixes for $30 a pop, so if I can sell a bunch of them a week, I'm dancing! However, I haven't been selling too many mixes as of late. So funds were wobbling slightly. Thank funk for these new DJ sets. Actually, thank funk for Chowder and Charlotte. Mighty couple. Beyond sound friends. Highly grateful for them going out of their way to hook me up big time. Seeing as they have now jokingly taken me on as their adopted son. (Although I jokingly joke back that they're more like my brother and sister. And then enquire as to how the incest is treating them?)

Myself and Chowder have decided to team up as a DJ duo for certain gigs. Eurotrash, as we're now called. Chowder knows a few folk who DJ and promote in some cool Hollywood clubs so the networking has been on and the gigs have been trickling in. Another DJ duo in particular - The E.C Twins - have been helping us out a lot. Booking us to play for a couple of hours before them. Money isn't the greatest but at least the venues are slick and as a wise clown once said: Better than a kick in the balls. Plus, we get to play house music so we're dancing!

Played a cool club last Saturday night, The Purple Lounge. Famous enough place in the Standard Hotel on the Sunset Strip. Club featured in "Sex and the City" and "Entourage" to name but a two. Very purple. Dizzyingly so. Purple walls. Purple bars. Purple couches. Purple lights. Thankfully, I am a big fan of purple. Go on the Purple Rain!

And I know, I know: A club is a club. They have them in Ireland too. Four walls and a sound system. However, DJing your first Hollywood club is pre-tty cool, if I do ape so myself. Nice boost for the ego. Bouncer tries to stop you going in. Promoter waves you through,

> "It's cool: He's the DJ."

Girls' ears in the queue prick up. Oh the wild haired guy and his smarter looking friend suddenly look interesting to ye now, is it ladies?! Even better, we rocked the Purple Rain! Clientele of posing guys and good-looking ladies were dancing. Up on the tables. Along the couches. Down by the bar. Place was going mental. Revved them up nicely for the two twins Marc and Allister to take them home. Hollywood circuit all the way.

Finished up our set. And then things went a tad... Hollywood? Waves of hype washing over us. Buckets of spoof dunked on our heads by all sorts,

> "You guys are amazing!
> ICANTBELIEVEIWASHERETOSEEYOUPERFORM!!!"

> "Ehh, pardon?"

Kind of odd. But I had a few drinks so I obviously nodded along in agreement and embraced their adulation. Next minute people are buying rounds and rounds of drinks. Taking photos. Posing. Smiling. Shot-ing. This is kind of a surreal buzz. Seems like they want to believe we're superstars more than we do. Leave them off. Be rude to burst their bubble and let them know it was our first time playing here. Reality off. Sur-reality on.

"Girls, ye want another photo?! Cheeeeese!!!"

One thing of note I realised after the set: Apparently a lot of girls have always wanted to be a DJ. Life ambition. If only they had someone to show them how...,

"Oh my Gawd can you teach me?"

Hmmm. Let me mull it over, you attractive lady. Here, why don't you stick your number in my phone. Oh and your friend who looks exactly like you wants to learn too? Mighty! Few lessons penciled in. All about passing on whatever knowledge one may or may not even have. Obviously. All that. Cough. Teach on.

So those gigs are a good old hoot. However, Charlotte has been hooking me up with far better ones: Fashion gigs. Never even thought of them. Thankfully, Wing Woman works with Ted Baker, an English fashion label. (I predict one day she will run the whole show at Ted Baker. Ye heard it first!) Big enough in the US. Stores all over the country. One close-by in Beverly Hills. Downtown L.A. And also in Newport Beach, Orange County.

So we're out one night in Barney's and Wing Woman casually asks me if I would be interested in DJing any of her fashion parties. Apparently they're big events. Magazines. Celebrities. Paparazzi. Usually they might get a well-known DJ to play at them but she can get me in if I'd be interested? Eh, yeah. Please. Jesus. Some dancer. Loyalty to her adopted Irish son! Which is why no matter how much she might abuse a barman for not pouring her a strong enough drink, I will always back her up. Then apologise and tip kindly on her behalf when she eventually leaves the poor man alone. Anyway first gig I got hooked up with was in Newport Beach. Costa Mesa, to be exact. Classy. Expensive. American. Blondes, beaches and fake boobs. Along with rich husbands to boot. Also discovered it was home to an abundance of cougars. Lots of older women on the prowl. How bad hammer, as a man might say!

Turns out the event was a big production. On in a mall voted the best in America. (By the looks of it, the mall with the best talent. And by the by, aren't malls just the essence of America. Big. Commercial. Smell like candy floss.) Party was sponsored by 944, a popular magazine in L.A. Sapphire Gin sponsoring the free booze. Waiters carrying around fancy food.

Basketball players showed up.
Some models.
Reality TV stars.
All those kind of celebrities.
Along with me. Over by the entrance.
Getting the whole place dancing. Quite a fun night. Success all round.

Next day Charlotte phones me up,

> "The manager of Porsche was here last night. Loved the music. Wants to book you all this weekend if you're available? They pay really well too. I bumped up your rates when they asked. You'll make a bomb."
>
> "Ehh. Yes please and thank you. Chalk me down! And don't worry Wing Woman, I shall be hooking you up with your fifteen percent! I swear. Wingaduu!"

So that's where I was all this weekend. Me and my baboon toe. Two days. Five hours a day. Long enough. But well worth it. Filling up the rent jar nicely. All from just one weekend! Fashion gigs are the way to go. Also gave me time to realize that Costa Mesa is a strange enough place. Throw in a crutch and an accent, and it gets even stranger.

Flocks of Freddie Cougars out on the hunt.

All sharing a similar facial expression. Not vacant. Or expressionless. Just one constant intense look. Joan Rivers everywhere. Face peeled back behind their ears. Eyes fully opened to the max. As if they were screaming silently at you. Scream on!

Walking through the mall looking for a restaurant. Well, more hop-along with the crutch. Concerned women stopped me along the way. Late 30's, probably older, but looked younger. After Howler my radar for guessing ages has improved. Plastic on. Asked me what happened. Could she help? No, I'm OK, thanks though. Is that an accent? Yeah, I'm Irish. Eyes light up.

> "Well in case you ever need help or anything at all, here's my number. Be sure to call. Anytime."

OK. Thanks for the card. Be rude not to take your number. I'll be in touch, Freddie! Found a restaurant. Queuing up. Thinking to myself. Jesus, America's a great place, isn't it? I'm a fan of this Newport place. That was a ballsy move in fairness to that lady too. Fan of her direct approach. Although should it be called a "boobsy move" for a girl? And then two older ladies walking by stopped when they saw my crutches. Again. What happened? Am I OK? One with her hand in mine. The other pursing her lips at me. Asked where I was from?

> "Oh I've been to Ireland. I lived in Switzerland for a while."

> "No way, odd that you mention it but so have I! Well, on the Swiss/German border."

So then we spoke about Switzerland for a minute. She then asks,

> "Do you play the banjo? Have we met before?"

Em, what now? Banjo? Starts rambling in Swiss German to me. Didn't get what she said. Looking at me with crazy eyes. Had me a bit freaked. Bizarre enough. Looked around to see if it was a wind-up. Realised I wasn't the person she met before.

> "But maybe we should get to know each other more. I'd love to meet again."

Wrote her number on a napkin and told me in German to call her sometime. Leaned in to tell me something else... Oh no - She's actually kissing me on the cheek goodbye. OK so. See you later. That was odd. Particularly as I'm guessing she was at least in her mid-fifties? And that's me being kind. At least that was the end of the oddness. Well, until I finished eating. Sipping on a coffee. Sitting in a booth. Back against the wall. Facing outwards. Foot kind of raised up on the edge of the seat. Old woman walks by. If she were an apple, she'd be a Granny Smith. Short grey hair. Wise eyes. Nice tan, in fairness. Sees the crutch. Throws me a look. I catch her eye. Quickly try to throw it away. Too late. Cracks me a smile. Ahh, at least she has teeth. God bless her tooth-full mouth. Try to bury my face in an empty soup-bowl. No joy. Dose. Stops,

> "So what happened to you then?"

Turns out Mrs. Smith is a physical therapist. Or used to be one. Before she retired. Perhaps she could help me though? Before I can say hubbulla, her hand is on my foot. Massaging. Rubbing. Asking if she could massage my toe better perhaps. She has oil at home. Very good with her hands. Did I like massages? Hmmm. Since when can you massage a broken toe better? And this is weird. Her rubbing me. Looking at me sexually. Am I being paranoid? Is she *tickling* my foot now? Ha-ha-ha. Yeah. Oh Jesus. Thankfully Charlotte had come looking for me to see if I was ready to go home. Swooped me and my crutch up, up and away from Mrs. Smith. Saved by the Wingaduu!

All in all ‘tas been a fun couple of weeks. Baboons. Cougars. And. Grannies. Hopefully I'll get booked for more gigs down in the O.C soon. Purely for work purposes. Obviously. Especially seeing as after all those gigs and my gibber, not one lesson was given. Tut. I blame the toe. Hindering this dancing clown!

Chapter 10

Buck On!

My publishers are vague to say the least. Vague contract. Vague when they pay me money. Vague deadlines. Just told me to write away. Send on the first draft. Around January, or February, or March. OK?

Good to have freedom, I suppose. Although when it comes to work, I like to have a deadline. Nay, I *need* to have a deadline. Otherwise I'll just spend my days procrastinating, adventuring and tweaking away. Kind of like how I've studied for exams all my life. In college we used to get a month off in April purely for study before the end of year exams in May. Full month!

Which I, like many others I assume, spent fanning about. Swanning between staying at home for the day and going up to the library in college. Dropping your bag off at a desk. Then just hanging around outside. Sitting on a wall. Mingling with friends. Chatting to strangers. Boozing on. Until the final week. When the monkeys hit the fan. And you realize,

"OHDEARJESUSIMFUNKED!!!"

But then you just study like a whurse. Through the night. All the next day. So on for the entire week. Cramming in every single morsel of information possible. Cover all angles. Show up at the exam. Bleary eyed. Bushy head. Regurgitate. Reinvent. Stumble out the words. And... You're dancing! Majority of the time anyway. Always one German teacher with a personal vendetta on her mind. Anyway, that is why I am a fan of deadlines. I think it was the great Jack White who said:

> *"Deadlines and things make you creative. Force yourself into it."*

Something along those lines. Couldn't agree more. Having "*all the time in the world, all the money in the world, all the colors in the palette, anything you want*" just make me ramble too far off track. My vague deadline is still a month or two or three away, so at the moment I'm more easing in. Doing my research. Reading books. Googling. Buying pens and paper and notebooks and notepads. Those kind of productive things. Just that so if and when anyone asks how the book is going, I can say,

> "Oh she's coming along nicely now, you know yourself, tipping away, ploughing through, shaping up quite well!"

Another thing I've been doing the past week: Dodging nutters. Well, one nutter in particular. Brittany. Hot. Blonde. Big. Boob. Small. Ass. Tick, tick, tick! And maybe slightly, em... Thick. Ah no, only joking. Cough. Met her one night after DJing in the Purple Lounge. Told myself and Chowder how she loves us both. We were her favourite set of twins. Huh? Oh right. You think we're the E.C. Twins? In her defense, we covered for them for the whole night so they weren't there. In her dumbness, they are identical twins whereas Chowder and I look very non-identical. Unlucky for Chowder, I hear you say. I know. He knows. Awful.

Anyway after the gig Chowder went home with Charlotte while I stayed on boozing with the bar manager and Brittany. All kinds of concoctions being formulated. Bar folk like to just try things out on me. "It's great, just drink it!" One in particular struck a chord: Vodka pickle. Shot of vodka. Chased with a slice of pickle. Sounds horrendous. But oddly works. Really well. Apparently it's a Russian drink. Go on the Ruskis! Besides tasting quite good, it also does the job really well. Four or five of them at the end of the night and I was pre-tty goosed. Brittany wasn't drinking, so offered me a ride home...

> "You want to give me a ride? Ride on!"

Outside to the valet. Brittany's slick Mercedes convertible pulls up. How bad?! In we get. And then it all gets a bit blurry. Fresh air and my mind don't mix too well after vodka. I remember we went back to Brittany's apartment. High up in a place called Shoreham Towers. Savage spot. Expensive as funk too. Unreal view of L.A.

Sea of lights all the way to downtown. I remember standing out on the balcony thinking (or else shouting),

"What do you do Brittany? How do you afford all this?!"

"My Daddy's rich. I'm going to be a fashion designer and a spokeswoman."

Oh right. Well done Daddy. I think you should be more of a looks-woman too. Brittany then started showing me photos of her in various magazines. FHM. Maxim. Maybe Playboy too? Seems she modeled as well. Or else just sent in photos of herself? Not sure. Could've been showing me gardening tool magazines for all I knew. Booze flowing through me. Too busy dancing around to some 80's music I had put on.

I remember Brittany trying to sober dance with me. Awkward enough. Then I remember her unclipping something on her shoulder. Her dress slid off to the ground.

They are HUGE and look very fake, almost too fake, was my first odd impression. I then remember thinking she's hot but kind of ridiculous looking too, in a good way I suppose, if that makes sense. As if she ordered her body out of a cartoon catalogue. But a sight which we should all see at least once in our lives. You just don't get that kind of thing in Ireland! And then the drink started pumping through me again. Thought off. Dance on. Over I go,

"My turn to give you a ride now Brittany! Hey hup!"

Got a bit dodge at one point. I slipped. Lucky we didn't end up going over the railing. Twenty floor drop would've been sore I'd say. At least she had safety bags to fall on. I would've been a goner. Although not a shabby way to go out, to be true! I do have a weird flashback that I'm not too sure of. I think Brittany dispersed a lot of knowledge. If you know what I mean? Let me try to explain in a civil manner... Remember those toys before, Super Soakers? Do Americans have those toys? Water guns. Squirted out a lot of water. I think Brittany was like one of those toys. Never seen such an amount come... out. Or felt the likes before. Like a thunderbolt of water shooting out of her. Thought she was taking the... Well you know. Besides a damp sleep, all good. Except when she told me,

"I love you."

“Eh, what?”

She did then laugh as well though. But still. That was odd. Next twenty-four hours I was peppered. Sprayed. Bombarded. Texts. Phone calls. Non-stop:

‘BRITTANY: I love you.’
‘BRITTANY: What are you up to?’
‘BRITTANY: Miss me?’
‘BRITTANY: I miss you.’
‘BRITTANY: Call me!’
‘BRITTANY: Where are you?’
‘BRITTANY: Can I come over?’
‘BRITTANY: I’m coming over!’
‘BRITTANY: Do you love me too?’
‘BRITTANY: Joking.’
‘BRITTANY: Miss you.’
‘BRITTANY: I don’t even *like* you!’
‘BRITTANY: I’m not usually like this.’
‘BRITTANY: WHERE ARE YOU!?!’

At first I laughed along with her. Texted back a few hardy hars:

‘ME: Good one.’
‘ME: You’re funny.’

To which she might reply:

‘BRITTANY: Do you love me too?’

Oh sweet Jesus stop, please. Asked her if she remembered I told her at the Purple Lounge how I wasn’t looking to go out with someone? She did? Oh, you don’t want to either? You were only joking all along? Great. Chill out so! And then I didn’t hear anything for the rest of the day. Nor the day after. So that was good. Thursday night I’m at home, writing away. Managed to get two chapters done and dumb. Happy days. As if on cue, I get a text from:

‘CHOWDER: Up for a pint in Barney’s?’

‘ME: Long day at work. You know what, I’ll come down all right. I’ll only have a water though. Sober on. See you in ten!’

Off to Barney’s I go. En route a text comes from:

'CHOWDER: Sorry mate, Charlotte just called over.
We're going to chill here instead.'

Tut. Dose. Hmmm. Might as well go home. Swivel around. Phone vibrates again:

'BRITTANY: Are you out? I'm going to Barney's,
don't you live near there? Come see me!'

Scratch of the head. Quick mull. Head calculates. Shouldn't really. She seems like a nut. No banter either. I'll leave it off- My wandering pondering pipes tell me to shut up. She's hot. Points me in the direction of Barney's. Fair enough, I'll pop in for a minute! Stroll in. Head for the bar. See Brittany jump up. By Hollywood's standards, Brittany is hot. By Barney's standards, she's un-real. Especially on a quiet night. Brittany's kitted out in tight jeans and a leather jacket. Boobs spilling out of her top. Guys at the bar are giving me dirty looks as she runs to greet me. My bad lads, tough life being Irish. Tip o' the! Sensible head gives my ponder pipe a high-five. Good work. Straightaway Brittany orders me a pitcher of Bud Light and a shot of whiskey.

"Ah no, I wasn't going to booze, just on the water."

Gives me a startled look.

"But you're Irish!"

Good point. Especially if it's on you. Cheers! While I'm pouring a pint, Brittany starts to grill me,

"Why haven't you asked me out?"
"Why aren't you obsessed with me?"
"Why aren't you in love with me?"
"Look at me!"
"I'm amazing!!!"
"You need a haircut."
"Why are you acting like this?!"

Presume she's joking, so I just nod along. Drink on.

"Sorry, Brit, I just don't."
"Calm down."
"I hope we can still be friends?"

Brittany's eyes dilate. Oh Lord. Is that fury? Nutter on my hands? Tells me,

> "Drink the shot and stop being such a pussy."

> "Well OK so, you didn't have to call me a pussy, I was going to drink it anyway."

Chug. Brittany calls for another. Barman starts to chat her up while she orders. I look around the bar to see if I know anyone. Recognise the guy sitting next to me. Craig Robinson.

> "Hey boss, big fan of *The Office*! How's it going?"

Looks at Brittany next to me. Smiles,

> "Not too bad my man, how about yourself?"

I look at my pitcher and shot,

> "Not too bad at all I suppose, could be worse. Although could be slightly better. She is a nutter."

Craig asks me what I do. Start rambling on. Told him my plan: Blog – Book – Sitcom – Movie. Asked about my book. Likes the sound of it. Wants to get an early copy. No worries boss.

> "Make sure you write me a good role in the sitcom too!"

> "Will do!"

Craig enquires,

> "What's up with the girl?"

> "Not too sure."

As I turn back around I hear her asking the barman how much he can bench,

> "More than him?"

Realise she's pointing to me. Ha. She certainly knows how to make me jealous. Looks over. Sees I'm not bothered. Seems to make her irate,

"Are you gay?"

"Ha.
No."

"Well then why aren't you all over me?!"

"Well, Brit, I have things on my mind."

"You should be all over me! What's wrong with you?"

"Honestly?
You seem to be a bit of a nutter.
Really hot but still, a tad nutter-ish.
All that love stuff is just weird.
I did tell you I didn't want a relationship."

"Well I don't either."

Awkward silence.

"OK so I think I'm going to go home. I've work to do.
Might get another chapter in."

Shocked look on Brittany's face. Thought I was going to get a slap. Instead, Brittany hands me a shot. Big thick dumb shot of whiskey,

"Just drink up Irish man!"

"Ha. One more and I'm gone so."

"I'm coming with."

"You're which now?"

"Take me home with you...
Now!"

"Pardon?"

"We're leaving. I'm coming back to yours. I want to see where you live."

Whiskey wakes up my ponder pipe.

"OK..."

"But I'm not having sex with you. Just know that."

Oh yeah. I know what that means. Ponder pipe is now jigging. Let's go dancing! Bid Craig a good duckaduu. Out the door we go. Get to my place. Ask Brittany if she wants a drink of anything? Come back from the kitchen and see her on my couch. Top off. Points with both index fingers,

"Don't you like my glorious boobs?"

Yeah, they're nice enough, bit too fake looking though... Ponder pipe tells me to shut up.

"I do. Duu."

"Well then rub them for me."

"OK so...
Ugh.
Actually.
Give me two minutes. I'm *bursting* for the bathroom!"

My bladder likes to intervene at certain times. Scuttle off to the bathroom. Off-load. Wash my hands. Knock on the door.

"Let me in!"

"Jesus, calm down, you'll wake up my roommate. Here, come in. shhh."

"What's wrong with you?! Are you gay?"

"Ha, no, I was bursting for the bathroom."

"Shut up and fuck me."

"Pardon?"

"Shut up and fuck me."

Off come her jeans. Now just in a tiny black thong. Bent over my sink. Emm... Rightio. Here we go. Ahem in. Ahem on! No vodka and pickle in me this time so I was more aware of what was going on. Brittany was an enthusiastic girl. Liked to moan. Like to scream. Liked to say,

"Spank me."

Quite a performer. All fake but a good performance none the less. At one stage she was giving it too much though. Kicked my wall somehow. Broke the hand-towel rack. You clown,

"Hang on, I need to fix that."

Go on the OCD. Brittany didn't hear me. Turned back around and bent over the sink again. I was a few feet away fixing the rack. Spat out,

"Smack my ass!"

"OK..."

Smacking with one hand. Fiddling with the rack with the other.

"Oh my God you feel so amazing. This is the best sex of my life! You are amazing. Feels so good!"

But I'm two feet away from you. We're not actually doing anything right now. For lack of a better phrase, I'm not in it to win it! How do I feel amazing inside you? So,

"Oh yeah? Right now. Tell me how good it feels. Really good, right?"

SMACK!

"So deep! So good. I'm going to cu---- OHMYGAWWWWD!!!"

All the while I'm standing about two feet away. Backing off to see how far I can go. Still throwing in the odd smack. As I said, fake but a good performer. Oscar nominee all the way. Finished up. Moved on. Knowing she was a spoof in the boudoir was a bit off putting, to be honest. I lie to myself enough, I don't need you to do it too. Although better than lying there like a dead fish, to be true. She did also say this while we were at it,

"You have a lovely- ...Ahem."

"Why thank you."

"Oh my Gawd.
I love it!"

"Cheers."

"I love you so much, Daddy."

"Sweet Jesus above.
Ehh.
Thanks."

Kind of had me a bit freaked. Such weird genuineness too. Had me looking for escape routes. Only the second time we've met. And you just broke my towel rack? I don't think I could ever reciprocate your love after you did that! Moved on to the bedroom. Fun was had. Although at one point mid-stream I did get a flash of brilliance,

"That's it! The tagline of my book! Hang on Brittany, could you get off a second me please. Need to write something down. Give me a minute."

So that went down well. Perhaps I have the Nutter label on the wrong person. Woke up the next day to a wailing in my ear. Brittany's iPhone screaming at me. No sign of Brittany. Heard a call from the bathroom,

"Is that my cell? Who is it?!"

"Eh, let me see."

MOM: flashing on the screen.

"It's your Mom!"

"OK. Don't answer, I'll phone her back!"

No worries. About to put the phone back on the pillow when I realised something. Wait. The photo that's flashing with the name MOM. Ehh. I know that photo. Looked again. Oh sweet funking Jesus. My brain wakes up with a shrill: THAT'S YOUR MUM?! I

KNOW YOUR MUM!!! My eyes scream into the pillow. Phone still ringing. Double checked. Yeah. Jesus Christ. Say nothing. Here comes Brittany,

> "Ha-ha. Good shower?"

Say nothing about her Mum.

> "You have a casting? Oh yeah, no worries. Do what you have to do."

Say nothing about her Mum.
My mouth blurts out,

> "You better hurry. You'll be late."

Say nothing I said! Don't let her know that you know her Mum and have her saved in your phone as "Howler". Don't let it out that her Mum gave you a...,

> "Ha-ha. Great night all right Brittany. Don't worry about the towel rack either I'll sort it out!"

> "Bye Irish man. Love you! Ha hee ha haa. And if you don't love me back, I'll kill you!
> Joking.
> Hah haaeeha. Bye!"

Locked my door when she left. Deleted Howler's number. Oh God. This is not good. I know she kept saying everything as a joke. But with the look in her eyes and the fact I don't think guys tell her the truth too often. Not really up to date with reality. And now she knows where I live. As does her Mum?! Funk me pink. This is odd. Actually speaking of odd there was no super soaker this time around. Hmmm. Strange? Shhh. No time to worry about that. I think I need to go hide. You know, what with these deadlines and all...

Chapter 11

Halfway House

Cheques: Received. Money: Lodged. Rent: Paid. Monkeys: Sorted.

For now, at least. Wuu! On the downside, I'm not too sure when I'll be working again. Open calendar for the next two weeks. Absolutely zero income shall be coming my way. Which is, eh, mighty. You know, for book writing purposes and all. Time to get the head down. Book written. Plough on with whatever it is I have planned after that.

All of which is why I've decided to come up to San Francisco for a week or so. Take heed of Rob's advice: Go somewhere quieter to work. Get the book done. At least the majority of it. Come back to L.A in a far more settled state of mind. Also better to go now before I get inundated with offers of stand-up gigs, DJ gigs and TV shows to act on. Along with the odd movie role of course. You know: Work, work, work! Plus, I did want a bit of distance between myself and the Nutter. Her friendly threats to castrate, maim and mutilate me if I didn't proclaim my love for her soon were getting a bit too squeamish for my liking.

Perhaps this should've been my very first port of call when I flew back to America from Ireland. If Cork was like my stint in rehab (quiet, peaceful, chilled, not too much going on), it's safe to say L.A is the complete opposite. Going straight back was like jumping in at the deep end. Two feet. Head first. All that, at the same time. Swimming in a sea of temptation. Battered by the randumbness of it all. Too high. Too fast. Too soon?

Cheap flights. Dancing. Good to go. Friday morning. Arrive up.

Intent on keeping my head down. No booze. Write on. Staying in my cousin Colin's house. The house which Colin and his wonderful wife Ursula leave every day to go to work. Meaning quiet abode all to myself. I'll get *buckets* done. This book will be finished in no time!

Actually, turns out Colin has the day off work. Swoops me up from the airport. Mighty. Save those pennies on cabs and trains. Driving back to his place, he casually asks if I want to go watch a soccer match? Ehh. Yeah. Sure thing. I am your guest. You did just pick me up. Be rude to say no. But I'm *not* boozing. Seriously. No! Where are we going to watch it?

Five minutes later we're strolling into his local pub. Oh Jesus. All his buddies in there. Spot my other cousin Kevin. About to give him a howdy and a high five when their buddy Brian grabs me,

> "Hey! What are you doing up here? Great to see ya!
> Drink this you feck!"

Thrusts a Bud Light into my hand,

> "Ah no, I'm all right, I actually wasn't going to go..."

I could tell by Brian's face there was no point going on. Cue their closer, Niall,

> "Here's another one to keep your left hand occupied.
> Now. Pipe down. Drink up."

My "No Boozing" stance lasted all of two minutes. What time is it? Not even noon and I'm double fisting already?! Tut. Weak, weak, *weak* man! Felt my spine give way. Rubber elbows twist around. Cold beers wink at me. Flock of happy Tipperary faces smiling. Hurry and start drinking, kind of smile. Ughatha-yay! All right... I'm in! Gulp.

This would be the start of a lengthy all day session. Also the start of me lying to myself: Work starts Monday, OK? You can take this weekend off and go out with your buddies but come Monday, no more. Deal? OK. Deal!

See the thing is my cousins and all their friends are sound out. As in *ridiculously* sound. All delighted I was back in America. Delighted that I got a book deal. Delighted I had come up for a visit. All delightfully buying me booze. Not even accepting ones in return. Perhaps they knew of my struggling artist ways. Or else they're just living up to their ridiculously sound statuses. Either way, the booze was flowing.

Mighty banter with their group. Far different small talk compared to L.A as well: GAA (Gaelic football for any Americanos on board, which is like soccer but you can use your hands). Hurling. Odd splatter of soccer. And... How are the women treating ya? Well, mostly different. Feels like I'm back in Ireland. Dark old Irish pub, Nelly's. Irish chéile music playing. Tin whistles and fiddles tooting over the airwaves. Some depressed old men in the corner but for the most the place is tipping along nicely. Move on to the Blackthorn up the street. Again. Irish. Dark. Chéile. Good hoot.

Day goes. Night falls. I start to get itchy dancing feet. Whereas most of these lads like to stay in the same pub and just booze on, I prefer a bit of a wander. An adventure. Head out and about. Meet new folk. End up in weird places. Unfortunately no one else is feeling as adventurous. Most are settled down. Girlfriends. Wives. Lovers. Me. Be. Single. Plus, I am nicely tipped up on booze, so my feet are going dancing somewhere no matter what. Right when I feel the group winding down and talking of going home, I'm fully going. Send out the group text to people I know in San Fran:

> 'ME: How's it going? I'm up in San Fran! Out tonight?'

Mostly replies of:

> 'RANDUMBER: Who's this?'

Couple of folk too far away. Tut. Hmm. Hang on... Ding! One dancer replies. Nikki. Small. Half Portuguese. Half Asian. Not sure which half is which. Big lips. Funky clothes. Hot sex hair.

> 'NIKKI: Already out downtown. Come meet me!'

Indeed I shall. Turn to the crowd in the pub,

> "Lads: I'm going downtown. Good duckaduu!"

Flag down a cab outside. Make a new buddy en route. Rick. Big beast. Swallowing up the driver's seat. Long hippy hair. Wearing a cowboy hat. Sound man. Although he did tell the most pointless stories ever. Rambling. Far worse than any of my rambles ever. Like the time he was going to Woodstock but never ended up going. As he was going to go hike through a desert instead. Or that time he and his buddy went to Ireland. But it was really just a cliff in California. And now he doesn't talk to that buddy anymore.

"Oh yeah, why's that?"

No reply. On to a new tale. Pausing for chunks of dead air just before he made his point. But never making a point. Catching me out when I was meant to laugh. Or not. Not too sure. I think he was just doing it all so he could take me on an extra loop or two. Drive that fare up, Rick! Jump out at Union Square. Night chill in the air. Big fan of the way San Fran feels like a proper city. As opposed to a smoggy sprawl. My rambling thoughts are interrupted by a car honking.

"Hey hup, Nikki?"

"Jump in."

Few seconds of awkwardness. Until she realizes I'm drunk. She needs to join me. Her friends are at a bar nearby,

"Want to come?"

"Oh but of course..."

Drives to a nearby parking lot. Pulls out a flask. Takes a swig. Hands it to me. Swig. Mank. Straight vodka. While I'm grimacing, she asks how I've been,

"How is your er, ha-ha... Cock-a-doodle-duu?"

Ha. Now I remember why I'm such a fan! Asks to see it. Thirty seconds later my chair is reclined and I'm in heaven. Staring at the ceiling. Notice a weird coffee stain. And she's back up for air,

"What time is it?"

"I don't know. Early. Plenty of time."

Checks her phone,

"We'll have to finish it later."

Tut. Dose. But. Fair enough. Go into a slick looking bar. Really classy. Surprisingly cool. Looked dead outside. Packed dance floor. Quieter by the bar. Big group of her friends at a table. Quick hellos. How's it going? They either instantly dislike me. Or. Can't understand my accent. Probably both.

"Anyone want a drink?"

Thankfully they all say no/ignore me. Thank funk. Big round. Bullet. Dodged.

Now usually the Irish accent is not that big of a hit up in San Fran. Maybe one of the reasons I prefer L.A. However, I got lucky with the bar lady who served me,

"I like your accent."

"Why thank you."

"Do you do shots?"

"I do."

"What do you want?"

"Anything but tequila. That funks me up."

"Sure thing."

Slides me over a big chunky tequila. Sweet Lord. You listened well. Three more quickly followed. Dumb all round. Bar lady started looking hotter. Flirting flowing. Must've been the lighting. As I'm declining any more shots, the guy next to me asks where I'm from. Ah to true.

"That's so awesome. I just flew back from England."

That's even more awesome.

"You do know they're different countries?"

He didn't care. Only cared we had a shot. OK cool, anything but... Salt. Tequila. Lemon. Although by now I was loving this fine Mexican spirit. Olé! High fives! And then I realized I might just be a tad bit goosed. Back over to Nikki and her friendly buddies.

Quickly realised Nikki was being less amicable to me in front of the group. Or else I was just drunk and imagining this to be the case. Felt the tequila was taken over me. Oh no. Speaking. Slurring. No one understands any of my self-proclaimed witty openers,

> "Here's a good one so... What does a gay hor... Actually... Here's a better one... What do you call a man with no sh... Ah shur, doesn't matter, you don't even underschtand meh do youu?"

Am I drunk? Or is it the accent? Drunk? Accent? Ashcent? Druuuunk aschcent? Drunk. Survival mode kicked in. Must. Go. Home,

> "Nikki, I must bounce."

Goosed. Thumbs up to the lads. And with that I was off. She was not happy. But I was too drunk to really notice. Survival mode! Out the door. Arm in the air. Taxis whizzing by. One screeches to a halt. Jump in. See a mane of hippy hair. I know that cowboy hat...,

> "Rick! No way!! I never thought I'd see you again. Ha ha ha. I missed you man. I swear. Seriously. Now. No. I swear. Ha. Take me home please Srick, shake meee shoome."

Rick took off. Flopped my head back on the seat. Closed my spinning eyes. And things went a bit hazy. Woke up in my socks. Jacket still on. Never good signs. Judging by how I woke up it appears I fell into bed. As in I'm assuming I fell and was lucky the bed was there to catch me. Did the check. Passport: Check. Wallet: Check. Phone: Blank. No... Noooo!!! Funk balls. Some ape. I need my phone. Why did I go downtown? Where's my phone? Come on flashbacks, hook me up... I remember texting Nikki in the cab. Cab pulled up outside Colin's. Still trying to type the text. Took out my wallet to pay. Put the phone down on my knee- No, on the seat. Got out of the cab. Closed the door. Saw my phone. Tried to open the door. Locked. Huh? Rick. RICK! Before I knew it Rick was gone. Drove away. With me chasing him up the street,

> "Stop Rick... Shop Shrick... RICK... YOU PRICK!!!"

Chapter 12

Some Mug

Hmmm. It's four in the morning. I'm in a recording booth. In a music studio. Drinking Guinness. Thinking up lyrics. Singing a song. Well, rapping, to be precise. This is odd. Oh, hang on. I can hear someone talking into the headphones...,

> "Let's go again."
>
> "OK. Could you slowdown that loop though? No, another notch... There we go. OK, let's do this. And a one, a two, a three and a duu..."

...

> "Yo yo hello, it's me, the lyrical master, don't you worry, oh no, I just started, we can go even faster... *A duuy duu.*"

Not too sure how I ended up here. Well, I'd say it's down to me not being able to say no. And I was guilt tripped. Super combination really.

So here's a thing I don't really like about coming to San Fran: I know lots of folk who live here and also a good few who live near enough to San Fran, as in an hour or two outside the city. So when I mention that I'm in town for a visit, I get asked to come visit these other buddies. Some are too far away so I can get away with dodging them. Others guilt trip me,

> "What do you mean you're not going to call out and

say hi? I let you stay in my house rent-free for two months. Do you not remember that?"

Yes indeed I do. Very kind of you to remind me. It's not that I don't want to see these buddies. Just that it's hassle. Already traveled up to San Fran. Now I must travel another hour or two? Mighty. And: I don't like when people make me feel obliged to do things. To be very true. Often my offers to meet these folk in the city centre somewhere are rebuked,

"Ah well you know we don't really go to the city. Too far away for us. But you just jump on a train and come out here. We'll have a night out!"

"All right. I'll come out for a night. Can't wait to catch up. Really. Can't. Wait."

Despite my phone dose the night before, I said I'd get this trip out of the way now before I culled all boozing and gallivanting. Plan was to go visit my buddy Jenny, her husband Chris and their friends out in Walnut Creek. On a good day it takes a tram and a train to get from downtown to Walnut Creek. About an hour and a half max. On a good day. Saturday was *not* a good day. Horrendous altogether. Detours all over the place. First tram broke down. Had to wait for a bus. This took us half way. Swapped to another bus. Finally got downtown. Missed the original train I was supposed to take. Next train stopped in Oakland for some reason. Meaning we had to change again. Hang around the dodgy train station there. Eventually my final carriage took me onwards.

Thankfully, I planned ahead. iPod on. Also made a quick shop stop when the first tram broke down. Bag of cans on. Both kept me tipping along. I actually like trains and trams too for the most part. Time to think. Look out the window. Check out the American scenery. Get a good "I'm in a big city now!" kind of buzz. Except when dodgy hobos stare you down for an uncomfortable length of time. But then you just crack open a can. Stare back. Say nothing. Tip on! Three hours later, I arrive in Walnut Creek. Stroll out of the station. Realise: Balls. Forgot I've no phone. There's no way Chris is still waiting to give me a lift to the bar. Mighty. Don't worry, my brilliant brain replied, I remember the name of the bar they're all going to – Redux! Good work, buddy! Off we strolled. After such a time-consuming, energy-sapping journey, Walnut Creek was under a lot of pressure to deliver a mighty night. Nice spot. Wealthy. Clean. Although a bit quiet. Hmmm. Find the club. Greet the short bouncer,

"How's it going?"

Stops me. Asks for I.D. Examines it. Tells me my passport isn't real. Not coming in. Oh mighty. Little-Man syndrome. Not a fan of Irish folk. Particularly those who wear scarves. Who could blame him really? So now stuck outside the club where everyone else was inside. Shaking my fist at the little man...,

"You prick! Do you know Rick?!

Thankfully I spot one of Jenny's buddies leaving the club,

"Marty!"

"Hey boss."

High five.

"Crap inside."

"Well then where are we going boss?"

"An Irish pub across the road!"

"Really? I've never been to one of those! Let's just go."

Order up. Look around. Dive bar. Good talent at least. Realise that they haven't had many Irish folk in their bar before. My accent is even more exotic here. Hard to use the words 'exotic' and 'Irish' in the same sentences but in these small towns around California it would appear to be true! Say the most mundane thing to any of these folk and they think it's hilarious.

"I have a cat who sits on a mat..."

"HA HAHA HA you're so funny!"

Some people get used for the looks, some for their money, and a small group of us for our accents! Unfortunately the place was also filled to the brim with American meatheads. Genetic freaks. Necks bigger than my leg. Most sporting blatant spray tans too. I imagine a lot like Jersey Shore. Kind of reminded me of the muscled up guys you'd see in West Hollywood except where they're happy and gay, these guys were angry and intense. Probably as they've yet to come out of the closet.

Few dirty looks thrown my scarf's way. So I decided to focus on two cookie-cut Britney Spears lookalikes sitting at the bar. Start telling them all about my cat on a mat... And then some guy's head is BOUNCED off the bar next to me.
Beer sprays all over my suave scarf. Tut.
Thankfully his blood splattered to the left.
Cue a scrummage of people. All jumping on. Half probably just enjoying the touch of another meathead on top of him. The rest giving it socks.

Fists FLYING.
Mass BRAWL.
Lights turned on.
Police called.
Marty and myself wisely left.

Met up with all the rest of them afterwards. Most pretty drunk. Doubt half of them remember seeing me. All in all: Tremendous night! Well worth the three hour trip.

Too late for me to get the BART train back. So went to Jenny's house and hung out with her brother Barry, who was in his home studio with his buddies working on music. All up boozing on. Asked me if I wanted to "spit some lyrics". Chalk it down, the Guinness replied,

> "Play that loop back again boss!"

Uuu'ing. Duu'ing. Butchering. Editing. Finishing up with two songs under my belt. Convinced they were great.

> "THESE COULD BE HUGE!"

Joking with Barry how funny it'd be if they were one-hit wonders. Actually believing they had the potential to be,

> "Seriously man, seriously, they're good songs. I'd buy that song. Seriously man. Seriously. I might be after a bit of drink, but seriously, that's a great song. Great hook. Seriously. Pardon? It's 6AM?"

OK. Bed on. Woke up feeling surprisingly mighty. Chat flowing out of me. Also the right amount of charm,

> "Better leave. Must get back to my cousins. They'll be worrying about me. Yeah. I swear, I'll be out again soon! Barry, spin to the BART? Mighty! Cheers boss. Let me know when you master those tracks too. I seriously think they're going to be *massive*."

Hangover finally kicked me in the bowels on the BART back. Goosed. Decided to get something to eat downtown before the final leg of the trip back to my cousin's. Quick roll in Subway. Ordered. Waited. Paid. Realised all the seats and tables were occupied. Dose. Asked a girl,

> "Would mind me sitting at the spare seat at your table?"

> "I *WOULD* mind!"

Shunned. Hmmpf. Seat wasn't taken. Just didn't want to be disturbed. Tut. Not happy with her. Perplexed where to eat my roll. Ordered it with the works. Overflowing. Messy handful of food. Standing in Subway wondering where to go. Hangover making my thoughts drift. End up outside. Strolling around the streets looking for somewhere to sit. Realise I'm in the dodgy part of downtown. Homeless people everywhere. Not the friendly-looking sort either. Mind getting distracted again. Pondering why Subway don't offer corn as part of their fillings options. You'd think they would? By now I was munching on my roll. I had also absentmindedly walked down an alley. One full of bums. Only copped on when one of them approached me. Thought he was asking me for change. Took out an iPod earphone,

> "Pardon me?"

Still didn't understand. Took out the other. Now I understood,

> "You want my food and my money? And the iPod? Hmm."

When hungover I've a really care-free state of mind. Plus, I was tired. Hungry. And I love my iPod. All of which combined to make me just shrug my shoulders, shake my head and say,

> "No."

Too tired to care what he was trying to do,

> "Just leave me enjoy my roll will you?"

I think I threw him off. So he added in more aggressively,

> "Give me your wallet now or you'll be in trouble."

Still too tired to take him seriously. Plus he was a lot smaller than me. Didn't look intimidating. All that he really had on his side was where we were – down an alley full of bums. Although he did look like a small crazy homeless guy himself.

> "Give me your change or else!"

Just felt like a poor attempt of being mugged. None of the bums had his back or seemed to care what was going on. Too busy talking gibberish to themselves. Perhaps if I was fully sober and more clear thinking I might've thought this was a dodgy situation. Presumed that he would be more aggressive if he was actually going to mug me properly, so I decided again to just decline his offer to mug me,

> "Not happening buddy. Too tired and spent a bit too much money yesterday to be mugged today. Sorry."

As I start to walk on, he yells out,

> "I have a weapon! Don't move brutha."

Shoves his hand in his pocket. Takes it back out. Thrusts it in my direction. Which is when I see he has nothing in his hand. Just shows me an empty palm. Sees he is caught. And then starts telling me,

> "You're crazy. I'm not going to hurt you. Could you give me some of your money for cigarettes, man?"

> "What's this? You're trying to be buddy-buddy with me now?"

Brutal attempt. Made me realise he was just the world's worst mugger. So I walked on. And little did he know he was actually trying to rob the world's newest and best rapper. Tut. Some mug!

Chapter 13

Clean Up on Aisle Me...

Read a good quote recently:

> *"Being happy is a habit. So is being sad. Choose one."*

Something like that. So good that I can't even remember it fully. That's the gist anyway. Got me thinking... What have I been choosing lately? Not so much between happy and sad. Who would choose to be sad? Cop on. Although then again, who would choose to be such a mess?

All over the place.
Unfocused.
Unorganised.
Forever catching up.
Scraping in the door.
Not where you want to be.
Disappointed in your performance, in yourself.
Constantly having The Fear tap you on the shoulder every Sunday night.

You know, kind of like how I've been. Maybe not on purpose. But still, subconsciously or not: It's been messy. Maybe I set the tone for myself coming through customs in LAX on my return at Halloween. Usually my replies are: "Yes sir, no sir, three bags full please-just-leave-me-into-your-fine-country-thank-you sir." However this time seeing as I had a long-term visa sorted, I was considerably more lax. Customs officer asks me,

"Here for work or holiday?"

"Ah well you know yourself, it'll probably take a few weeks to settle in so it'll be a bit of a holiday at first but then after that I'll get around to doing some work - unless the holiday is *too* unreal and no work gets done! You know?"

He did not. Looked at me oddly. Monotone reply,

"If you want me to stamp your work visa, just say you're here for work and nothing else. Otherwise, holiday only."

OhdearJesusGodAlmightyapologieswhatwasIthinking,

"Work. Thank you. Sir."

Scraped in the door. I'll know better in the future. Perhaps it's my inability to juggle has something to do with my mess like state? Multi-tasking has never been a strong suit of mine. Appears I've lead myself to believe I'm unable to write and live in L.A at the same time. Juggling work with the inability to say no to invites can be tough. Not that I'm complaining, as I've said. It's heaven. Although I imagine heaven is serene and peaceful. Maybe it's more like hell. Combination of the two. Heaven but the devil is in charge. Strange as well that I can't juggle seeing as I used to be the chairman of a juggling club. Seriously.

U.C.C Juggling Club. Well known fact, really. First year of college my buddy Colm and I decided to try out a new sport for a laugh. Surely we can chance some free pints out of it, we probably thought to ourselves. Signed up for the juggling club. Went along to the first meeting. Only five of us showed up. When it came to decide who would be in charge I ended up as chairman and Colm was the treasurer. Just like that.

Tenure lasted only for about an hour though. We all had to fill out a form with our names and addresses. Turned out that two of the guys there had no addresses. Homeless, it seemed. One French guy. One unknown nationality. Funnily enough, they were the only two people who could actually juggle. Few weeks later I saw them busking on the main street of Cork. Full hat of coins collected too, in fairness to them. I wonder if Colm was informed of their bounty? Those unknown nationalities, always the sneaky ones, to be true.

Anyway, that one meeting we had was the club's first and last. My juggling skills were doomed from the get-go.

Back to the now. Fair to say my book-writing trip to San Fran got off to a *shambolic* start. Drunken adventures. Rap songs. Mugging attempts. Lost phones. Horrendous opening two days. Amount written: Zero. Sunday night: Riddled with The Fear. Crawling all over me. At least on the Monday I decided to get myself back in order. No more being a chaotic clown. Sense on! First things first: Phone. I'll just ring the taxi company. Ask for the lost and found. Hope they have my phone. Not going to be a lengthy affair. Small molehill, that's all, no need to make a mountain out of it. Good plan. Until I realised there was no one else in my cousin's apartment. No phone at hand for me to use. No way for me to ring the cab company. By the time anyone would be back the lost and found office would be closed. Have to wait another day. Oh no. My molehill was growing already.

Actually no, funk that. Just buy a new phone. Can't waste a full day on this. Need to sort it out and settle my mind. Off to RadioShack I go. Powerwalk on!

Muttering to myself along the way. How are some people so organized? Why can't I be like that? I've yet to sort out my social security number. Or go to the DMV to get my licence. Should I hire a car? Lease? Buy? Or can I even afford that anymore?! What else is on my to-do list? I need to sort myself out. Might not get as annoyed by people who are so together then as well. Everything in its right place. Perfectly efficient. Freaking me out. Kind of like morning people. Chirpy. Productive. Constantly telling me what they get done before the hour of eight in the morning. Do they want me to give them a medal or something? I go to bed late. You get up early. Well done. Although maybe I should join their group for a while. Become one of them. Organised. Clean up my mess! Except I am a morning person too myself. My wit is at its sharpest then, oddly enough. And I'm a night owl. Daytime is really when I suffer... Around now is when a few things happened. Tried to avoid a flurry of Asian people coming towards me as I crossed the road. Attempted to step on to the footpath. Kept on powerwalking. Dumb-diddly-dumb.

CLIP the curb.
Tweak my groin.
Leg spasms.
Down I go.

Tumble.
Fall.
Flat out on the path.

Surrounded by old Asian folk. Looking down on me. Just lying there. Gazing up. Started asking me questions in Chinese. Or Cantonese. I can never tell. So I just kept lying there. Wind knocked out of me. Back to being a mess. Splashed out on the pavement. Down. Was I out? Deep sigh. Resignation. Until I was hauled to my feet by an old Asian couple. Both only up to my waist, height-wise. Giants in my book though! Patting me on the shoulder. Presumably telling me I was fine. Dusting me down. Felt my tweaked groin. Helped me clean up my messy self. Staying with me until I gave them two thumbs up. Waved goodbye as they scurried across the road. Skipped onto the path on the far side with ease and comfort. Putting me to shame. At least I realised I was leaning up against something that I forgot even existed in this world: A payphone! A telephone that I could put money into and phone the cab company and see if they had my phone and in turn hopefully save me spending more money and time on this particular mess. And guess what... They had it! Betsy. Appears Rick had dropped it in this morning. What what?! He wasn't a prick after all! Gave them my address. Waited for a driver to drop it out to me. Just have to pay the taxi fare. Happy days. Until a guy showed up in a normal car. Asked him how much was the fare?

> "Oh I never turned on the meter. I have no meter. You could buy it back for thirty dollars though."

You feck,

> "Fair enough."

Cheaper than a new one. Thanks for the extortion,

> "Tell Rick I said cheers for dropping it in too. I had him all wrong. Would you believe I thought he was a prick!?!"

The extortionist gave a laugh,

> "Ha, don't thank Rick, he tried to shop it around to the other cab drivers. Nobody wanted it though."

Basic phone really. Lucky it wasn't a smart phone or in all honesty

I wouldn't have got it back. At least he was honest in that regards. Shower of dodgy cabmen in every other possible regard though. Lesson of the day: Not having a smart phone is not so dumb after all. Dumb on Turning point to say the least. Flying ever since. Work going. Book flowing. It is true what they say: Hardest part is starting. Until you get to the next part. Not sure what that is yet. But at least I'll get there.

Also met a fellow author the other night. Friend of my cousin's who in turn happens to be friends with Dan Brown. Golfing buddies. Offered to caddy for himself and Mr. Brown the next time they played a round. Politely declined. Good at least to ask him a bucket load of questions that have been bouncing around my head. Signed a five-book deal with Random House. Telling me that they were pretty hard to deal with at times. Vague. Unresponsive. Old-fashioned. Slow... No way! So are *my* publishers! And Random House is probably the best in the world? This oddly puts my mind at far more ease. I thought it was me. Nay: It's them!

And now I must sleep. Alarm is set for six in the morn. Up early tomorrow. Go for a jog, walk the dog, read a book, answer a few emails and write four chapters. Morning bird all the way. Oh, and I've decided to get back down to L.A as well. My stint in the halfway house is over. DJ gigs are calling me home. Time to cop on.

And on another good note, the Nutter has managed to nullify herself too. Kept texting me asking what was wrong with me. Then asking if I was gay. Finally she proudly figured it out one day:

> 'NUTTER: OMG. You're married. That's why you're so weird. Is she German? Is that why you speak German? Does she live here? What's her name?!'

Kind of teed me up. Gave me the escape route. So I said:

> 'Yes. This is true. We were on a break for a while. But now we decided to give it another go. She's in the process of moving to L.A.'

So the Nutter and I could no longer be. She took it well:

> 'NUTTER: I hate her. And you. What's her name?'

> 'Gertrude... my German wife.'

No reply since. So at least that's sorted. I think. Let's hope. As I said, I'm really starting to cop on! Although. Just got an email from Chowder. Appears The Man is back in town. Wants to meet up. Have a night out. Quiet one. Hmmm. You know, I have been working hard lately in fairness. Maybe I'll go for just the one...

Chapter 14

Lobster and Basketball

Eat what I have to so I can drink what I want!

So after I graduated from my masters, I also graduated from my university soccer team. Mighty years playing for U.C.C. (also known as University College of Cork). Tip top o' the banter, to be true. Well, for the majority. No need to go into the other minor details here. Ahem. Anyway, banter at the next team I joined wasn't the greatest. So I just stopped playing soccer regularly. Ergo, my weekly exercise regime was out the window. Unfortunately, I've always felt that there's a fat man inside of me waiting to burst out. Maybe I'm wrong, but my paranoia told me there were signs. (I remember when I was younger back in Ireland, I was on TV once singing Christmas Carols as part of a school choir. I signed up purely to get out of class. Little did I realise I'd end up on a national TV show because of it. Although I have always thought I can sing too. Deluded from a young age. Anyway, on TV. Singing. Falsetto, of course. After it aired that night, my Gran turned to me and said,

> "Well done Mark, very good. Although I must say you look very fat in the face on TV. It really does add the pounds. You're not that fat, are you?"

So that was nice. Me being a Telly Tubby and all.

> "Ehh... ehhh... ehhh... It's just because I was wearing a turtleneck and it was *roasting* in the studio so my head was red and must've looked bigger than it is so that's why you think that - all an illusion!"

Just one incident that springs to mind. So. Where was I? Oh yeah. No more soccer training...) As a result, despite not being a fan, I decided I had to start gyming it up. Little did I know that this really didn't mean too much unless you became a healthy eater as well. So I decided to only eat healthy food. Or at least healthy in my eyes. Read up about it. Sussed out what was what. Switched from a breakfast, lunch and huge dinner to six meals a day. The whole shebang.

OCD kicked in. Juggled around. People gave me grief when I shed some baby fat. Usually those who themselves probably struggled to shed their own baby fat. Finally I kind of figured it out properly. And I've been a healthy nut ever since. Well. Besides ketchup. And. Booze. My two cheats, as the health nuts say.

Flagrant cheater when it comes to the odd booze or four. Whereas I'm strict *beyond* belief when it comes to food. Quite odd. Even more so considering my Mum barely drinks while my Dad has never touched a drop in his life. In fact, my Grandad's a pioneer too. I come from a long line of non-drinkers I do believe. Great little family tree side ramble here. Hi Grandad! Now. Where was I? Oh yeah... Eat healthy. *Booze on*! God only knows what kind of alcoholic concoction you'd have to give me where I'd have to say no but offer me a sandwich made with white bread and I will without fail simply smile and decline, telling you that unfortunately I'm lactose-intolerant. (For some reason people leave you be far easier if they think something's wrong with you, as opposed to,

> "Ehh, I'll be OK I'd say, thanks, I don't eat white bread. I will drink whatever liquid is in that sock over there though."

And I know, I know: Lactose-intolerant doesn't even make sense but most people don't know that. Say nothing!) Since I've been back in L.A, however, this strict totalitarian way of eating has once or twice gone out the window. Kind of. Whenever I go to ridiculously lush and top of the range restaurants, I decide to let myself loose. Sample the fine cuisine. Well, the healthiest option they have at least. Can't just ask them for a toasted chicken sandwich on wheat with some ketchup, please and thank you.

My fine dining experiences have thus far been related to The Man being in town. Fan of the high life. Worked hard to get it. Also kind enough to share that high. Quite a dancer. Back again this weekend for a few days. Just wrapped up some business in Texas.

Now time to unwind for a few days. And by unwind, I mean go live it up! So Saturday night we all went to a restaurant called "XIV". Michelin-rated chef. Celebrity hotspot. Jeans ironed. Best shirt on. Limo pulls into the car park. Porsches. Ferraris. Bentleys. Phantoms. Army of valets. Extravagant flower and bush displays. Red carpet. Lit up. All jump out. The Man and the Jackie. Charlotte and Chowder. And. The fifth wheel: Me. Adopted leprechaun all the way!

Limo drives off. Down the red carpet we jig - well, I kind of hobble along behind. (Did I tell you I did more damage to my toe? Dropped a plate on it. Kicked a wall. All in the same motion. Mighty fun.) Paparazzi outside. Pretentious inside. Mighty! In we go. 'Plush! Lush! Casual! Elegant...' were not the first batch of words to pop into my head as we strolled in. More the second batch of four words. 'Funk, she's quite hot' were the first, in reference to the hostess. To our left was the long, marble countertop bar. Chandelier dazzling overhead. Cool buzz around the place. Lighting had everyone looking well. Dim. Not too dark. Looked around. Full of well-looking people.

Place looked like you were inside the banqueting hall of a castle. Leather furniture. Couches. Tables. Bookshelves. Big huge Rembrandt-looking oil paintings on the wall. Pheasant feathers everywhere.

We're brought to our table by the hostess who looks like a Covergirl. I'm seated on a low old-fashioned Victorian style couch with a leopard skin rug thrown over my lap. As you do. To even off this fancy buzz feel, The Man orders a round for everyone. Get 'em inta Cynthia, I whisper inside my head. Observing my surroundings as I sip on the first Tanqueray and Tonic. Oh Betsy. This gin tastes savage. SMACK of the lips. Bit too loud. No one heard. Ahhh. This is the life.

Not too sure what I'm looking at when a menu is handed to me.
Hmmm...
Snapper Sashimi?
Sustainable Shrimp Scampi?
Niman Ranch Lamb Tagine?
Passion Panna Cotta?
What. The. Funk?

> "Charlotte! What in God's name are these things? Which is the closest to being a healthy chicken dish?"

Chowder's laughing at me already. Or else just drunk. Perhaps both. Tell me she'll take care of it for my order. Mighty. Order on. The Man asks me if I've ever tried caviar.

> "Nay, not yet."

Orders some for us. Recommends that the next time we do this, we do it properly.

> "Oh yeah, how's that?"

> "You order just caviar and champagne. That's it."

Sounds interesting. Like an oral adventure. Pencil me in for next time! Take a spoon of caviar when it arrives. Odd little pellets in my mouth. Not too bad though. I've only had porridge and a chicken sandwich all day too, starving. Take another spoon for myself. Chowder's laughing again.

> "What's going on? Huh? How much did that cost?!"

Someone mentions,

> "Six or seven hundred dollars usually, for the good stuff."

Jesus, no way. And I'm shoveling it down like porridge. Ha. My bad. Just one more spoon and I'm done, I swear! Waiters start arriving non-stop with all our dishes. I think I get lobster and scallops. Not sure exactly. Plates everywhere. It was savage though. Bottles of wine and champagne wash it all down nicely. While Chowder is busy entertaining Jackie and Charlotte with his Derby ways, I'm having a mighty laugh with The Man. Fellow adventurer. Kindred spirits. Instant bond. Banter flowing. Similar life outlook. Although I must say when it comes to style, The Man dresses like he's a few months ahead of the rest of us. Sharp as funk. Asked me how the book was coming along.

> "Not too bad. Juggling scraping by with writing along. Tough enough at times but all good. Look where I am now. Can't complain!"

Told me his tale of how he got into the oil business. Started with nothing. Struggled for years. Barely surviving. Eating beans and toast in a tiny cold house back in England. Kept the head down.

Worked on. Climbed the ladder. Slowly built his empire. Got the breaks. Company went global. Now reaping the rewards. Travels the world. In style. Enjoys life to the fullest. Keeps working hard. Creating it all himself from scratch, which was the most impressive thing to me. Complete dancer in my book. Drunkenly tell him there's always room on my couch if he ever needed somewhere to stay. Just in case. You never know. So that was very nice of me.

> "Oh - along with ten bottles of gin!"

I added with a wink. The Man can drink. Chowder pops his head in between us,

> "What are you two gay boys talking about? I think Pam the Driver is going to be outside in thirty minutes. Should we finish up?"

Girls order a desert. The Man orders three Avernas. (Sicilian liqueur. Delightful after-dinner digestif. Obviously. Ahem.) While my tongue is being danced on, I notice it's still early for us to have finished up,

> "How come we're done earlier than usual actually, Chowder?"
>
> "Did I not tell you mate? Ha! Wait until you see, it's wicked!"
>
> "See what?"

Averna. Down. Pay. Up. Bundle. Out. Limo. On! Half an hour later, we arrive at our destination. Downtown? Never been down here- Ohnoway! Take me out to a ball game, take me out to a show! Oh yeah, sorry, I thought that was for basketball. Staples Center. L.A Lakers. First basketball game I've been to! And what's that Chowder, we're in V.I.P? We have our own table. Where? Hyde Lounge. As in the nightclub. In the stadium? Brand new. Just opened? Unreal slick? Oh. Yes. *Betsy!*

In the gate. Through the door. Up to V.I.P. Greet the bouncers. Past the velvet rope. Push through the curtain. Step inside. And... Oh sweet Jesus. This is mighty. First thing I see: Basketball court. But it's a good bit down. We're halfway up the stands. And this is just like a nightclub. Bar to my right. Dance floor to my left. Tables all round me. Again, plush all round. Leather chairs. Leather couches. Leather walls. Blue lighting. In fairness, these places do hire good designers. Savage looking. Although all one really needs is a bit of leather with the right lighting and we're dancing! Class view of the basketball court. Great views all round really. These places also do well with hiring models only to work for them. Barbie-looking waitresses. Ken-looking barmen. Vacant looks and white smiles all round!

Hostess-Barbie brings us to our table. Right at the edge, overlooking the court. People craning a look to see who it is that got the best table in the place. I sneakily have a look around to see if I spot any celebrities myself.
Apparently Chowder was sitting next to David Beckham last time he was here. Quick scan: Hmmm. No sign of any celebrities I know of. Hoping Shaq or Michael Jordan might be here. All I see are hot women. Tut. They will have to do. Waitress-Blonde-Perfection comes over,

> "What can I start you guys off with?"

The Man replies,

> "Bottle of vodka, bottle of gin, bottle of Jack and two bottles of champagne to begin with please. We'll see how we are then..."

Seems like we arrived at halftime. Not sure who we were actually playing. (We, as in I immediately jumped on the Lakers bandwagon.) Being honest, I saw very little of the game. Too busy looking around inside the club. Stood with my back to the court for most of the time. Too many times I thought I was out clubbing, only to turn around and see someone dunk a raindrop behind me... Oh yeah, there's a game on! One thing I realised is that when you're out with The Man, people tend to assume that you yourself might also be "The Man". Little do they know I'm just a man-boy-ape-clown. If even that. An Irish gem.

However, if that's what they want to assume, assume on! Might have been a reason why so many girls seemed to be lingering nearby. On top of this, I was on a crutch. Not sure what it is but women love crutches. *Love* them. Not quite up there with being Irish but they do get an urge to take care of you. Looking at you like you're a hurt puppy. Give out an Irish bark on top: Giddy up! I knew a broken toe would serve me well somehow. All about the positives. Maybe I was just having a great time and my gibber was in full flow but I've never actually had so many good-looking women give me their number without asking for it,

"Call me sometime."

Writing down their number as they eye up the table full of booze next to me. Apparently a sign of wealth and success in America is how many bottles you order in a club. Even had Tila Tequila give me her digits. I say even as I thought she was a lesbian. Not sure what she is really. Vietnamese girl who's famous for being famous? A reality star? Talented lady. Although I obviously took the number gleefully. Wait until I tell everyone back in Ireland! *She* was cracking onto *me*!?! It feels like only yesterday when I was back in Cork wasting my life on the couch watching her on VH1. And now she's asking me for a DJ lesson?

"So can you, like, teach me how to spin?"

"Yeah, you just put your finger on your head and twirl around."

"You're fun-nee, call meee..."

This is amazing! I'm going places!!! Or else I might just be a tad drunk. Hmm. While the inner Irish boy in me was dancing around and jigging with delight by being surrounded by such beauties, the older outer me who now lives in L.A so let's pretend like we're used to this, decided to just observe a while.

Really is quite a sight to behold the textbook beauty in L.A. Almost looks like an assembly line at times. Everywhere you look there are girls with high cheekbones, skinny yet curvy bodies, big trout-pouting lips, flowing hair, perfect white teeth, permanent smiles and dead eyes. The best money can buy. Women are key to the nightlife. Make the place tick. Shipped in to make a buzz. They provide their looks. Men supply the money. Tit. For. Tat. In return they – at the very least - expect champagne in full flow. As opposed to in Ireland, where guys do buy girls a drink but if they come up and insist on one before talking to you,

"Buy me a drink now."

The typical reply is,

"Funk off. Your round first."

Then again, maybe these are all the thoughts of a now drunk me. Started playing a game of eyeing up with a girl at the table next to us. Tall. Cool. Funky hair. Looked like a model. Turns out she *was*... Winner of America's Next Top Model few years ago. Caridee,

"I like your height."

"Why thank you lady, I've been working on it for years."

"What do you do?"

"Writing a book. DJ'ing."

"You're a writer and a DJ?"

Hand touches my arm. Hey hup, bit of interest here.

"Give me your phone!"

"OK."

"You must call me. We should hang out. I like you."

Well then, that sounds like a nice plan. Almost blew my cover when I whipped out my phone to hand to her. Ha. It is quite horrendous. Like a little suitcase. Told her it was my Irish one. Ahem. Distracted her with,

"We're behind in the times over there shur you know yourself OK so I'll be in touch, ciao."

Game finished up. Curtains were shut. DJ started playing music. Turned into a full on club. We were all a tad bit goosed at this point though. Decided to head back to the SkyBar. Night cap. Blurry. Hazy. Booze. Basketballs. Savage night. Can't beat a bit of the high life! Although, it wasn't all Walt Disney. No happy ending. Tut. Home alone. And. When I checked my phone the next day, I had zero replies to my wonderful gibberish texts I sent out after the Lakers show. I'm sure they're all just slow texters. Definitely. That's it. Can't all be fun and games, I suppose. Well, sometimes it can. When The Man's in town at least. And eventually they all did reply. With the exact same text:

'RANDUMB GIRL: Who's this?'

Ha. As I said: Some man-boy-ape-clown.

Now then. Crippling cruel depressing gin hangover off. Porridge on!

Chapter 15

Wigs, Wine & Weirdos

> "Oh God. Why am I holding this man's hand?"

'Twas the night before Christmas Eve and all was...

Dead.

First Christmas away from home. Away from the family. Away from my Mum's mighty Christmas dinner. Aww. Poor little Merrick. Woe is me. All week I've been constantly asked,

> "Will you not miss going home to Ireland for it?"

> "Well, it would be preferred, but I'll just have to make do."

Making sure to add,

> "And besides... In this economy? Hm."

That part usually confuses them enough to ask no more. Besides, I'm sure Cork will miss me just as much. Only the other day did a buddy Diane tell me,

> "Oh, eh, *yeah*. Christmas just won't be the same if you're not here. Like Disneyland without Mickey Mouse, so it will."

So that was nice. Being compared to a mouse. Mighty. Anyway, last night I did the 12 Pubs of Christmas. Woke up this morning. Still full to the brim with Christmas cheer. Plan was to go to Charlotte's for Christmas dinner. First, mass. Must go to Catholic Mass on Christmas Day, my Mum would kill me if she found out I didn't! As it happens, two churches right around the corner from me. Go on the Google Maps. Hop out of bed. Bounce off a wall. Christmas clothes on. Scuttle around the corner. Blessed myself going into church. Found a seat. Sat down. Kneeled down. Stood up. Realised everyone else was still kneeling. Back down. Spaced out. Joined in. Humming prayers. Head spinning slightly. Saw a sign on the wall:

METHODIST

Hmm? What does that mean? Looked around. Slightly odd. Something feels off. Red-eye-balled the folk around me. Stared at the rainbow flag above the priest's head. Hmmm. I think this appears to be a gay and lesbian church? Did I miss something? Asked a spiky haired lady next to me... Oh right. I am in the wrong church. Balls. Across the road I go.

Double blessed myself going into the right church. Forgive me Father. Although it did kind of look the same. Just that it said Catholic on the wall. Phew. Lucky escape. I almost worshipped the wrong version of God! Looked around. This feels more like it. Now we're dancing. Seems like mass at home. Looks like it. Just an amped-up version. More open. People taking their worshipping up an odd notch or two.

In Ireland everyone at Mass looks solemn. Serious. Annoyed? Polite. Forced? Wary. Here, everyone was smiling a lot more. Big huge smiles. Joyous delight. Looked like they were on something. Lucid. Filled with the love of God, no doubt. Boondock Saints style going on. People almost shouting out prayers. Intense. Lots of sideways head motions too. Everyone looking at each other. Some folks' heads almost spinning a full 360 degrees. Kind of all looked like Chuckie, that psycho puppet from the *Child's Play* movies. Got me a bit freaked. Should I have combed my hair? Not to worry. Time to say some prayers. Zone out...

So Christmas has kind of snuck up on me. Maybe it was the roasting hot weather all last week. Perhaps the fact people are apparently not allowed to call it Christmas. Must call it "The Holidays". In case they offend someone. Who? Why? What? Funk that. And where?! Highly odd. Although I think it's mostly due to the lack of hearing Wham and The Pogues on the radio. Kind of feels... Hmmm. I won't say different. Usually that suggests its worse. As in, if a girl has ever said to you that,

> "Well that's not usually how I do it. It was, eh... ahem, different..."

Do you think she's implying it's a good or bad thing? Exactly. Great analogy. Thank you. Let's just say that usually Christmas is the time of year when the actual day of the week is irrelevant, whereas here in Hollywood, Christmas Eve felt just like a Thursday.

However, I did have one secret weapon up my sleeve: Good old 12 Pubs of Christmas! One of my favourite traditions back in Cork. Group of buddies from my university soccer club all meet up. All ages. Eighteen to forty-five. Brave first-year freshers – young, dumb and full of shots - to old, old, *old* school players out pretending to be doing some last minute Christmas shopping. Wife hiding. Young wishing. Reliving the glory days! Off we all go on a pub crawl. Pint per pub. At least twelve. Additional shots are *encouraged* but optional, of course. It is also preferable for the group to stick together as much as possible. Keeps the banter levels high. Finally: No girls allowed. Lads' night out and all! Well, until the twelve pubs have been completed at least. After that? Dance. *On!* (If you still can, obviously.) Fun. Drunk. Messy. Mighty! Some clown (ahem) brought a whistle along one year. Older folk taking too long in each pub. Half an hour time limit implemented. First SHRILL of the whistle indicates five minutes to go,

> "Drink up!"

Second shrill means we're moving on. Usually accompanied by the grumbles and tuts of said older crowd,

> "Is that Hayes again? Would he ever shut up with that FECKING whistle. Ruining my FECKING pint for FECK'S SAKE! Some FECKING IDIO- "
>
> "Shh. Pipe down. Drink up."
>
> SHRILL SHRILL! On we all go. Outside to the cold air. Christmas decorations lighting up the narrow street.

Into the next pub.
Order up.
Repeat the banter.

Whistle on.
And away we keep going.

Drink flows.
Bellies warms.
People relax.
Fun begins!

Pub One: Orderly. Sociable.
Pub Three: Warming. Up.
Pub Five: Banter. High.
Pub Eight: Merry. Very.
Pub Ten: Tad. Messy.
Pub Twelve: Drunk. Skunks.

By now everyone is arm-in-arm. Traipsing the streets. Odd football chant or song being flung out into the cold night's air. Biggest gap between bars at this point so a few good men get lost along the way. Those that are still dancing carry on through. All roads lead to The Castle, a tiny old fashioned pub in the middle of Cork City owned by a woman known only as Mary. Magical place where cell phones are banned, the toilets consist of a wall and drain out the back, and the night usually ends with a sing-song of some sort. Low on frills. High on banter! Into Mary. Last pint before vodka. Pub. Everyone. Full to the brim. Loud. Proud. Goosed. Swaying. Singing,

> "Do You Like Cake?! Whatkindofcakedoyoulike?!"

SHRILL of the whistle is piped out. Dirty looks thrown my way. Pint. Down. Hatch.

> "C'mon! Must make the club. Thirteenth pub. Final port. We can do it. Plough. On!"

Arm in the air. Scarf around the neck. Charge back out into the cold winter's night. Whatever happens after that, who knows? One of *the* mightiest nights out of the year! Well. Until the next night. Giddy up them steps! All of which applies for Cork at least. In L.A? Ahem... Horrendous. Calling a spade a shovel, close to zero interest in the Hollywood 12 Pubs of Christmas. Most people were out of town for Christmas. Those left in L.A, all a tad depressed. Single. Driven. Lonely. Stuck here on their own. Hope. Gone.

Zero.
Christmas.

Spirit.

Most folk thought my invite was just a spam email, I was trying to sell them something. Didn't get it, even after I explained it fully. Well done all round. This led to me breaking my first rule: No girls allowed. Ergo, mass email sent out to any I knew. Wonderfully received. Again. Most text with:

> 'RANDUMB GIRL: Who's this?'

The rest thinking it was a date...:

> 'RANDUMB WEHO-ER: Love to meet for a drink. Movie afterwards?'
>
> 'RANDUMB GIRL: Sounds lovely. Nice quiet drink, just the two of us.'

Did you even read the email? Movie? Quiet drink? This is 12 Pubs! What part of "the more the merrier!" was lost in translation? In the end it was just myself and Charlotte to start off with. Fellow Tiny Timmy spending Christmas in L.A for work. New wing-woman for the night. Wingaduu!

Pub One: Chaya (technically a restaurant). Poor start. I was slightly late. Charlotte tucked into a bottle of wine on her own. Oh Jesus. Time for me to catch up. Quick drink. Chug. (One pub in and I'm chugging already? Never a good sign. Just a great one. Wahey!) SHRILL of the whistle. Balls. Clown must adhere to clown rules. Where next?

Pub Two: Barney's. Quick pitcher. (Two pubs in and I've gone from pints to a pitcher already? Sweet Jesus.) Also realised finding twelve pubs within walking distance was going to be tough. Particularly when one of you is wearing heels. I won't say who...

Pub Three: SkyBar. Met a guy named Boris. Refused to acknowledge that his country (Yugoslavia) no longer existed. So that was fun to prod. Kept spitting out disgusted sounding Russian. At one point I thought he was going to go KGB on us but instead he bought us all another round. Cheers Boris!

Pub Four: Took a chance. Taxi to Hollywood. Boris included. Bad call. Every pub shut. Christmas Eve. Disaster. Buzz wearing off. Back to Barney's. Boozed on. Charlotte. Goosed. Taxi. Home.

Barney's again. Boris asleep at the table. Mighty. Final pitcher. Night done. Booth. Boozing. Solo. No sing-song. No after-party. No buzz. At all.

Meager three pubs of Christmas. Tut. At least I got the twelve pints in. And I even managed to make mass. So here I am. And now I see everyone's standing up. How long have I been kneeling? Pretty sure I'm still drunk. Stand. Up. Pray. On. Scanned the church. Odd looking Asian woman in front of me. Wearing a wig. Set of false teeth. Arms dripping with lots of gold bracelets. Keeps waving at everyone around her. Including me. For some weird reason beyond my control, I keep waving back every time. Wink. Thumbs up. Underhand wave. Couldn't stop doing it. Copped on as to why: Definitely still full of Christmas cheer. Maybe why I was so fascinated by her wig too. Kept sliding around her head as she spun left and right. Had to use a lot of self-control to not reach out and touch it. Looked for someone else to look at.

Tweaking older looking mother and daughter decide to leave. Wonder if I can too? Nay. Very early. Wailing Mexican woman across the aisle giving it socks. Blatantly singing the wrong words of the hymns. Good effort though. An even later straggler interrupts her to squeeze in on the pew. Very big Amazonian woman. Might be a man. Quite the mix at Hollywood mass. Realise the old guy next to me is also wearing a wig. Must be the fashion at this time. (My hair can look particularly wig-like when I wake up from a night out too though, so I blended in well.) This old dude had a magnificent perm going on though. Slightly lop-sided on his head as well. Probably as brilliant/horrendous a wig as I've ever seen. Particularly when morning drunk and curious. Pray on...

Dear Lord, forgive me for my- Actually, 12 Pubs wasn't all that bad. Did meet those two sisters in Barney's the first time around. Elle and Shawnie. New Yorkers. I was a fan of Elle. Blonde hair. Blue eyes. Nice lips. Rock and roll style. Bridget Bardot/Kate Moss look going on, to be true. Glint of a chancer in her eyes as well. Shawnie looked more Portuguese. And far was more wary of me. My accent. My hair. Maybe the fact I was taking a shine to her sister. Probably all of the above. Tried to explain the 12 Pubs concept to them. Not a clue. Also struggled to grasp my accent. Confused looks all round. Surely I'm not slurring already? Hmmm. Time to gather my thoughts. Asked Elle what she did,

"Model."

> "Oh yeah, any campaigns... Pardon? Calvin, as in Klein? Lin- as in -gerie?"

(Oh dear Betsy! Ahem. Play it cool...) On the downside, I never got her number. Whistle shrilled. Clown. Although I did manage to tell her about Sigur Ros and how she must listen to them. At times they can be an acquired taste, but I felt she would like their ethereal Icelandic rock ways. Asked me to send her some songs... So that's something. And now everyone is sitting again? Or are we kneeling? Down I go.

Pray. Hymn. Pray. Come to Our Father time. Notice people starting to raise up their hands. Opening them out. Just like the priest was doing. Saw the people in front of me holding each other's raised up hands. Getting ready with the priest to start praying. Felt an urge to show God I was paying attention. Time to join in and do the same. Mouthing the words. Closing my eyes. Raising up my open hands. As I thought it was the norm to do, I started to hold the hand of the person next to me. Before I remembered who it was, too late: Old dude in the wig. Felt his clammy hand grip mine. Opened my eyes. Wigman staring at me. Smiling an odd, lucid smile. Holding on for dear life.

I should've really looked around more before I grabbed hold of his sweaty paw. Seeing as when I did a few moments later, I saw a fair few people weren't holding hands at all. Mostly only families doing that. One or two older folk. Plus me and Wigman, who by now was almost fully facing me. Praying at me. Slowly mouthing words. Ignoring the altar. Lifting my hand up as far as he could reach for some reason. Very odd experience. Got odder. Thankfully communion time saved me. Had to release me. Up I go. Just as it was my turn to be served, I realised I'd completely forgotten what to say after you're giving the communion. (Amen. Easy to see how one might forget it.) This caused me to panic. Blank. And say,

> "Thanks a lot for the communion, Father sir, bless you."

Priest looked at me oddly. Asked,

> "Are you from I-r-land?"

Which is when his American accent developing an Irish twang.

> "Ah shur, Father Seamus, I am!"

"Great to meet you, laddie!"

Father Seamus seemed delighted to hear my gibber. Handed me a chalice. Encouraged me to wash the bread down. As I was last up to receive communion, told me I might as well finish it off.

"Looks like you could do with it..."

Wink. Yeah, gasping. Need some water. So I drank up. Good chunk. Gulps. Audibly chugging from the chalice at the end. Father Seamus tipping up the cup to help me get the last few drops. Realised then it was wine. Not water. Oh yeah. Topping me fully up on Christmas cheer. Rollover jackpot. The minute I handed the chalice back I felt it: Oh Betsy. Now I'm drunk. Father Seamus, ye have me goosed!

Walking back down to my seat the wine had put a pep in my step. Noticed that everyone was shaking hands with each other. Hugging one another, like a big happy family. I thought the sign of peace had already happened but maybe I got it wrong. Started shaking hands with everyone on the way back. Hugging the Asian lady. Patted her wig-head. Back to the seat. Shook Wigman's hand again. At first he gave a surprised look. Back for more? Odd smile came back.

"Oh Jesus."

Fr. Seamus wrapped up the proceedings. Felt the wine kick in a bit more. Just in time for a song. *Silent Night.* Everyone bellowing it out. Me included. Singing for Ireland. Like an ape tenor. I had no sing-along last night. Muted bird. Sing on!

Mass ends. Point up at the priest. Seamus, buddy, see you at Easter! Salute the Asian lady. Call me sign. Dodge the creepy wigged wonder. Frozen smile of delight on his face looking at me. Licking his lips. Wiggling his eyebrows. Time to scuttle on. Left the church. Time for dinner. Charlotte's here I come. Meant to be there now. Need to get a cab. Mighty: Hail one down straight away. Pulls in way down the street though. Start walking after it. Next minute I hear,

"Heeeeyyy!"

Turn around. Wigman. Who's he calling? Now waving wildly. And then running. Towards me. Oh Jesus. What's he after? Need to get out of here. Power walk on!

Power-power.
My present for Charlotte slips out from under my arm.
Dose.
Look back.
Momentary panic.
Should I abandon it?
Can't deal with the wigged weirdo.
Need to get to the cab!
What to do, what to do?
Sprint.
Grab.
Present.
Balls.
Wigman has caught up to me.
Dose.
Grabs my hand as I pretend not to see him,

> "Heeey! I was calling you. Did you not hear?"

> "No sorr- "

> "Have you ever modeled before? Would you consider it?"

> "Ha, what?"

Threw me off. My dumb ego gets sucked in. No no, Wigman, never. That's funny though. Didn't expect you to say that. Funny man. Wish him a,

> "Merry Christmas!"

Smile. Swivel. Walk. Wigman walks alongside. Tells me he is a producer of some sort. Works with all the big model agencies, so he says. Asks if I've ever heard of Tyra Banks? Implies he discovered her. Sure you did, old creepy man in a wig.

> "Sorry, not really interested in modeling, unless of course it was hand-modeling?"

Me and my brutal jokes... Wigman grabs my hands again. Examines them front and back. Caresses gently. All right, this is enough now. Got to go get my Christmas dinner on. Wigman rubbing my hands and slips me his card,

> "Call if you change your mind. Or if you ever need anything. Anything at all. Give me a call."

"OK. Cheers... Joe."

Joe smiles. Straightens his wig. Winks. And trots off back up the street. So that was kind of odd. Not the typical start to a Christmas Day really. Slightly different, to be true. Better? Worse? Who knows? I do know that I had a surprisingly mighty day in Charlotte's abode afterwards. Savage feast. Charlotte can cook. Tasty turkey named Terence. Ate too much. Drank a little. Got some slick presents. All in all, quite a dancing day. Although, early night. Charlotte had work the next day. So I walked back to my abode. Wondering what was going on back in Cork. Christmas Day. All my family in my Nana and Grandad's. House lit up. Fire roasting. Everyone toasty. Happy days.

Nice empty house waiting for me here. All to myself. No Christmas décor or happy lights to greet me. Cold enough too. Had a cup of tea on the couch. Watched some TV. Read a bit of my new book *Tales of Ordinary Madness* by Charles Bukowski. Fun read. Full of cheer. Ahem. Went to bed. All felt a tad depressing. Slightly different buzz this year. But we won't dwell on that. After all, I did make a new friend: Joe!

Who, it turned out, was a fan of orgies...

Chapter 16

Milk & Sugar, Orgy Joe?

Christmas in L.A is weird. And also highly disappointing. Which is why I might be still going on about it. Whereas in Ireland we gear up for it, here the whole place just winds down. Almost to a grinding halt. Everything feels dead for a change. Kind of weird too as Christmas is full on advertised beyond belief. Commercials everywhere. TV non-stop. Christmas specials. Christmas sales. And then almost every person doesn't really give a hoot about it. Not the folk in L.A, anyway. Care more about work.

Adding to the festive spirit has been a few days of rain. Gasp. Dark. Drab. Dreary. Depressing. L.A folk really let the rain affect them. A lot. In fairness there were big bulbous buckets of gushing water. But still, people here can barely cope. Melt away at the sight of rain. Cars crash. People panic. Everyone. Freaks. Out.

Back in Ireland the Christmas spirit freaks folk out in a good way. Pumped for the turkey, boozing and presents! Here: Wet moaning non-believers. Zero buzz. The week or two before Christmas I was pretty busy. Mind distracted. Dodging nutters. DJing in Orange County. Writing down in my well. Ploughing through. Trying to get myself sorted. Tried not to think about how this was my first Christmas away from home. How will I survive without my Mum's mighty cooking? More importantly, how will my family survive without mighty me?! So tough for them all. Going to miss out on all the fun and banter with buddies too. Dose.

Back home, Stephen's Day (day after Christmas) is maybe my third favourite day of the year. Everyone's off work. Wake up late. Leftovers for lunch. Leftovers for dinner. Almost even better than the day before. Soak on ye delightful juices! Pubs open up again. (Gasp! They shut down for one full night. How did we survive?!) Family time has been put in the day before, so you're now free to go out and booze on with all your buddies who are in town for Christmas. Savage. All this continues on until January 2nd. Non-stop banter. Booze. And promises you're never touching another drop after the session last night. Not a week for the weak! Here, Stephen's Day was slightly different. Charlotte was working all day. No one else around. Leftovers were in her apartment. So I had a toasted sandwich for lunch. And porridge for dinner. Delightful.

Even worse, once Christmas Day is over, that's *it* for most people. Decorations yanked down. Tree thrown out the door. End of. Move on. Next holiday? Valentine's Day. OK. Up go the heart signs and chocolate roses. Chris-who?! *Funk* that. Christmas is not done yet! Undeterred. Decided to keep some Irish traditions going for the week. Now that I had DJed a good few gigs recently, I had some shillings in my pocket. Also: I'm horrendous at saving. Ergo, the past week has been a drunken blur.

Went down to Barney's on my own Stephen's night. Bartender started lashing out free booze to me. At least one person had the Christmas spirit! Trying out new concoctions. Cocktails. Shots. Personal experiments. Getting me drunk. Everyone else as well. Didn't realise that all those drinks were being added to a tab. One that I had opened. Apparently. No recollection of opening it. Tad drunk. Couldn't remember my address in the cab home. Might have got kicked out and about. Woke up. Rolled over. Discovered that there was a Jehovah Witness in my bed. Hmmm... Oh! I remember you from playing pool.

Nice girl. Randumb drunken pillow talk. Filled me in on how the religion works. Cult-like it seems. Used to be a door knocker herself. Until she had to flee. Escape in the middle of the night. Couldn't hack it anymore. My head started spinning around this time. Passed out for a coma nap. Woke up. And she was gone. Did that just happen? *Pretty* sure it did. Hmmm.

Chowder returned from England so I met him early the next day. Offered me a beer at breakfast. Tasted nice. So we had a pitcher for dessert. Continued on. Day turned to night. Hustling randumbers at pool. Drinking shots with Johnny Knoxville. Gibbering with girls. Bumped into Elle and Shawnie again down there. Apparently I had bought them a round without knowing. (Funking barman going to town on my tab!) Elle was looking dancing in all black. Shawnie was looking at my hair with disgust once more. At least she was on a date so that kept her busy. And meant Elle was a spare wheel. Cue more shots together. And then...

Not sure after that. Pretty sure we ended the night wrestling around on the street outside the pub. Then she tried to choke me with my scarf. Then our lips danced. And finally, she ran away up the road. As in sprinted. Still not sure why. My breath was minty-fresh. Must be something else. No clue. Still don't have a number for her either. Wrestling and choking - Good or bad signs? Hard to tell. Intrigue on!

Woke up wondering why there was still so much cash in my wallet. Although no credit card. And no sign of my key. Clueless. Cardless. Keyless. Mighty. At least I found my key (in the door) and my card (behind the bar). Still clueless as to why Elle sprinted away like a mad woman. I know it's all about the chase but still. Think I might be going slightly delirious too. Staying up until 6 in the morning. Felt guilty. I think it was from a need to justify taking a few days off and boozing on when I have so much to do and so little funds overall. Tut. Tried to write. Wrote nothing. Spent the hour between four and five in the morning sitting in a chair next to my bed wondering if I should just go to bed. Not actually going to bed. Just wondering. From five to six was spent looking at the blank screen of a turned off computer wondering how you might know if you were going delirious? Do you just become delirious? Or is there a point, like sober to drunk, when you think: Hey hup, I think I'm delirious. Either way, repeating the word delirious over and over in your head is a pretty effective way to send you on your way to deliria town.

Decided no more boozing. Holiday over. Work back on. Time to get my house in order. Need some food actually. Up to Trader Joe's. Bright fluorescent lights piercing my hungover head. Moving at lethargic speed. Ughatha. Ambling aimlessly down the wrong aisle. Picking up frozen food I'd no interest in. Felt a tap on my shoulder. Looked up. Oh Jesus. It's Joe. Not Trader. Wigman. Weirdo from Mass. Straight away I noticed his nervous demeanour, very Woody Allen like, just with an added bucket of perviness on top. Fidgeting his hands. Twiddling his fingers. Reaching out. Putting his hand on my arm while reminding me who he was,

"Hey, the Irish guy, am I right? Merrick?"

Don't think I realised on Christmas Day just how much of a creepy old man Joe was. Full-on sleaze. Surprised he was wearing pants.

> "Oh yeah Joe, how's it going? Kind of busy now, not sure if I'm up for the modeling malarkey either before you ask, have a good one..."

Joe murmurs something at me. Tut...

> "No Joe, I wouldn't be interested in swimsuit modeling."

Go away please Joe. You're creeping me out boss. With that I ambled off again, back down the frozen food aisle. Away from hands-on-Joe. Thinking it was kind of weird that I've never seen Joe before in my life yet now I see him again so soon. Was Joe following me? Hangover making me paranoid. Might have seen him a few times and just avoided eye contact. Joe followed me down the aisle, repeating the word,

> "Swimsuit"

Said goodbye again to Joe, told him I had his number, might be in touch. Perhaps when I'm in my eighties and suddenly get an urge to model a swimsuit.

> "See ya Joe!"

Joe realised I was giving him the slip. Or else got lucky. Started dropping names. My dumb ear stopped me. Sucked me in.

> "Nnnaaeeeh, have you heard of Tom Jones? Sonny & Cher? Jay Leno? Jerry Seinfeld?"

Did make me subtly swivel on a sixpence.

> "Yes Joseph, I have heard of them. Why so?"

> "I've worked with all of them. Produced their live shows. That's what I do."

Funker. Now I was stumped. Was Joe being legit? Or just a spoof? Throwing out names in the hope one would stick.

> "I might be of use to you. Depends on what you do? Are you married? What do you do?"

Hmm. Asking me was I married was odd, if he was legit. Which made me think again he was a spoof. But those names at the end did interest me. (Jerry Seinfeld!) In an attempt to suss Joe out, I told him I did a few different things,

" ...But at the moment, I'm mostly a dancer."

I thought telling Joe I was a dancer would mean very little. Just throw him off. Not a dancer in the dancing way. Dancer as in a chancer. However Joe's eyes lit up,

"I started off as a dancer! I've produced so many shows in Vegas. Biggest shows in town! Everyone knows me there. Showgirls all love me. You'd love the showgirls. Are you married? You'd love the showgirls... OR the guys who danced. Either is fine. Whatever you like. Girls OR GUYS. Whatever it is you're into."

Joe's pervy way of talking made me realize he was definitely just a dirty old spoofing man.

"Wigman, I better get on with my shopping. See ya later."

"Hey, don't go, I could help you with your dancing. You'd love the showgirls."

Kept swift-walking away. Out of that aisle. Fruit section is more open. Joe talk-following all along telling me all about the showgirls. And the guys. Whatever I preferred. Kept repeating it. Tried to tune him out. Realised he was a bit of a freak. Just a dirty old man in a wig following me around the store. Pretended to suss out the potatoes. Joe creeping up next to me. Now asking if I liked orgies.

"For funk's sake, what are you asking me that for?"

Particularly odd coming from a guy his age, grandad like. Uncomfortable buzz. Even more so when he started to tell me his favourite positions. And the things he liked to do. This one time in his house by the lake. Or another time in his house in the hills. All the time going into graphic detail about body parts. Just wrong. Hearing all this made my hangover way worse,

"What are you on about? Freaking me out, Joe.

Making me dizzy! Don't want to hear anymore."

Joe managed to look stunned, surprised and upset,

"Why not, do you *not* like orgies?"

"Sweet Jesus. Joe. Please shut the funk up. Leave me alone. I don't like orgies."

Well, maybe I do. Never been in one though. And not up for trying, especially after hearing you describe them in such graphic detail. This had no effect whatsoever on Joe. Instead he told me his favourite sexual act/position. Very nice of him. Let's just say, Joe was a fan of dipping. Teabag into a cup, kind of dipping. Or, Joe added,

"I also liked to be the cup... And have balls dipped onto me."

I'll say no more. I've said too much! Final straw. Felt an urge to physically remove Joe from my vicinity. Old man though. He was going nowhere either. So I just put my basket of food down on the ground. Told Joe,

"I am more of a coffee man these days. Will you look after my basket while I go get a trolley?"

Out the sliding doors. Left my food behind. And just go home. Away from Trader Joe's. Away from Orgy Joe. Away from that disturbed little man in a horrible wig. On that lovely note, that's enough about my first Christmas away from home. First Christmas here in L.A. Quite a treat. Felt like a one-night stand. Over. Done. Dumb. Kicked out of bed the next day. Screaming: It's over. Get out. NOW! IDIOT!!!

Same as how all one-night stands end, right? *Anyway...* At least I survived another year. Stumbled into the new one. Now then. Time to finish this book before I go mental. Down the writing well I... Go!

Chapter 17

Crazy in Logic

To paraphrase a certain Hunter S. Thompson, he of the mighty *Fear and Loathing in Las Vegas*:

> *"If you're going to be crazy, you have to get paid for it..."*

Mighty quote. Good logic behind his madness too. All I've been doing is: Book. Book. Book. Starting to take its toll. The more I speak to people who work normal business hours, the more I get the impression they think I'm going crazy. Particularly when I mention the hours I now operate. My night owl is soaring at the moment. Sleeping times flipped on their head. Up all night. Asleep all day. Going to bed when it's bright. Getting up when it's dark. Curtains only needing to be opened for about a ten-minute period. That's crazy, I'm told. Would you not try to sort it out? Why don't you change your routine? Makes far more sense! Tut. Night. Day. Write. Right!

Perhaps it's time I just stopped talking to these folk. Although I can see their logic of how it kind of looks illogical. There is, however, a method to my madness. During the day, people are awake. At night, people usually sleep. Ergo: Less distractions. More writing. See. Logic. Dumb by day. Alive at night! At least the book is being churned out. All about the cave-like lifestyle. Must go into hiding to get work done. Living in my head. Running around my mind. Scanning notes. Going back over stories. Reliving these tales. Strangely: Living vicariously through myself.

Resulting in sporadic mood swings.

Frustrated.
Pumped.
Happy.
Annoyed.
Delighted.
Dumb.
Over and over.

My mind being stretched and pulled.
Flexed to the max.
How could you do that then?
Waste *so* much time there?!
What were you thinking?!
Clown!
Quite a strange buzz, to be true.

Firm believer in the phrase: Laziness is the root of all evil. Now starting to think that logic might be the root of most of my problems though. I think it stems from the maths side of my brain. Maths was my favourite subject in school. Given a problem. Use some logic. Figure out a solution. Used to be quite good at this too. My brain does actually see the logic in things. Just not all the time nowadays. New routine has been developing on a nightly basis. Sit down. Write. Brutal. Nothing worthwhile. Lump of useless words. Could be lazy. Just go with that. Hand it in. Job done. Thankfully nay. See. I know there's good stuff in my head. Problem is it's *way* at the back. *All* the way at the back. Needs to wade through a marsh of messy dumbness in order to push itself to the front. Stories taking their time to come out as you might want them. Reach a point halfway through the marsh where it's slightly closer to the back than the front. Stops to take a breather. Decides what to do? Plough on? Or just go back? Hmmm.

This breather is usually when Logic shows up inside my head. Brings along Buddy Doubt. No friend of mine. Complete muppet of a man. Logic, why do you always bring him to the party? Told you I can't stand him. Appears at the worst times. Out to cripple. Logic stands up for Buddy. Doubt tries to get a word in...,

> "Look, why not just stop here and go with what you have? I mean, really what's the point? Just get it over with?"
>
> "Doesn't matter what you write! Just leave me and Logic into the party and you can finish up!"

At which point I sit in my chair in front of my desk. Put on some house music. And wrestle Doubt,

"Ya dirty whure! Get out!"

Finally after a good old battle: Buddy Doubt, kicked out. Strong old funker at times. Although look, now the good stuff has started to flow. Betsy! As long as I can keep Doubt out, I'm dancing! My sanity will stay intact too I feel without Doubt around. Just need to get it done. I think that should work anyway. Never too sure. Might just all be the ramblings of a clown who's stuck down a writing well, slowly losing grip on reality. Hard to tell in L.A at times... Who exactly is the crazy one?

Prime example. Walking to the laundry place earlier around the corner from where I live. Strolled past a homeless dude flailing his arms. Shouting out. Asking me for,

"Money. Cigarette. Vodka. Anything!"

Few yards further down the street I was greeted by two girls. Also flailing their arms. Shouting out. Asking me,

"What are you doing? You're cute. Gotta light?"

"Eh, no. That homeless dude probably does though."

Which is when they stopped flailing. Stopped looking through me. Started looking at me. Oddly. Informed me they were just rehearsing for a scene they had for class. Two actresses attending the acting school around the corner from me. Oh right. My bad? As far as I see it, they're all in the same boat. None of them are getting paid to act crazy. In fact, the girls are even worse as they're *paying* to act crazy. Homeless dude is far more sane in my eyes. More coherent flailing of the arms too. As I said, hard to tell what's going on at times in L.A.

Although I did meet far weirder on that little excursion: Dude in the laundry place. Looked like a Hells Angel. Big. Burly. Handlebar mustache. Leather jacket. Staring at me while I folded my clothes. Kept staring, while he also started to rub his crotch. Not looking away when I saw what he was up to. Asked him,

"Are you all right?"

Replying in a high-toned effeminate squeal,

"I'm very all right."

Then kept on rubbing. All righty then. Weirdo. I bid you a duu. Time for me to go back down the well. At least I'm getting paid to go crazy down there. Must say though, I'm enjoying it. Submersing myself. (Not seeing a Hells Angel touch himself.) Feels good. (Again, writing the book!) Working on. Being productive is good for the soul. Although I have noticed how easy it is to lose grip on what's going on in the real world. Waking up to find out I've no clean socks. Nor jocks. Plenty of T-shirts though. Well done me. Regimented eating disappearing. Running out of food. No milk in my fridge. Forgetting about the six meals. Making myself disappear. Big, wild, cave man head up on me. Haircuts? Shaving? Ha! No time for such trivial nonsense now!

Which is why I'm starting to resemble a captured Saddam Hussein. Also forgot that I need to find somewhere new to live pretty soon. Lease is up at the end of the month. So that's something big I need to get sorted. Or else I could be homeless. Wandering the streets. Dazed. Confused. Looking like Saddam. Wilder version. Beady-eyed. Wearing just a T-shirt. And dirty socks. Out flopping about. Asking strangers for milk. Or a loan of their jocks. Now that would be the life! Something to look forward to if nothing else.

Until then: Logic off. Write on!

Chapter 18

In Me Back Door

At the advice of my mighty mother, I have been trying to get out of the house more. Can't just stay indoors all day and night writing. Apparently. Only person I actually see in person lately has been my roommate Tara. And she's been quite depressed. Or depressing. World is against her, kind of malarkey. If it's not one thing, it's the other and if it's not the other then it's something else, as she might say. Over and over. Again and again. Dragging me down with her. Making me want to go back to bed. Escape under the blankets.

Except I can't really. As it's usually about half past five in the evening and I've only been up an hour. Seeing as I went to bed at eleven in the morning. As I was up all night wading through a marsh, wrestling Buddy Doubt, and writing a book. Did I mention I'm operating odd hours these days?

Anyway, whenever I can I've been getting out of the house. After breakfast. Before work. About five bells. Around the time when Tara returns from work. Coincidence. Giddy up! Out the door. Dodge on. Found a good little spot around the corner to go to as well. Tea shop next to the laundry place. Little hippy spot with a chilled, far-out-man vibe going on. Big, inviting couches. Dreadlocked girl behind the counter. Bangladesh music playing. That kind of place. Cool spot. Although that's not really the reason why I go in there. Always an ulterior motive. So I'm at the laundry place. Always filled to the brim with babbling weird dudes. Some of them are just pacing around ranting at themselves. Twitches. Ticks. Everywhere. Others just give me odd looks that I can never tell if they want to fight me or funk me. Hard to say. Weirder when they give me a look like they want to do both,

"What are you looking at?"

"Huh?"

"You like this?"

"Heh?"

Very odd.

This particular night there are one too many nuts eye-balling me up and down while I wait for my socks to dry. Decide to stroll outside. Delighted I do. Swivel to my left. Who do I see strolling into the tea shop: Elle. The girl who ran away from me at Christmas and then returned to choke me with my scarf before we kissed like two drunks rolling around on the ground. *That* Elle! Looking well too in her knee high boots and scarf. (She was wearing jeans and a top as well but it was the boots and scarf that caught my lazy eye.)

Hadn't seen or spoke to her since that particular night. No number. No Facebook. No joy. Go on the weirdos in the laundry place! Hooking me up serendipitously. Elle's ordering up while I'm bundling in the door. Clear the throat. Squeaky first attempt. Sound like Mickey Mouse,

"Hiii..."

Cough. Ahem. Cough. And then,

"Hiya boyo! Remember me?"

Cue an odd look. Eyes narrow. Widen. She does. In like Flynn!

"Did you just call me a boy?"

"Ah no, no no, just an expression. Same as how's it going?"

Forgot my humour is lost on people at times. And isn't funny the other times. Spoof on. Elle replies,

"Interesting. And it's going well, girl. Thanks for asking."

Takes her drink and looks for a seat. Quick order of some herbal fruity tea. Try to rectify what appeared as an opening insult.

> "Mind if I join you?"

Elle has sat on the biggest couch in there. Too tough to say no. Plonk down on the couch next to her. Immediately three things occur to me. One: Elle is hot. Two: I'd be up for kissing her right now straightaway. Except. Three: I am sober. Arggh. My good old Irish ways. Cue me getting awkward. Flustered. And then start babbling on about music,

> "Did you listen to Sigur Ros yet? You have to, seriously. For some reason I think you'll like them."

Elle is just nodding along. Trying to figure out my accent. What I'm saying. Or how to get away from me. Not too sure. Confused expression the whole time. After about ten minutes, Elle gets a phone call. Her sister Shawnie is having some sort of car crisis, she needs to go.

> "Are you sure? She'll be fine I'd say. Just stay another ten minutes? I've got socks to collect and work to go to myself. I was just getting warmed up too! No?"

No joy. Must leave,

> "It's been great though. Nice seeing you. Best of luck with the book."

Tut. Balls. Chance. Gone. Despite Elle insisting that she's fine, I walk her outside. Suggest we should be tea buddies more often. Smiles a Bob Hope smile back at me,

> "Yeah... Sure... Busy at the moment though. Maybe some other time... OK. See ya."

> "Sounds good! I'm around most days this time. Let me know when suits. I don't have your number or anything but just let me know or I could meet you here or I'll just start coming here now so maybe I'll see you here again sometime, if you're lucky of course!"

Nice and awkward. As was the handshake I instigated to say

goodbye. As she turns, leaves and starts slipping away, I blurt out,

> "Actually, you should eh, definitely give me your number and I can text you on some of those songs I mentioned. I think you'll be a fan. And if you're not, I'll *never* bother you again. How good an offer is that?!"

Too good to turn down it seems. Elle laughs. Gives in. Puts her number into my crap little dumb-phone. Oh Betsy. Now we're dancing! Elle has to go. Her sister is phoning again. Runs off. And my gibberish texts begin:

> 'ME: It's me! Your new tea buddy! Tip o' the, top o' the. Run off. Run free! Wuu duu!!!'

Obviously I get no reply. My gibber in writing seems to scare off American girls. Except if they're nutters. Mighty. Next day. Same again. Hmm. That's odd. Something must be wrong with her phone. Or are my texts even getting through? I'll text and ask if my messages are getting through. That's always a smooth move. Try in vain to cancel the text as it sends. Too late. Nooo! Some clown. Whenever I try, I am really quite brutal. Although... Hey hup! Reply:

> 'ELLE: Yes. I got all your messages. Sorry, really busy. Email me the songs please. Gotta go. Bye.'

Well that was a bit curt, wasn't it? And we're going from texts to email? Never a good sign. Don't worry though, I forgive you! Oh balls, why did I send that? Delete. Cancel. ABORT! Too late. Sweet Jesus. All right. Emailed the songs. That's done. Back to me listening to Tara's woes. All I heard was: (Clap clap) Radio silence (clap clap) radio silence (clap clap). (I hope you sang that line to the tune of Queen's Radio Ga Ga!) Until, about a week later. Two in the morn. Gearing up for Buddy Doubt to call over. Beep beep. Who's this from I wonder...:

> 'ELLE: I just listened to the songs. They are amazing! Can you make me a CD with more, please? I could meet you in the tea-shop tomorrow?'

> 'ME: Well would you look who it is... Coming crawling back... Using me for some CDs!'

> 'ELLE: If you can't then it's fine, I just really like them. It's cool, I'll hunt them down myself.'

> 'ME: Oh yeah, no, I was joking, I can, see you tomorrow. Good duck!'

Next day. Same time. Same place. Left my bat-cave. Met the Elle. Looking dancing. All smiles. Loved the music I sent her. I took the plaudits on Sigur Ros' behalf. Cheers lads! And then myself and Elle just gibbered on to each other. For a change, I wasn't the only one rambling. Two babbling brooks. Conversation was flowing. It was weird too. Usually I'm very good at not letting girls in fully. As in I'll have banter with them but if I cop on that there's no immediate connection, I just entertain as opposed to talk. If that makes sense. I wonder if that's why some girls I used to see might still like me or stay in touch so much. Maybe they know they hadn't been fully let in the door. Or didn't cop on how to let themselves in. Then again, maybe I'm delusional and they all really can't stand me. I wonder which? Delude on! Elle, on the other hand, just strolled in the backdoor of my head. While I'm busy keeping an eye on the front door, Elle was in the kitchen making a cup of tea for herself. Hey hup, what's going on here? Who let you in? Oh the door was open. Didn't think you'd mind. And I didn't. It was beyond mighty being able to talk *to* someone, as opposed to the norm in L.A - just talking *at* one another.

Even mightier, Elle was the first person I met in L.A who I felt I could fully relate to. She too was on a similar journey. Living in the unknown a lot of the time. Not only was she a model, also an actress and a singer. Booked big campaigns, appeared on TV shows, had a record deal. On the flip side, she also had periods of nada. Lulls. Struggles. Waves. Highs and lows. Fellow Buddy Doubt wrestler. Also a fellow dancer!

Elle was also the very first person I met in L.A who I thought: She's going to be a star. See I've met a load of stars here already. By that I mean people who have - in the eyes of the public - made it. Whatever that really means. Successful. Top of their fields. And then on the other hand, I have also met a legion of spoofs, clowns, apes and idiots. All of whom will gladly tell you they've made it, the next big thing, a star, the one! But in reality none of them are really even close. Preferring to talk than putting the effort in to walk.

Anyway, this is how Elle and I came to be tea-buddies. Started meeting regularly. Going for strolls around West Hollywood. Just talking. Having a laugh. Getting cerebral. All in all, quite mighty! Pleasant change, to be true. Becoming buddies with Elle also made something very glaringly obvious to me: I am horrendously brutal at making a move sober. As in beyond bad. I actually can't remember the last time I kissed a girl for the first time, sober. Not really the Irish way. Sober kissing. Pretty odd, I know. Even worse was my attempt with Elle. One day we're out for a stroll and it starts bucketing down out of nowhere. Close enough to my abode so I say let's run there. Off we scuttle. Get in. Not too wet.

> "Want to watch some TV?"

So we're watching Fox Soccer Channel. I'm telling Elle all about Everton, the main team in England that I support. Explaining the woes of being an Evertonian. Elle asking me,

> "Why do you support them if they're not that good or never win anything?"

> "Not too sure. I blame my Dad. He supports them. Passed on the curse to me."

Some repeat of an Italian Serie A game comes on. Elle seems interested,

> "Let's watch some of this, tell me what's going on."

> "Mighty. Would you like a drink? I have some vodka, gin, whiskey, tea or water?"

Water it is. Go to the kitchen. Survey the situation. Hmmm. I wonder should I make a move now? Looking mighty. I do want to kiss those lips. But I'm sober. How am I going to do it without looking like a wally? Just go out and do it. Subtly. Be smooth. We can do it! OK brain, I'm in. Let's go! Return to the sitting room. Sit down on the couch. For some reason my body chooses the furthest side away from Elle. Jesus, nerves are getting to me. Start having a conversation with my brain,

> "How do I do this again? Should I pre-warn her? I'm coming in. Just close your eyes. Relax. It'll all be over soon... That kind of thing? Or do I just do it? Brain, what's the protocol?"

> "Well, clown, remember that time years ago when

you tried to kiss a girl, sober? And you told her you were now going to kiss her so she better back off and leave if she didn't want you to? And then she backed off and left. And told you the next day you should've just shut up and kissed her? Remember that? Well just shut up and kiss her, you clown!"

"OK so. I'll do that. Hang on... Jesus, brain! My ponder pipe is fully up dancing. Can you control that a minute? She'll think I'm some sort of perverted nutter. Simmer it down! And maybe turn down the perspiring too. I'll have to wipe down with a towel soon if it carries on..."

Subtly slip a mint into my mouth.

"All right, brain, I'm ready. She's sitting on the edge of the couch. Her lips look hot. Here I go!"

And then I proceeded to do a big wide lunging swoop from the far side of the couch. My left arm swung around. My eyes closed. My head threw itself towards hers. Just as I thought I was landing I hear,

"So what's this offside rule thing?"

Eyes open. Lips retreated. Arm still swung. And I ended up just LUNGING onto Elle. As if I was saving her from a bomb explosion. GET DOWN! Cue a what-the-funk-is-going-on-here look from Elle.

"Oh sorry there, just had to get the remote control next to you. This game isn't the best. Let's see what else is on. Apologies for the wrestling style clothes-line I gave you. Almost head-butted you too. Didn't mean that. Accident. My bad. Is it hot in here or *what*?!" Ha ha. Oh look, stopped raining, sun is back, that's great news. Ha ha. How about those Red Sox?"

Elle turns to see if my weather report was true,

"Oh great. I better be getting going, told Shawnie I'd meet her for sushi. Thanks for the soccer lesson! See ya, tea-buddy!"

I know: I did well, very well indeed. Ahem. Quite the smooth pepper I am. Few hours later I get a text:

> 'ELLE: Did you try to kiss me earlier? My sister thinks you did.'
>
> 'ME: Ha! No. What are you on about? We're buddies! Your sister is crazy. Tell her I said she's crazy. Jesus. She's crazy. Well, I better get back to the writing. Tea on soon. Ciao ciao!'

Tea-buddy all the way. At least I'm getting out of the house. Out of my head. Just need to get out of my own way next. Then my Mum will be delighted!

Chapter 19

FIRST. EVER. SHHH...

Did I ever tell you I'm a fan of the crust? The heel. You know, the start and end parts of a loaf of bread. Whichever name you want to call that rose. Lot of folk don't like it at all. But I'm a fan. Particularly when it's toasted. Tasty. As. *Funk.*

So when I went to prepare a celebratory meal for myself last night, I did not mind that all I had left was one slice of bread crust. Horsed it into the toaster. Checked the fridge. What else do I have for this fine meal? Hmm. Fridge. Bare. Naked. Tut. Although, I do have two baby tomatoes left. Wonderful. Anything else? Sniff. Balls. Toast. Burning. Burnt. Ah Jiminy. Not to worry, I shall make do. Nothing can sour this mighty celebration!

In the end, I had: One burnt slice of toast. Two sliced tomatoes. And. A glass of gin, to wash it all down. Mmhmmm. Tasty. Horsed it into me. Two bites. Two chugs. Gone. Quite the feast. Quite the celebrations. Standing in my kitchen. Alone. In my underwear. Betsy. Momentous occasion! Rejoice! Could've been a burnt sock for all I care. Especially as moments earlier I had finally finished a full draft of my first ever book. Wuu huu!

Rambling. Boney. Skeleton. The first draft.

According to Hemingway: The shit one.

Or as a clown might say: The brown sugar one.

Thanks to a mighty shower epiphany, the last sentence had been bouncing around my head for a while now. Gist at least. Problem was filling out all the bits in between that and the first sentence. About 80,000 words or so. The closer I got to writing that last sentence, the slower I found myself writing. End is in sight. So obviously I need to sabotage myself somehow. Not really knowing if I'd make it until I actually got there. My mind fighting itself. As if the marsh man part of my brain, Marshall - another dope - had been woken from his slumber while I was busy getting the bulk written. Oh Jesus, what happened? You're almost done?! My alarm never went off!!! Nooo! Can't let you finish! Must. Funk. You. Up!

Marshall tried his best to pull up the reins. Yank me back by my wild mane of hair.

Too late.
Dancing over the first hurdle.
Wrote out the last sentence.
Instantly a cloud disappeared.
Fog lifted.
All the clutter dispersed.

Buddy Doubt. Funked out. Along with all the other dudes. Just left.

Shoulders.
Relaxed.
Face.
Smiling.
Willie Beaming. Like a delighted clown. Go on the baby steps! Learning by numbers. All worth it. Because now, technically, I've a draft of my book. Happy day!

Not to worry, I'm sure Doubt, Marshall, and all the other apes have just gone out for a pint. They'll try to get back. I also know how good the draft isn't. Yet. Which is good, I think. Big list of things that need changing. Big list. Big. List. Biiiiiiig list. You get the drift. I have a chunk of work left to do. Still though, I've figured out it's far easier to go back and re-write and tweak, than just write something for the first time. Obvious enough. Obviously. Just maybe not so much when you are writing and wading through the marsh at the same time. Wriding, as some like to call it. Speaking of wriding, the past few weeks I've been asked by various Irish newspapers and magazines to write articles for them,

> "Tell us about your life in L.A. Give us some juicy stuff. What's been going on lately?"

Hmmm.

> "Want to hear about me being down a writing well?"

> "Ehh no. We want celebrity stories. Famous people. Drop lots of names. Gossip. Be our Irish Perez Hilton!"

I think these requests flare up my narcissism to an almighty high,

> "Why do you want to hear about what *they* do? *My* trivial life is *waaay* more interesting. Especially when I tell you about what's been going on at the laundry place lately – Cra-zy!"

To which I get the response,

> "We don't care about that. And by that I mean you. We just want celebrity name-droppings. You've met famous people there, right? Tell us about them. Otherwise we'll leave it off."

Tut. Bastards. Need the money. Need the exposure. Like a cheap whure hunting down a grubby dollar, I cave,

> "OK so, I'll sort something out."

Thankfully, Friday supplied some ammunition for me to meet them halfway. Finished my burnt toast and tomatoes. Washed down a glass or two of gin. Did some laundry. Sent out a few texts to see what was going on, who's out tonight? Chowder and a few of his buddies going to a pub nearby, The Den. Charlotte too. Sounds good. I'm in!

Back out into the real world. Time to reacquaint myself with life. What is it one does again? Oh yeah, get dressed. Realised I had no clean socks or underwear. Put on a wash. Slight incident in the laundry place. So, par for the course, I'm late. Balls. Scuttling along. Up the street. Head down. Skipping along. Around the corner from the bar, two girls stop me. By screaming. Inform me that,

> "You're Russell Brand!"

> "Ha. No. Not the first time. But sorry, wrong guy."

I wonder if he gets that he's me, a lot? I'd say so.

"All right girls, I'm late. Ciao ciao."

See that the girls have no clue what I just said. Only that they hear I have a weird accent. Which makes them think that they're right about who I am.

"YOU ARE RUSSELL BRAND! We just heard you were closeby and now you're here!!!"

"Well isn't that a nice story. However. He's not me. I'm not him. Please leave me be. I'm late. OK so - Quick photo."

Smile. Flash. One more. Again. Flash. They SQUEAL with delight,

"THANK YOU RUSSELL!!!"

"No worries, always a pleasure to meet my fans."

Brand out. Off on my merry way again. Get to The Den. Cool spot. Across the road from the Chateau Marmont. Chateau is pretentious, posing and too cool. The Den is chilled, up for a laugh and feels like a proper pub. Den on! See Chowder, Charlotte and a gang of Chowder's buddies. All boozed up already. Time to catch up. Chowder greets me with a hug,

"Wuu huu! First draft finished!"

"I know, mighty, booze on!"

"My round mate, I'll get us some shots!"

"Cheers boss! I'll be back in two, quick bathroom stop."

Walk into a full bathroom. Stalls. All taken. Cubicle? As I go to push open the door and walk in, a guy walks out at the same time. Both on the front foot. Walk into each other. BUMP. Noses. Literally. Eskimos.

"Sorry mate."

"No worries boss."

Look up. See who it is: Russell Brand. Ha. No way. So that's why those two girls were insisting earlier.

"It's you."

"It's me."

Realise I'm standing in his way.

"My bad."

Step aside. He passes over the cubicle baton to me by making a joke about the smell.

"Wasn't me mate, but do enjoy..."

So that was nice. The warning. Not the smell. It reeked. Head back up to Chowder. Shot. Chug. Up for a stroll? Place is buzzing. And packed. Baby steps strolling around. Decide to go outside to the beer garden for some air.

See Russell Brand again. Give him the old 'Phew, what a smell' action. Looks away. Doesn't see me. One of the two. Chowder is pretty drunk and telling me there's a load of people here I should talk to. Yeah, there are a lot of people here. What are you on about?

While Chowder is twirling his head around, I start chatting with a girl next to me. Compliment her funky nerd glasses. Asks me what do I do. Chowder jumps in,

"He just wrote an *amazing* book. You must check it out."

Good work by the Chowaduu. Some man for a prop. She feigns interest,

"Oh that's great, can't wait to read it."

Spoof. Good actress in fairness. Actually, I recognise her now. She was in *The Office* for a couple of seasons. Quincy Jones's daughter!

"How's it going? Your Dad produced Michael Jackon's *Thriller* album. Just thought I'd remind you... How mighty is that?!"

Laughs. Me away? No no, she's laughing. Asks,

> "Where you from?"

> "Ireland."

> "Oh my Gawd I love Ireland."

Guy next to her joins the conversation. Asks me,

> "What part are you from?"

He's been. Tells me about his road trip around Ireland. Big fan of the place. Or else the accent. Not too sure. Mid-some-tale-about-the-Ring-of-Kerry he's interrupted by people asking for a photo with them. Odd. Turn to the girl,

> "Rashida..., who's he?"

> "Ever hear of Doogie Howser?"

> "No. Sorry. I'm from Ireland. What's that?"

Took another look... Oh, I know who it is now. Neil Patrick Harris. He's in that show *How I Met Your Mother.*

> "Are ye friends?"

Before she could answer, a birthday cake appears next to us. Everyone bursts into song. Automatically join in, obviously...,

> "Happy birthday to you! Happy birthday to you! Happy birthday dear..."

Turn again to Rashida,

> "Who is the you?"

Points over to a big smiling guy...,

> "Oh, that's Jason Segel..."

> "Happy birthday to you! Yay!"

Blow out the candles.

"Speech. Speeeeech. SPPPEEEEECCHHH!"

I said that last one too loud. People turning around to see what clown was bellowing at them. Looked behind me too as if it was someone else.

"Chowder, pipe down!"

It was then when I took a proper look around. Place full to the brim with actors and comedians. Cast of *Knocked Up*. Andy Samberg and the likes from *Saturday Night Live*. Few folk from *The Office*. Main people from *30 Rock*. *Parks and Recreation*. *How I Met Your Mother*. Now I see what drunken Chowder was telling me. Jesus, if you wanted to write an article for a celebrity obsessed country, this was the perfect spot! Chowder comes back over,

"Mate, you should tell these people about your book. Get an in with them."

"Hmm. Don't think so. Doesn't make sense to me."

Points to Anziz Asari next to us.

"Go, tell him. He'll love it. You'll never know what happens."

No. Not up for that plan. How is that meant to work? I wrote a book that isn't even out yet but maybe you could hook me up with a sitcom or a starring role on the one you're in?

"Nay. I'm going back inside. I've no business out here."

Not sure why, but I got in a mental huff. Jealous of their success? Perhaps. Gin? Probably. Dumb? Yes. As I'm making my way back in towards the bar, I get stopped by Doogie Howser. Introduces me to the guy next to him. Presume it's his brother.

"So you're from Ireland. How amazing!"

"Yeah, it's a mighty place. Ever been?"

"Of course, we did a tour together."

"Oh right. Family trip? Did your parents go too or which?"

Gives me a confused look.

"Family trip? What do you mean by "parents"? You're funny."

"I mean you're brothers, right? You look alike."

Cue a SQUEAL of laughter. Endless. My turn to be confused. Until they inform me they're married.

"Oh right. You're a couple. Ha. My bad."

Although for married men they both seem to be big fans of the Irish accent. To change the topic, when asked about my book, I start rambling on about this other book they must both read: *The Road Less Traveled.* Deep conversation. Mighty book. Pimping it out big time. Instead of my own unreleased one. So that was dumb. Might've been the guys who could've hooked me up with my own sitcom too. After that, the night petered out. Went home. Alone. Drank some gin. Recapped the night. Basically I was in a pub with a lot of other people, the majority of whom happened to be well-known actors and comedians. I kind of spent a long time chatting to a gay couple about their passion for Ireland and my passion for a book. I also think they invited me back to a pool party at theirs. Not sure if they meant what I thought. Think I chose to be dumb and act clueless. Dodged on. Just like I'm not sure if Quincy Jones' daughter was in fact chatting me up. Or if I shot that all down with my high-pitched squeals of *Thriller.*

Oh and some girls screamed at me for being Russell Brand. And then ironically Russell Brand warmed up the toilet bowl seat for me in the pub. All in all: Good old night? Not sure. Depressing hangover the next day says: Nay. Personally, I prefer the story of why I was late in the first place. Not every day you get locked into a laundry place with a guy who looks like Meatloaf and another guy whose favourite band was definitely Queen. Automatic door of the Laundromat locked. Imprisoned. Three amigos. How do we get out? Oh Jesus. Panic. Handbags.

Flailing.
Freaking.
Yelping.
Worlds.
Crashing.

Thankfully I had a bag of Guinness cans with me that I had bought for drinking at home. Offered them around. Calmed everybody down. Finally Meatloaf figured out that the automatic lock might not have even been locked all along. Thinks that the door was actually just a bit stuck? Perplexed. Who knows? Who cares? Freedom. Balls, I'm late for The Den... Crap story really. Far more interesting is how I got to find out that celebrities don't smell of roses. Amazing! Who would've thought? At least I got an article out of it. And also realized how much work I still need to do, to get where I want to be. Wonderful.

Now then, time to sort out this pile of sh... Brown sugar. Ahem. Wride off. Tweak on!

Chapter 20

Dirty Old Hunt

If you were to think about it, you might say I'm a bit of a swinger. Dabbled on both sides of the fence. Men. Women. Sometimes both at the same time. Recently though, it's been all women. Personal preference. Lifestyle choice. No need to judge or anything. Then again things do change. Looks like I'm going back to the lads' side for a while. Pressured into it. Necessity. Otherwise I might've just ended up on the streets. Wandering. Homeless. Bumming around. Time to bite the bullet. Bit hard. So I trawled. Crept. Pounded. Knocked. Grilled. Interrogated. Stripped bare. Felt hollow. Mission accomplished at least. Happy days!

I am of course referring to my mission to find somewhere new to live. Swinger when it comes to whether I've lived with guys or girls before. What else would I have been on about? Tut. Ah come on, get your mind out of the gutter! So about a month ago Tara rang me from work,

> "Really exciting news! Are you at home?! OK, stay there! I'm on the way. This is huge! So excited for you!!!"

Oh Jesus, I thought. What's this? So nervous. So excited. This must be huge despite having no clue what it's about!!! I remember Tara said she knew someone who knew someone who might be a T.V executive and she was going to talk to them about me and my book. Did she talk to that person? Had she somehow sorted out a sitcom deal for me? Oh Jesus. Yes! WHAT ELSE COULD IT BE!?!

Funk me pink.

Hang on, calm down.
Deep breaths. Wait until Tara breaks the news to you herself. Then you can go funking wild!

Tara arrives home. Smiling. Happy. Winking. Tapping her nose. Whatisitwhatisitwhatisit??! Balls. She must go to the bathroom first. Ten minutes later. Toilet flushed. Returns. I'm in the kitchen. Acting cool. Pouring myself a celebratory glass of gin in anticipation.

> "Oh hi Tara, didn't see you there. Good day at work? You mentioned something about having news to tell me...?"
>
> "Yes. Are you ready? OK...
>
> I found us a new place to live!"
>
> Tara throws her arms open,
>
> "Ta-da!
> It's an amazing house in the Hollywood Hills! Perfect for you to write, chill, up in the hills, so quiet and best of all, you can pay the exact same rent as now. I'll cover the extra cost. I really want you to move in with me. Will you, will you, will you?! I love having you as a roommate! How amazing is this??!"
>
> "Huh? What? No way? That's *it*?"

The butterflies in my stomach belly flop to my bowels. Quite clearly my mind works in weird ways. Maybe I'm that hungry (desperate) that I can fool myself about anything right now. Ugh. Give me that gin. Slug. Ha. Smile. Nod. Compose. Squeak,

> "So, eh, anything about a sitcom at all...?"

Now it's Tara's turn to give me the confused look. Awkward kitchen moment. And then we proceed to normal small talk about the new abode.
See the truth was, I no longer really enjoyed living with Tara. Really nice offering me her spare room when I arrived back in L.A. Started off grand. Buddy-buddy. Short-term agreement. Just until I find my feet. Play it by ear. But then I went down the writing well. And lived in my own little bubble. All the while, Tara got more and more depressing. Always something wrong. When really we all deal

with the same stuff. Daily basis. Complaining about something. Someone. Nothing. Sweet Jesus, please stop! Worse still each complaint was followed with,

> "Not that I'm complaining, I'm a positive person but still why does it *always* happen to me..."

Well if you say that, what's with all the complaints? I would quietly scream in my head as I absentmindedly nodded along. And must you constantly moaning, bemoan and drone? I'm trying to live in a bubble of joy! Speaking of moaning, overhearing Tara having... ahem... in the room next to me with only a thin wall as protection - another nail in the coffin. Just couldn't hack it all. Got to the point where I kind of dreaded Tara coming home every day from work.

Cherry on top, Tara then started seeing some English guy, John, who thought it was hilarious to put on a mocking Irish accent every time he was over. If you know me, you have free licence to mock me until the cows come home. For example, I remember back in third year, my buddy Vinny Motherway and I were mocking to and fro. I think I asked him why his head was so big (quite a square head to be fair) and in return he said,

> "Good one, Toaster Head."

To this day, that is my favourite insult ever. First time I ever remember being speechless. Some call on the spot! (I obviously examined in the mirror and Vinny was right: Long, narrow head – it really does look like a toaster!) Although, maybe that's just funny in my toaster head. Bad example. Anyway, all banter when you know me. However if I don't know you and the first thing you do is mock me, I will probably think: Who's this ape? Keep doing it and I will tell you,

> "You're *some* ape."

So that was also nice. Wanting to punch that fool of a man. Anyway, enough was enough. Still very grateful that Tara gave me a lift to Ikea to buy my writing desk and all, but in the end I had to tell her I wasn't up for moving to the hills. It's not you, it's me, kind of thing,

> "I need to be in WeHo for writing reasons. And other stuff. Are we still cool?"

No. We were not. Tara took offence. And then told everyone I was horrible to live with. Couldn't wait to get rid of me, although for no specific reason. Just as you do. Sound! Felt the wrath of a scorned woman. Toasty and awkward.

Perhaps I am only bring this up now as I have a thing against people who moan constantly. I once had a friend who was mostly my friend because we were friends since we were young. All she would do was complain. Constantly exasperated. Permanent state of disbelief. The world owes her something! Blame others if anything went wrong. Jealous of everyone. Bitching behind their backs. That kind of thing. All very exhausting to be around. Dangerous too. Trying to lay seeds in your own brain. The world owes you too, you should act like me! Jesus. It doesn't. Get away from me. Only solution is to cut them loose. Weight off the shoulders. Sagging energy set free. Felt mighty. Cull on. And I was telling the truth as well: I am a fan of West Hollywood. Only good part of L.A that almost feels like being in a city. Besides downtown. But that seems dodge and dead. Although if I was pushed I'd have to say WeHo doesn't really feel like a city at all. At most an oddly laid out village. Full of the Village People. However, at least places are within walking distance here. Shops. Bars. Gym. Nightclubs. And most importantly for the next part of my overall plan: Comedy Clubs.

If I was to move up in the hills; farewell to all that. Besides going over to your neighbour's house, you must drive everywhere. Need milk: Drive: Need booze: Drive. Need gym: Drive. Want to walk somewhere: Drive. Basically I'd be moving to a new way of life. Which I'm not really up for at the moment. Too busy on my current mission. Trying to mold and craft a jungle of thoughts. Wriding along. Wrestling Doubt and Marshall to the bitter end. Right now I can barely decide between having grilled chicken or stir fried chicken for dinner. Having to decide about changing daily way of life? Bob Hope. As a wise clown once said: Go with thy gut. Decision made. The Hills: Apologies. Boys Town: Sticking with ye, lads! WeHo on!

Unfortunately this decision meant I would have to do something I swore I'd never do again: Go back to "him". Craig. And his lists. Best. Worst. Website. Ever. Double edged sword. My first voyage to L.A lead me on many highs and lows. Pretty sure every low can be traced back to Craig. Probably most of the highs too. Craigslist has lead me down so many merry paths before. Maybe one legit classified ad out of every ten. The rest: Scams. Scams. More scams. Nutters. Weirdos. Freaks. Psychos. Stolen. Dodge. Until finally, just before you've said never again, you give one more try, respond to one final ad and then: Success!

That one success usually gives you enough rope to go back again the next time. Making you think Craig will change. I can make him. You don't understand. That *one* time. We were golden. You haven't seen him like I have. He can be really nice! Lured me back once more. Time for some apartment hunting. Scour. Scrutinize. Suss. Just have to find somewhere nice that's furnished, with affordable rent, a sane roommate and within a few streets of where I am now. How hard could that be?!

Checked the "Rent" section. Always makes me feel cheap. Rent boy. When am I going to start owning?! At least the initial signs were good. Early contender. Gabi. Leasing out her second bedroom. Looked slick in the photos. Pool and gym in the building too. Price: Only slightly more expensive than what I pay now. First one in, could be a winner! Appointment made. Called over. Knock knock. Door opened. Dose. Never presume... Gabi turned out to be an older guy. Never met a male Gabi before. Gave me a tour of his manor. Highly flamboyant man. Whisked me around the place with fine flair. Offered me a seat on his rouge couch. Small talk. Pointless. I had already signed out in my head. Place looked *way* smaller in person. Flattering photos. Nodding along while Gabi tells me about the computer firm he works for. Then asks me how I spend my Sundays,

> "Would you be in or out of the house?"
>
> "Huh? Not sure. Why?"
>
> "Usually my boyfriend spends the day here on Sundays. Would you have any issue if you... heard us?"
>
> "Heard you doing wha- Pardon?"

Oh right. Naked Fundays? Hmmm. I'll be honest. I don't want to hear anybody doing that. Guys. Guy and girl. Cats. Dogs. Maybe I'd be OK with girl on girl but I'd have to listen and decide. Anyway, cheers Gabi but this might not be the best option for me. I'll be off. Doors locked. How do I open it? Say hi to,

> "Roger is it? Three's a crowd. No, I didn't mean I want a threesome Gabi, gotta go. Enjoy Naked Fundays without me. Meter is up on my car. Yeah, I know I said I walked but I lied. I drove. Love to drive.

Drive on. There we go. Good duck!"

It was never going to be that easy. Wouldn't be the only time I was asked about "that" kind of thing either. Not the whole naked part. More the personal sexual preference side of things. Aural carry-on. A dirty old house hunt overall to be true. All very interested in it. Talking to complete randomers about sex. My usual habits. Their typical ways. Something to consider, I suppose. Some seeing how far they could talk about it until I got up to leave. L.A is a *throbbing* pulse. Day two. Found a place right on the same street. Girl asked me to meet her in Starbucks down the road. Thought nothing of it. Until. She tells me,

"It might get a bit weird now."

"Why's that?"

"Well, it could be weird if we start dating."

Sweet Jesus.

"Gotta go. G'duck!"

Second appointment. Nice spot, one street over. Couple renting out a spare room. Meet the girl who put up the ad. Instant sexual buzz from her. Also tells me *straightaway* that,

"My boyfriend is my BITCH!"

"O?
K?"

"We can have all the fun we want. He just cleans up after us."

"Pardon me? What do you mean? You mean you really like Irish guys? You want to do what with me? Ha. Sorry."

Boyfriend and all. Plus. You seem like a whure to be true!

"Oh Lord is that the time? Gotta go."

Good duck! Two apartments. Two romantic offers. Never got to see the inside of either place. Craig - What the funk?! You're at it again!

Next place was pretty slick. Savage looking Spanish style country house. Secluded. Only an eight minute walk from everywhere. (I was timing all the walking distances - vital!) Cheaper than everywhere else as well. Obviously some sort of sex-den-orgy-abode going on. As I walked up the driveway flanked with piles of dirt and cement, I hear someone call from a top window,

"Hey, keep an eye ou- "

Before I knew it, I was POUNCED on by a horse of a dog. Huge beast. Bowls me over. Straight into a pile of dirt.
JUMPS on me.
Licking.
Breathing gusts of dog breath on me.
Slobber. Dripping. Stunk.

"Sweet Jesus get him off! HEELLLP!"

No joy. Along comes horse two. More slobber. Almost French kissing me. Pinning me down. Save a clown! Double teamed by two *beasts*. Helpless. Flailing in muck. Craig? WHAT'S GOING ON?! Finally the owner has run downstairs. Pulls the horse dogs back. Laughs and tell me,

"They really like you."

"Thanks. I like them too. Ha-ha. Ha. Haw."

So then we all laughed. Picked myself up. Horses start BARKING again. Making me nervously laugh out loud some more. Also wondering if I posses some of the devil in me. Dogs like to pounce. RUFF-RUFF-RUFF-RUFF!!! Owners thinks it's great fun. Ha, yeah, me too. Smiles on the outside. Freaked on the inside. Big beasts! At least the married couple who owned the mansion seemed really nice. Something was up though. Smiling nervously as we approached the front door. Complimented their house:

"Savage looking! What's the inside like...
Oh."

Skeleton. Gutted. Bare. Falling apart. Owners were doing it up.

"5 year project. It'll be restored in no time."

"And when did ye start?"

"Last week – No two weeks ago."

Asked would I mind the noise and the commotion? And my room would have no proper floor either.

"It will though. Soon. Come on, what do you say Merrick, are you in??"

"Ehh..."

Doubtful. But I already knew this the minute I was raped by your two horses. Thanks though. Gotta go... G'duck! Slobber. Off. Hunt. On. Next day. Another place nearby. Two friends renting out a room in a house. Looked good. Spanish style. Fully furnished inside. Cheap enough as well. No horses. Everyone wearing clothes. Hmmm. This could be good. And then we all sat down on the couch. And the first two questions threw me off.

"Would you have your own toothbrush?"

"I... would.
Is that the right answer?"

Launched into how they needed respect for their toothbrushes. Last roommate had no respect. Always used their stuff. OK. Don't worry. I have my own. Next question...,

"Do you do heroine?"

"Ha. Pardon?"

"Are. You. Into. Heroine?"

"I. Am. Not. Why so, do I look like I am? Thank you."

Turns out the guy of the abode was a recovering heroine addict and didn't want to relapse. Launched into another tirade about the room's previous occupant, Peaches. Apparently Peaches had just moved out/pulled a runner. Left them in the lurch for rent. Peaches had all sorts of problems. So then Peaches just ran away. No more Peaches. Peaches is now in London.

"Do you know Peaches? You're both Irish."

"Peaches who?"

Oh that Peaches. No. More of an apple man myself. Sounds lovely though. Her Dad Bob seems sound in fairness. Yeah, you'd think I *would* know him, what with us both being Irish. Never bumped into each other - I know, weird, right?! Ireland is just one street where everyone knows everyone. How have we not?!

"OK so. I'll be off.
Yeah, I'll definitely let you know soon if I want to move.
I'll be in touch. Gotta go... G'duck!"

Day four: Met a Russian girl whose apartment reminded me of a sterilized hospital ward in some barren part of Deutschland. Harshest place I've ever been. White. Grey. Plastic. Hardness. Everywhere. Protective covering over everything. She wasn't the most fun either. Felt like an interrogation the whole time. Thought at one stage I had her with a joke but realised it was just a momentary twitch which rippled through her face. So I bid her a fond farewell. Day five: Three duds. Too small. Too weird. Too "bro". Held some hope for appointment number four though. Emails were flowing back and forth. Very eager renter. Googled the address. Walk over to the place. No sign of anyone. No answer on any door. Return home. Check email. Hmmm. Apparently the landlord *just* moved to Nigeria..."On God's mission". Wants to do me a deal though. He will give me the first month rent for free but I just have to pay him the next 3 months rent up front? Oh and I don't actually get to see the place before I decide, he'll post me the keys once the money is lodged.

"Really? No way! Amazing! Sweet Lord, where do I sign? Actually, can I pay even more money, you FUNKING IDIOT CONMAN?!"

Ughatha. Waste of a walk. Shattering my high hopes. CRAAAAAAAAIIGGG!!! Almost gave up at that stage. How bad would living on the streets really be? Hmmm. Bad. Number ten on! Saturday afternoon. Heading over to Chowder's place to watch a soccer match. Quick trawl of Craigslist before I go. Spot a place near Barney's. Looks mighty. Email. Reply. Set up an appointment. Be there in ten! Forward the place to Chowder for his sage advice... Dose. Re-read the ad. Read it wrong. Hopes now not so high. Seeing as rent was too high. Chowder recommends I might as well have a look though. Over I go. See it's a nice place. Nice street. Inside looks good. Place looks like a home. Feels like one. Nice big spare bedroom. Bathroom to myself. Fireplace. Big huge TV. Nice couch. Dining room. Balcony. Dancing all round. That's it. This is it. My new abode. Now then, time to somehow sort this out for myself.

Owner seems sound. Big. Persian. Jew. Schlomo! (Looks like a Persian Ronald Reagan.) At first I can tell he's put off by my hair and foreignness. Eying me up and down. Wary. Until I crack a few jokes. Whip out some Irish charm. Win him over. Sorted. We both figure out that the other person seems normal enough. Schlomo, ever hear of Naked Fundays? No? Good stuff. No man-on-man action. Not that that's bad, just that it's more preferable if no. Time to lay my cards on the table.

> "Schlomo, I like the place, I like you. This is what I currently pay rent-wise. That is also my limit. I know that's a third less than what you're advertising this place for, but that's all I can afford to pay. If this interests you, let me know."

Schlomo says that's too low, tries to haggle. I unfortunately can only haggle lower if he wants? No room to budge. Tell Schlomo to think about it. Let me know soon though, might be moving into this lovely place with two beautiful dogs, so time is ticking. Haggle. On. Leave and head to Chowder's place. En route, I get the call,

> "All right you Irishman, let's do it.
> Trial month at first."

No long-term commitment? Ha, even better. Go on the Schlomo! Now we're dancing. Giddy up that there gift of the gab that be in my mouth. Wuu huu! And. A. *Duu*! So despite economic restraints and Craig flinging curveballs at me from all angles, I've somehow managed to upgrade my living arrangements. And, cherry on top: I now have a pool. *Betsy*! Hunt off. Pool party on!

Chapter 21

Salmon Flavoured Steak

Want to know an amazing fact? I think it's exactly one year ago to the day since I arrived in L.A to set off on my randumb adventure. First time around. Fresh off the plane. Green as could be. No idea what exactly I was going to do. Clueless, one might say. One might then wonder: Just how many immense strides have I made since then? How settled am I? Surely I've a bucket of clues now? Ahem... Woke up with cramps in my stomach. Never fun. What did I eat last night? Actually, no. This is more the feeling of dread. I know what that is: My flow of income. Balls. Money issues. Still haunting me. Why doesn't more money get horsed my way?! Ughatha Christ Almighty.

Decided to skip breakfast. Might be time I start rationing. Stomach was too busy flipping cartwheels as is. When you have a blank work calendar in front of you, it's kind of slightly worrying. Waking up every Monday morning not knowing if any money is coming your way that week - Funking dodge. My one reserve is the rest of the book advance I get once the final draft is sorted. But still. I need some regular flow. As it is, I live in a cycle of bangs, ebbs and nos. Sporadic to say the least. Money comes. Flows. Disappears. Ebbs back. Grows again. Disappears. Over and over. Month to month. Land of the unknown. Hunting down spurts. Find a trickle. Relax a little. Carefree. Ish. Until it's time to pay rent. Almost zero again? *Whaaat*? New month. Blank slate. Start again. Which is why I now have this throbbing pulse in the back of my head. Not good for the mental well-being.

Time to go back to basics. Or is it scraping the barrel? Who cares. Need to generate something from somewhere. Craigslist: Anything?

Start horsing out emails to people. Spent the day making phone calls. Follow ups with places I've been DJing. For one reason or another these have all been hit and miss lately. Purple Lounge is maybe twice a month. Fashion gigs are seasonal. Other clubs and bars are slow to respond. Just have to wait. Could sit. Too depressing. Head out. Start knocking on doors. Bars nearby. No joy. Tut. Regular flow of income, I do not remember you at all.

Thank funk for the gym. Some place to clear the head. Lift the fog from the mind marsh. Even if you're not doing much. Just being there seems to be enough at times. Distracted by the weights. Lost in thought. At least it got my appetite back. Good work, gym!

Fairly uneventful trip. Well, just the end was slightly odd. I prefer to shower at home. Various reasons. One: Showers here basically show your silhouette to everyone in the reception area. Men's on one side. Women's on the other side. See what is going on now and again. Friendliness. Touching. Cahoorting. Only ever on one side. Never the women's. Tut. So to avoid naked weirdness I just don't shower there and avoid eye contact with certain nuts in there.

Unfortunately I did go into the changing room afterwards to weigh myself. Threw my towel and bottle of water onto a bench by the scales. My inability to throw a towel on a bench kicked in. (Even if I place a towel on a bench, it will invariably slip off. No clue why but it does.) Slipped. Instinctively went to grab it. Another towel dropped on the ground by it. Again, instinctively picked it up. Hand it over. Look up. Naked dude. Giving me a weird naked dude smile. Realised he'd thrown his to the floor. Holding both towels for too long as I handed his one back. Smiling at me. Staring into my soul. Seeing if I would smile back. Must be code. Asking if I was going to shower? Sweet Jesus. Get away. Ran off.

While I'm drudging home, my cousin Colin phones me. Wedding coming up in San Fran soon. Fills me in with the details. Asks me if I got the email? Which now? The one with simple question. Very simple email, in fact:

'For the meal, did you want salmon or steak?'

I'm the only one who hasn't replied. Need to make a decision. Two names. Pick one! Which irrelevant answer will I go with to this innocuous conundrum? Something I struggle with at times. Once took me a week to choose a generic iPod case. Decided to talk out my meal options to Colin on the phone. Leads me to spiral down.

Spitting out indecisiveness,

"Meal?
Eh. Salmon.
No, steak."

"Steak."

"Yeah, definitely salmon."

"Go with steak."

"I'll have salmon."

"Steak."

"Salmon. Any chicken?"

Pause.
No Reply.
Then.

"Salmon."

"Steak. Definitely."

"Definitely."

"Which one?"

"Oh, eh, I forgot. What are the options again?"

"OK, I'll take another day or two to think about it.
Thanks."

Hung up. Started debating with myself. I'd like steak but salmon would be nice too especially if I'm going to be boozing. Don't want to get *too* full is the only thing. Sleepy after the meal and all that. But then I wouldn't have to eat all the steak really, I could leave a bit behind. Although I have a problem with leaving food if it's in front of me. Don't want to waste it. Hmmm. Should I ring my cousin back, find out what else comes with the meal? How many courses I wonder? Starter? Veg? Potatoes? Desert? Actually, would choosing the meal now, determine what type of wine I'll be drinking as well? Because I'd prefer white. But with steak? That's red. I don't want to look like a clown and seem like I don't know what wine I should be ordering. I wonder if I should just go with the salmon? Which reminds me: I must buy a suit. Which also reminds me: I must sort out my flights. Which reminds me: Where am I going to get money? All right, focus: Steak or salmon? I wonder. Hmmm. I wonder. I wonder what I wonder? I know what I'm wondering: Am I a *funking* idiot who's losing his mind?!

By this stage I was pacing around my kitchen muttering to myself. Started getting dizzy. Need air. Went outside. Looked up. Star gazing. Saw a savage lunar halo in the sky. Pretty slick. As if the moon was a light bulb in a big black ceiling, surrounded by a lampshade ring. Made me forget my inner-monologue ravings. Chilled me out. Thank funk. Realised it wasn't like anything major had happened today to have me in such an odd mood. Although maybe that was it. Nothing major happened. What am I actually doing? Some sort of stalling? Perhaps I've been using the book as a front. Allowing me to avoid the real world. Now the book is almost done, people are asking what I'm going to do next. As if I should have something bigger than the book to move into straightaway. Because these things are easy and are just placed in your lap. Right?

Well, I know the immediate next thing I'll be doing: Move to a new apartment tomorrow. Converges nicely at the same time of the month. Time when I get cramps, mood swings and cravings for a salmon flavoured steak. Monthly. Pains. Known. As. Rent. Oh hello, Fear, long time no see. And here's Doubt, back again. Perhaps this moving malarkey is what has me unsettled. Didn't realise moving was such a stressful thing.

On the upside, at least I'm travelling light? Two suitcases. And a desk. Tara has everything else. Moved to her new abode today. My house is now a skeletor. Bare. Empty. Nada. Coming back tomorrow for the bed in my room. Also kindly left me a fork and a bowl. All one needs. Although the lack of any seat in the apartment is far more annoying than I imagined. Which is why I'm now currently sitting on a wooden step at the top of my stairs. Trying in vain to borrow my neighbour's wireless. Won't reach as far as my bed. Keep losing the signal. Gone are the days of borrowing milk and sugar. And I think he may have turned it off on me – Yeah. Just disappeared. Wuu. Mighty fun. Nice empty apartment. No food. No TV. No internet. Just me. My thoughts. The Fear. Doubt. And a dash of self-pity. Beautiful combination!

Rambles have kicked in. Not too sure what my point is again?

Year on? Still as bizarre. Maybe that's it. Today might have just encapsulated a whole year, give or take a few degrees of satisfaction/frustration. Circles. Knocking. Thinking. Gym. Music. Issues. Stars. Black hole. What am I doing here? Last minute, comes good. I hope. Is that my point? Let's just say yes indeed it is. Well done me. Stalmon on!

Chapter 22

NAKED FAT MAN... SIT DOWN!

Despite me having minimal belongings - desk, two suitcases, two bags of food – moving is quite a stressful time. I can now understand why Tara was in tears the day she had the movers in moving all her stuff. Two dodgy Hungarian guys. Triple charging her. Harsh enough. Felt bad. I thought I was good to go. Chowder was going to give me a spin. Throw my stuff into his car. One trip. Zip over to my new abode. Move in with Schlomo (or Moe as I now call him). Done. And. Dancing! Except: My desk was too awkward to fit in the car. Meaning one trip with my luggage and food. Then Chowder had to go meet Charlotte. So it was just going to be one trip of me walking back, carrying my desk? Ten minute walk only but still, awkward as funk. Especially carrying it on my own. Where are those dodgy Hungarians when you need them? Tut.

Thankfully, Moe swooped in. Saved the day. Ford pick-up truck. Offered to hook me up. Just throw the desk in the back. Are you sure? Go on the Moe! Big Ronald Reagan head up on him. Mighty man! The moving part wasn't really what stressed me though. Nay. Minor irk really. Main reason I think moving is so brimming full of stress is that you must start a completely new routine. Which is a particular balls when you're surprisingly routine driven. Comes as a shock to most folk but despite my outwardly mess-like carry on, I'm really organised, very clean and extremely tidy. Pretty much OCD. Take my room. Everything in its right place. Bed always made. Desk dust-free. Pens arranged. Books lined up. T-shirts folded. Jeans hung up. Runners in a row. Good to go. People are always amazed that it's my room when they see it. I'd say this comes from my Mum. Making sure I cleaned my bedroom when I was young. Say I wanted to go outside and play soccer...,

> "Mum! I'm going to play soccer... I'll clean it when I come back... No I will... I promise...
> MUMMMM NOOOOO...
> OK so! For sugar's sake! I'll do it now! Ughatha!!!"

Must have dawned on me one day, If I just have it clean all the time, I can play soccer all the time! OCD, here I come! My self-diagnosed OCD got bad for a while actually. Particularly when I was living in a comfort zone before moving to L.A. Far too much time on my hands. Brain had nothing to do. Just started playing tricks on myself. If you're going to eat some almond nuts, you have to eat exactly fifteen, no more no less. No actual reason - Just because! If you're going to walk into a room through this door and walk around the table that way, you're going to bloody well have to leave the exact same way or else something bad will happen! Same with the volume on the TV or radio, it must always be on an even number or else you'll start getting a headache and mentally freaking out! On the upside, it did lead me to saying prayers every night for everyone I know, so that nothing bad will ever happen to us and we'll all live until at least one hundred and five years old and also none of us will ever get herpes. So that was nice.

At least moving to L.A has kept my mind busy with other things. Actually, while I'm telling you about why I am like I am, I've also never heard my parents swear either. So that's probably why I don't freely swear now. Well in my writing at least. In case you were wondering what the Frederick Funk was wrong with me.

Anyway, back to my original mighty point: I like to be organized. Moving is the opposite feeling of that. Buckets to get used to. Lots of small things. Particularly when you move in with someone else. Get used to their ways. Don't want to impose. Get used to the new smells. New sounds. New route to the bathroom. Seats are in different places. Where are all the spoons? TV is now over there? Weird remote control. TV channels laid out differently. All that. I like to move around and travel. However when I pitch up my tent I try to maintain my own routine as much as I can. Having that with me wherever I go keeps me sane. Losing it makes me otherwise.

My new abode might just be the quietest place in the world too. Deafening. Empty chasm. Not use to it. Old place always had screaming neighbours or crying women of some sort. All those sounds that kept me company while I worked into the night. Now: Nada. Silence. Screaming out at me. Silent shouts. No longer talking to myself. Instead whispering. Having to go outside to listen for traffic or the likes. *Any*thing. Just to make sure my hearing is still working. Even the street is silent. Made me feel like I'd have to whisper if I was on the phone out there. Seriously. Ridiculously. Quiet.

I'm still getting a feel for the place too. Polite. Ease into it. Moe works a nine to five. Don't want to be loud while he's asleep. Up night-owling. Tip-toeing around the apartment. Not sure if the T.V is up too high? I wonder if the kettle boiling is making a lot of noise? Jesus Christ, sounds like a foghorn. No hot beverage for me. Maybe just an iced tea. How about the toaster? Way too loud. Sweet Lord. Toast is not happening either. I'll just sit down. Actually, don't want to make noise pulling out the chair at the table. Loud enough earlier today when I did it. Sitting is gone too. Leaving me standing in fear in the middle of the kitchen. Enjoying my slice of bread and cup of cold tea. Afraid to move. Enjoying the silence. Hear something.

"What's that?"

Breathing.
Loud.
Oh.
It's me.
Why am I bellowing breaths?

Clocks.
Ticking.
Amplified.
Tocking it out.
Voices in my head turn self-conscious.
No longer screaming at me.
Eerily whispering instead.
Far worse.

You always have to worry about the quieter type of nuts. That counts for in your head too. Always the ones who do the damage. Quiet. So quiet. Freaking me out. Maybe I should've moved somewhere else. Somewhere not so quiet. I miss the suicidal neighbour in my old place. Miss her depressed crying cat even more. Plus the couple who would loudly break up and then make up on a daily basis. I miss their various screamings.

"What have I done? What was I thinking?!"

Worst night's sleep in a long while. Some ape. Surrounded by monkeys. Hushing them. Screaming thoughts in my head. Tossing. Turning. Freaked. Needed to talk to Moe. Can't handle living in quietness. Need to be able to make some noise. Sat around all day. Moe comes home from work. Sees a worried looking me,

> "Something wrong? What happened?"

> "Don't you give me that, Moe! Something *is* wrong and you bloody well know it!!!"

Burst into a pile of gibber. Rattle out all the marsh thoughts. Issues. Gripes. Concerns. Rambling on and on. Until finally Moe stops me:

> "I haven't been in the apartment for two days."

> "Say which now?"

> "I stayed at my parents. Gave you sometime to get used to the place."

No one was here when I was tiptoeing around the kitchen the night before. Night and day before that...? Nope. Home alone.

> "Oh. Right. Good work."

Quite. The. Ape.

> "Ha ha, that stuff I just said - only joking Moe!"

Decided then I need to get rid of all the money-monkeys running around. Cash in on my gold bonds. Time to get the second installment of my book advance. Inject something into my flaccid bank account. I had told my publishers that the first draft I sent them was just an idea of how I wanted the book to be. Basically I just needed it to be done so I could send them something. My plan was to fix all that and send it to them again saying: Oh, here's the actual draft I meant to send. Use this one instead, ha ha.

Great plan. Although it did mean I had to go back down the well again. Yay. Now I don't want to bore you with what it's like to write a book. However, I would like to give you one insight. Slight glimmer of what it's like for me.

For arguments sake, let's just imagine that my head is a room. At the moment, it's bare. Almost fully empty. (Hard to imagine such a thing, with regards to my head, I know, but try.) All the furniture has been taken out. Except for one chair, which is in the middle of the room. And there's also one guy in the room, who represents my attention and discipline. Running around like a mad man. Naked for some reason. Hyper. Riddled with ADD. Spouting out gibberish. Pouring. Wide-eyed. Rambling. Fat too, representing my inner fat man I assume.

Now and again I can calm naked-fat-man down. Trick him. Get him to sit on the chair. Coax him to tell me a story so I can write it down for everyone else to read. Naked-fat-man starts off. Reenacting the tale. My fingers start typing. Tapping away. All sounds good. Getting places here. Until. I hear a noise. A distraction. Something catches my eye. Turn my back for a second... What's going on over there - And then he's gone. Naked-fat-man jumps up. Runs back around the room. Rattling on about something new. Won't finish the story he started earlier until I can get him to sit back down again. Starts drooling when I tell him to cop on. Flapping his lips up and down with his finger. Fully lost him. Tut. Why did I look at those shiny balls?! So the key is getting him to sit and stay in the chair. Plant him in that one spot. Rein him in. Make him talk. And talk. And keep going. Until I have enough out of him and I've fully finished writing my first book.

Great analogy, I think you'll agree. Any analogy with a naked fat man usually is the best. At least that's the gibberish I told Chowder today. Trying to explain why I won't be doing anything else bar finishing this edit. In case it would take me out of the zone, so to speak. As I had naked-fat-man glued to the seat. Talking the way I wanted him to gibber. No more shiny balls. Although if I had just used the word 'zone' earlier, I probably wouldn't have needed all that other gibberish above. Bit late now. Chowder also thinks I either have deep psychological barriers. Or else I'm just the world's biggest procrastinator,

> "Why not just write?"
>
> "I am! I'm trying to. Look, you don't understand. Don't worry though, I have a really clever new plan: Not-going-to-bed-and-sleeping-just-for-the-sake-of-it-when-I-could-be-up-writing plan."

So far it's working splendidly well! Woke up on Monday at about noon. Since then I've stayed up until the wee hours of this morning.

Which would be Wednesday night/Thursday morning, kind of thing. In between, just the one hour of sleep. Out of about forty. Slept in my chair. Regimented sleep. Quick kip. Otherwise the slumber would've been too deep. And I would've missed my one DJ gig of the week, up in the gym.

Oddly, I thought I'd now be in full on zombie mode. Surprisingly not too bad though. Besides just looking like one. Coffee. Music. Keep me going. Keeping me dancing. Maybe not fully dancing actually. More floating. Lucid. Mind transcending. Odd buzz. Out of it. And in some mighty way: Fully into it. Probably not the healthiest of living. But it's working for the writing. Getting some proper gems now. Everything I've been meaning to say in the way I wanted to say it is all coming pouring out. (I think.) Who cares if I feel like I'm slowly going insane and look like complete crap? Book on! On a positive plus, at least this writing routine I'm back into has settled my moving nerves down. Made me realise my new abode is pretty savage. Almost have it to myself. Quietness is good too. No one can hear me. No distractions. Just a quiet street as well. Doesn't mean that the street above and below have changed. Not now living the quiet life, which seemed to concern me a bit. My mind started asking me: Won't the stories dry up if I'm not in the thick of things? Nay. Ape. You're a hundred yards either way. And it turns out the place isn't stone cold silent either. Started to hear a lot of rustling in the bushes outside my window. At first I thought it was the Nutter. She's been texting/threatening/declaring her love for me again:

> 'NUTTER: Ok Irishman, what is up with this German wife of yours?'

And:

> 'NUTTER: I know you've moved. Is *She* with you? Gertrude, is her name Gertrude? I will find you.'

Then:

> 'NUTTER: I hate her so much, I hate her name and I hate you. You must divorce Gert so you can love me.'

Also:

> 'NUTTER: Love you. Might kill you. Hahahahaha... kidding or... heehee...'

Most worrying part was that she knew I moved and knows where I live now. Had me slightly concerned for a while. Until I realized it wasn't her in the bushes. Just two stray cats, who it appears take turns in raping each other. Horrible, soul-crushing cat cries.

Echoing around my head.

Ah well, can't have it all my own way I suppose. At least my fictional wife Gertrude is safe for the time being. One less thing to stress about it. Wuu! Shh.

Chapter 23

No Homo. Just Euro!

Eventful enough two weeks, to be true. First off, I got in a fight with my publisher. Mighty fun. Editor read the first draft I sent. Claimed to be a big fan. Only needed a few minor edits. Almost good to go. My view was slightly different. Well, it is the gist but I just need to change parts here and there throughout to make it flow better. Parts could be culled or edited too. His email insisted:

'No no, it's fine. Just slight changes.'

'No no, I think I know, it's my book, I must just make these minor changes throughout and then it'll be fine.'

'No.'

'Yes.'

'No.'

'Yes.'

'No.'

'Yes!'

And so on. For too long. Eventually they tried to hardball me with:

'Look, it's our way or the low way. You can make a maximum of twenty changes. That's it.'

That struck me as odd:

> *'Why a maximum of twenty? Is it so you'd have to do less work? Trust me. These changes will make the book better! I hardly want to make it worse??'*

No reply.

So I took that as I could change as much as I want in twenty different chapters. Particularly as they also tried to tell me:

> *'...this includes any typos or grammar mistakes you see.'*

> *'Huh? What? Why don't you want it perfect? WHAT'S WRONG WITH YOU?!'*

No reply. Eventually I emailed someone else in the company:

> *'Look, what's going on?'*

> *'Just don't change the whole book. Only needs a few changes.'*

> *'Look, can you lodge the rest of the advance in my account please? I need the money. I'm almost done.'*

> *'Well, just make the changes you want to make and then we can do that.'*

So I narrowed it down to about forty changes. Including grammar or spelling mistakes. Sent it off. And the money was lodged. Thank funk. I can come back to the changes later. Money. In. Sanity. On. That sprinkle of money in my account gave me a little bit of a boost, to be true. Pep back in my step. Come on to funk! Snap out of this lull.

> "Get yourself some more income!"

I screamed at myself every morning. Before I went out knocking on every bar and pub door within a thirty minute walk radius of me.

> "Hi there, how's it going? Just wondering if you might want to try me out as your new DJ?"

"No."

"Howdy! Just saw you opened up recently, might you need a DJ by any chance? I DJ in other bars around the place too."

"No. What language are you speaking, mang?"

And so on. For too long. No. Nope. Nay. Come back tomorrow. Manager isn't in. But I can tell you the answer: Go away. Get out. Don't come back. Just know: It's a no from us. Some laugh. Great old hoot. If you know what I mean. On the upside, I did manage to DJ two nights in the Purple Lounge on my own. Let's ignore that the money was minimal. And the place was pre-tty dead. Manager was just throwing me a bone I think. Sound of him. Not going to be a long-term banker though. All the same, between the book advance and the two nights of jigging, I was keeping my nose just above water once more. Swallowing buckets for a while. At least I could buy some milk for myself again. All about the pluses!

Speaking of, The Man swooped into town for a weekend with his better half, The Jack. Went out on the Saturday night. More finest of dining. Limos. Five star. And mighty banter. Welcome relief. Fine feast. Charlotte and Chowder fell asleep at the table. Work-related illness. Nine to five jobs can make one weary it seems. So The Man (looking sharp), the Jack (looking glamorous) and I (looking well-fed) went to the SkyBar and boozed the night away. The two of them have some stamina for the boozing. Barely a few hours off a jet and I'm the one keeping up with them? Life and soul of the party! Hey hup... And then I got a text:

'ELLE: Hiya boyo! Long time no see.'

'ME: Are you back from New York?!'

'ELLE: Yeah, fashion shows all done! Just got back today. Are you out?'

'ME: I am indeed. Come here! Actually, hold up.'

The Man and The Jack tell me they're off to bed. Jet lag finally kicking in. Elle was out with her sister so going to be half an hour still. Arranged to meet in Barney's instead. SkyBar is a tad out of my range if I'm trying to woo a girl. Barney's I can booze on. Down to Barney's I go. No sign of Elle yet. Time to play it economical. I'll order a pitcher. Safest bet. Bud Light, please, two glasses. Find a seat. Plonk myself down. Where's Elle? I'll just have the one while I wait. And wait. And by the time Elle shows up, the lights are on and the bar is almost closed. Oh, and I've chugged the pitcher.

> "C'mon we go back to my place! I just live up the road. We should listen to music! Plus: I have tea!!!"

Elle laughs at me,

> "OK, just for a while."

> "Yeah, perfect, quick cup!"

Outside we go. Cold air smacks me full in the face. WHACK. Goodnight Irene. Can't remember much. Still grand walking and talking and all that. Just my memory is dodge. Back to my place. Kissing. Touching. Feeling. What about the tea? No tea! Wayhee! Burst in my bedroom door. My shirt comes undone. Fling off my runners. Elle's dress comes down. Standing in her black Calvin Klein underwear. Step back and admire,

> "Sweet Jesus Betsy! Come over here you."

Boots off it seems. OK so. I sit on my bed. Elle puts one boot up on my knee. Some sight. I try to slide it off. No joy. Pull it. Nothing. Yank the boot instead. No give. No give. It gives! I flop back on my bed from the force. Laughing. Boot in hand. Smile on my face. This is fun! Head bounces off the bed. And then... Hmmm. And then I do believe I fell asleep. Passed out. Potato. Tomato. Some clown. Woke up. Next morning. Where am I? Why are my pants on? Oh balls. Is Elle here? Did I leave her out in the kitchen holding my teabags? Were we in my room? Did we? Was she? Did I dream that? Nope. I did not. Reality flashback. Dose. Text Elle. No reply. Kept plugging away. Eventually a reply the next day:

> 'ELLE: Don't worry about it. I shouldn't have come back. It's fine though.'

> 'You don't sound fine. Seriously, I was goosed, sorry. I have narcoleptic ways at times!'

> 'ELLE: It's OK. I just didn't realize. Now I know.'

> 'Know what?'

'ELLE: Are you gay?'

'Huh?'

'ELLE: It's just that's the only reason I can think of as to why you'd bring me back to your house, strip me down and then just leave me standing there.'

'Ha, no, I was just drunk!'

'ELLE: It's cool, don't get me wrong, I was trying to figure out if you were gay or just being European.'

'Ha. No - No homo. Just Euro!'

Well actually, just an Irish clown who boozed on and then drank a pitcher at last call. My homing device sent me to bed!

'ELLE: OK. If you say so.'

So that was mighty. Got the "lets-just-be-tea-buddies" vibe after that. Balls. Probably contributed to the bad dose of monkeys which followed that weekend. Although that might've been more the gin monkeys. Took their time to detox. Needed them to fly away out of my system. Just hung around. Trying to break my brain.

Living a surreal high life at times is savage. Unfortunately, a change of location doesn't change things much when you're living in your head. Still stuck in the same place no matter where you are. High life seems fraudulent when I come down. Tend to forget about reality when you're high as a kite in surreality. Perhaps it's time for me to say goodbye to gin too. Tastes savage... And then the next day arrives. I know now why they call it Mother's Ruin. On the upside, I did book a mighty gig this coming Sunday. Porsche is back! Gives me some breathing room for next month too. Break even and beyond! Although I can't really save too much money. Must go to San Fran tomorrow. Colin's wedding. Sorted me out time and time again when I ever go to San Fran. Have to go. Can't say no. Plus, my family are all going to be there. First time I'll be seeing them in about six months? First time I'll see them in California too. Not big travelers, distance wise at least. Big trip. Pumped to see them!

I'm also going to use the trip to try and fix my slowly breaking brain. Worrying too much about the future. Gnawing away at me.

Bleak enough. Where is my next dollar coming from? What if I can't pay rent? What if I don't find more gigs? What if? What if?! Hush. Shh. Calm down. Everyone struggles. Stop being an ungrateful ape. Focus on the good stuff. Enjoy the high times. Live them up. Appreciate. Deal with the bad gibber. Which is why I've decided I won't be telling anyone about my inner turmoil. Lock it up! Things could be worse. Who needs money? Well. You do, you clown. Ah hush, brain. San Fran on!

Chapter 24

Shuu Huu!

Some difference between San Fran and L.A. Night and day. Particularly with all my relations in town. Different but mighty. Reality in a good way. Feels like I'm back in Ireland. Abnormally normal. Back to living daylight hours. Getting up before nine in the morning. Everyone going to breakfast at a restaurant. Don't want to be the only one missing out. Make the most of it and all that. Full days spent out doing tourist stuff with everyone. Somehow making me more tired than folk who flew for 14 hours. Book lag worse than their jet lag? Some clown!

Big crowd made the trip from Ireland for Colin's wedding. My Mum and Dad. Mighty seeing them. My sister, Sarah. Good hoot with her dry humour. Aunts, uncles and cousins on my Mum's side – Margaret, Frank, Sheila, Dimitri, Niamh! Plus a bucket load more friends of the family. Majority of folk from the wonderful county of Tipperary. Consists mostly of green fields, farms, pubs and castles. A place where 's' is pronounced with a 'sch'.

> "I'll have a pint of Schtella please, your finest Belgium brew!"

Proud smugglers too. Sneaking in copious amounts of Irish teabags to the country. I'd say each person brought at least one box's worth, buried deep in their suitcases somewhere. In case of an emergency…,

> "Can't bate a cup of tay!"

Unfortunately some also brought bottles of fake tan. Tut. Hello, old foe. Even brought the weather with them. Humid. Raining. Drizzling. Looks like it'll ease off. Three minutes later: Pouring down again. Rinse. Wash. Repeat. Irish weather all the way. You can take the wedding out of Ireland, but you can't take the Irish out of the weeding. Or however that saying goes. Morning of the big day: Controlled confusion. Most folk staying in the Hilton in downtown San Fran. All meet in the hotel lobby. No one really sure what's going on. Irish women scurrying all over the place trying to figure it out,

> "Where exactly is the church?
> How do we get there?
> Why is this cabman blatantly taking us the wrong way?
> Streets are numbered!
> Ah be Jesus. Divil a bit!"

Finally. Find the church. Nerves. Tears. Kick off. Wedding. Mighty. Groom's phone rang. Ha. Almost mid 'I do'. Colin, you may kiss the bride, Ursula... Mr. & Mrs. White! Congrats! Group photos. On to the pub. Nelly's here we come! Ham sandwiches. Chips. Chicken nuggets. Washed down with buckets of booze. Everyone back on the bus. Reception time. Hotel on! Sing-a-long en route. Everyone already on the way. Long session in store. Arrive. Mingle. Main meal. Speeches. Health. Happiness. Followed by... Seventy-nine more buckets of booze. It. Was. *Flowing*! Bar actually ran out of beer at nine o'clock. Tut tut. Frantic cries for it to be refilled. Music. DJ. All sorts of dancers. Felt like a country disco. Black Eyed Peas took care of the rest. Full on. Irish wedding. Some laugh.

First time seeing the power of *I Gotta Feeling*. Cult like. All ages. Breaking down barriers. Stampede to the dance floor. Drunk. Sober. Young. Old. Dance on! Or: Just stand at the bar. Watch them all dance. While you sip on. Also pretty Irish. First time boozing with my younger sister too. First time experiencing random guys not knowing it was my younger sister. Which was different. *Different*-different. Oh yeah, no worries, chat her up away, I'll definitely not care. Ye fools. Funk off!

All good really. Although I'm pretty sure in the bar we went to afterwards some randumber tried to get stuck into me. I was a tad tippled and didn't cop on. In my defence, his girlfriend started chatting me up at the bar. His angry bone kicked in. Tried to start a ruckus. So that was nice. At least I had a mini army of Irish people backing me up. I think it was a combination of my cousin's friend Susie berating him and my two aunts who started belting him with their handbags that made him eventually regret him starting on me. In fairness to our weird race, Irish folk are as genuine as you could possibly ask for. Including the handful who eyed me with suspicion. Repeatedly asking,

> "You're Colin and Kevin's cousin?
> You?
> But... You're different."

I could see that they genuinely didn't like the look of me. And by the look on their face they were also genuinely dying to ask,

> "Are you the queer of the family so?"

Fair enough. Country boggers. Can't handle my "quare" hair for some reason. Makes them uncomfortable. I wonder why. Waffling on with them. Waffled on with a guy from L.A as well who was now living in San Fran. Told me all about the "Seven Year Struggle",

> "Seven years to become a success in L.A. How long have you left?"

> "Only about the six or so."

Mighty. Lots of waffling over the weekend actually. At least it was the good kind of gibberish. Waffle in L.A is the draining kind. People spinning lies for the most basic of things. Almost every conversation laced with a hidden agenda. How to get ahead by talking to you. All the time. Tiring enough. Hanging out with Irish folk there's none of that. Slower pace. Faster wit. (Not a slight against my buddies in Tassel town. Just the other randumbers I may meet day-to-day. I. Swear. Ahem). Different topics of conversation on the agenda here:

Gaelic Football.
Weather.
Parishes.
Prices.
Politicians.
Idiots.
Economy.
Fish.
And.
Obviously.
Tea.
Endless chats.
Endless cups.

People coming and going, in and out the door all the time in my cousin's abode. Always the same greeting,

"Cup of tea?"

"Era shur, why not?"

Rude not to! So you chug your half-full cup of tea. And then hand it over for a fresh one. At least eight times a day. Seriously. Unless you're Irish, you might not fully get the gist.

We.
Adore.
Tea.

Even when we're drinking tea, we'll have long chats about... Tea! Only one agenda this weekend. Out in the open for all to see: Let's all have a laugh! Although there was some nervous laughter thrown in too. Coming from my corner. Along with a few inner cackling ones. Not so good. Bizarrely, shoe shopping triggered this off.

Chowder – a *mighty* man – hooked me up with a slick suit. (My only suit was back in Ireland. I was kind of goosed. Nay money to buy a new one and all.) This left me only needing a pair of shoes for the wedding. Basic enough thing to do for me so: Buy a pair of shoes. Easy. Right? Well, yes. Unless you have shoe issues and also have an inability to make choices that have very little consequence. Plus you're hungover? Struggling big time. Seem to psychotically enjoy torturing myself. Shoe store next to the hotel. Saw a pair I like. Could be the ones. Well, maybe I should take a look around other places first. See if I find anything nicer. Or a better deal. Time to exhaust every possible outcome. Ended up doing circles all over downtown.

Every.
Single.
Store.
Must find the best deal.

Best choice.
Worst choice.
Best case.
Worst case.
Full on basket case.
Mind racing.

Weighing.
Confused.
Back and forth.
Numerous shoes.
Just has to go with the suit. Why so hard?!

Reminding myself that I don't even like shoes. I can't remember the last time I wore a proper pair of shoes. Graduation? Not a fan of shoes ever really. Remember the time I kicked a curb and my shoe burst open but it was just before I was about to start work in a clothes store so I couldn't go home and change so I had to spend the day at work with half a shoe and half a white sock sticking out and then I went and bought a big pair of metal-rockers boots with a metal heel for some reason and then I went home and stepped on my sister's toe and broke it and she had to go to the hospital? Remember all that?? No wonder you don't like shoes! Will I not just buy another dark pair of runners? Or how about this white suit shoes? White is might. Right? This one? That one? Or should I buy a cheap pair now just to wear them this once? Any old pair really. Cheap as can be. Could give them away afterwards. Is that not a waste then though? Don't be foolish and waste your money. Think about it. Maybe I should just buy a good pair that I might wear in the future? If so, I might as well buy a pair I like.

Better.
Go.
Look.
Again.

I'll just do another seven laps of Union Square and recheck every store I've already been in six times. Shoes are mental! No wonder girls are nuts! What do I like again? Oh yeah. Forgot: I don't like shoes. Especially when I think I just re-broke a toe or two squeezing into those pointed pair. Asking sales assistants. Asking security guards. Asking other people shopping,

> "What do you think?
> Which ones.
> Which shoe?
> Please tell me. Tell me what to do?!"

Then I get a loud,

> "SHUU HUU!"

"No no, don't tell me to SHUU HUU!"

Stumbled into Barnes and Noble for a breather. Go hide amongst the books. Wandering around trying to decide which shoe style was in fashion. Stumbled upon the Irish section. Picked up James Joyce's *Ulysses*. Fine sturdy book. Opened a random page. Read a few lines. One caught my eye...

"He laughed to free his mind from his mind's bondage."

Took this as a sign. JJ knows how to cure me! So I started laughing,

"AH HA HA HA HA Haaa Ha."

To myself. At myself. Out loud?
No clue.

Got a few weird looks from a couple of bibliophiles. My brain felt lighter at least. Bought *Ulysses*. Felt like I had achieved something, somehow. Well done me. Finally. Hours after I first embarked on my shoe-shopping voyage, I decided to give up and return home. Outside the hotel. Bumped into my Dad who had been out exploring with my uncle. Asked me if I,

"... bought a pair of shoes, yet?"

"No. Not yet. I bought this funny book though. Told me to laugh. Ha haha."

"Come on, I passed a good shop earlier. Let's buy you a pair, my treat."

"Jesus, Dad, you're a lifesaver... I know this shop! First one I went into this morning."

Upstairs we go. Took my Dad about two minutes to decide.

"How about these ones?"

"Ha. They're the first pair I tried on about five hours earlier."

Mighty work by me. Truly mighty. Done. Purchased. Sorted. Go on the David Hayes! All reminded me of the steak or salmon conundrum

I struggled with a few weeks before. Never could decide. In the end, my cousin just chose that for me too. Steak. Great choice. Tasted unreal. Shoes: My Dad was the one who helped me out. Great choice as well. I really do like them. All of which made me think that I must be some sort of funking ape. Need to hire a decision maker. Before I melt down. Need a slap in the face. Or else just to cop on. Innocuous story really. Pretty pointless. Or so I thought. Turned out to be a warning sign. Unfortunately. Seeing as the day after the wedding, the shoe incident would pale in comparison.

Frazzled brain.
Going insane.
All. About. To Get. Dodge...

Chapter 25

A Breakdown of the Breakdown

"Hello everyone, my name is Mark and I am a nark.
Great news: I'm staying another night! Isn't that just super?! Wuu huu! Doesn't that make everyone else's night as well?! Yes?!
No.
OK. Still. Plan on!"

Delighted. Sat down at the table. All out for brunch near the hotel. Me pleased as punch. My plan had come together nicely. Changed my flight. Stay up an extra night. Rent a car at LAX. Drive straight down to Porsche in Newport Beach. Make it in time. Good to go. Just cost me an extra little whack to change my flight. But well worth it. Even if I am broke. Family on!

Smiled across the table at my aunt, Sheila. Just-made-your-night-now-Sheila, kind of smile. Confused expression back at me. I-know-you're-dancing-inside, wink back. Happy days. Until. Actually. Hang on. Balls. Hits me: My driving licence. Don't have it with me. Left it in my apartment. Only have my passport. Meaning I won't be able to rent a car at the airport now. Only accept a driver's licence. Sweet Jesus. Nooo! Sheila now looking at me with concern. My face full-on contorting.

Newer plan needed. Ughatha. So I'm still in San Fran. Meant to be going back to L.A tonight. Gig in Porsche tomorrow. Forgot there was a post-wedding party on here tonight though. Unreal laugh so far. Woke up today. Day after the wedding. Looked around. Realised where I was. Realised my trip was almost over. Realised I was heading back. All felt kind of soon. Rushed. So I changed my flight to tomorrow morning. All good. Except now. No licence. Funk. Maybe. I did see that early flight leaving at 7 AM. Could get that. Get a taxi back to my apartment. Rent a car by my abode. Drive down to Newport. Still make it on time. Just meant I'd have to leave the hotel at 5 in the morning to get to the airport.

Thought about it for a second. Besides a few hours sleep, I was now going to get only about six extra hours in San Francisco. That's my new plan? What kind of plan is that?! Going to cost me a couple hundred dollars too with the extra taxis and to change my flight again. Jesus Christ, I don't have a couple of hundreds to spare! What should I do?! Newer plan? Or. Revert back to the old plan? Just leave in two hours as originally planned? Hmm. Either way it's vital I make the DJ set in Porsche. Only source of income in three weeks straight. Need the money. Badly. Oh Jesus. I can feel it.

Brain.
Jitter.
Wobble.
Decision.
Time.
Crunch.
Ticking.

Telling no one of my inner dialogue. Fielding questions of how things are going in L.A. Aunts and uncles telling me I must be doing great. Not really being able to say much back.

Just sitting in the hotel lobby.
Gawking.
Gaping at people with my demented eyes.
Mind darting all over the place.

Trying to evaluate: What do I want to do? What do I need to do? Money versus memories. Should I stay or should I go? Hmmm. Torn one way or the other. Polar bears running free. Both choices are the right choice. But both are the wrong choice? Polar opposite reasoning. I know. Let's just subtly ask *everyone*. Anyone at all who has an ear. Weigh up all the pros and cons. People giving me the same answer,

> "Ah we'd love you to stay, you *should* stay but if you need to go you *need* to go... but we'd love you to stay."

Split decision.
Sweet Lord.
Equal measures.
Polar bears.
Logistics.
Desires.
Money.
Memories.
Can't decide.
Can't figure it out.
Shoe flashbacks.
Circles.
Again.
Head.
Twirling. Spiralling. Breaking. My brain!

Finally make a decision: I'll decide in ten minutes. Too confused. Dumb. Hungover. Ten minutes, I'll know. OK. Comes. Goes. Still nothing. Except brain frying. OK so, maybe the next ten. First, I'm going to dinner with my parents. Just in case I do leave now. I'll decide at dinner. We head to a pub around the corner. Packed. Too many people. Too much noise. And either I'm paranoid or my parents are giving me worried looks,

> "Are you OK, son?"

> "Ha ha, yeah ha, fine fine. Just a bit tired. All good."

> "So have you decided what to do?"

Brain busy melting inside. Tongue twisting. Unfortunately out loud.

> "Well makes more sense to go as planned. I'd like to
> stay for the party though. I'll stay. OK.
> No. I'll go. Sense. Go. Party. Stay. I'll stay.
> Or did I just say go?
> Pardon.
> What would I like to eat?"

No clue.

> "Chicken.
> No. Actually.
> Salmon. Please.

Actually.
Joe the waiter, can I ask you...
Should I stay or should I go?"

Parents now giving me *very* worried looks,

"Do you have a third option?" Actually. I'll stay. Decided. Oh right. Let's just eat dinner, ha ha. So, how's everything back home?"

"Yeah, L.A is amazing.
Can't you see I'm amazing?"

"Everything's amazing. Everything's going so well.
And I'm going to stay.
Pardon?
That's the time?
I wouldn't make my flight now anyway.
Left it too late. Ran out of time.
Staying. Best choice. Stay.
OK so. I better go. Get ready for the party.
See ye back at the hotel!"

Left my parents bewildered at the bar. Felt like my brain was crying out for help. Didn't want to melt down in front of them. Just walk quickly back to the hotel. Go hide in the room. Pull yourself together. Post-wedding party to go to. Reason why I changed my plans in the first place. At least I made the right choice to stay. Nonsensical choice. But good choice. Settled. Done. Here to stay.

"Pardon me, sir..."

Concierge outside the Hilton stops me,

"Are you still leaving today?"

"No, no I'm staying. Anyway, I wouldn't make that flight in time now as it is. Joe the Waiter said it was too late, so eh, that's it."

"I can get you to the airport in time but you must leave now."

"What, wait? Wait, what?
I'm staying though.

Am I?
I'm not?
What?
OK. Hang on.
You think I should try and get the flight?
Serious? Or are you just saying that so I will tip you?"

"Both."

"OK! Great plan! Hang on."

Ran. Room. Packed. My sister's on the bed watching TV, chilling out. Said goodbye. Think she thought I was just going to the lobby. Bolted out the door. Ran down the hallway. Bags half open. Chowder's suit over my shoulder. Bumped into my parents who were just getting back from a stroll after dinner,

"What's going on? Where are you off to?"

"Oh I'm leaving. Flight to L.A."

"Why? I thought- "

"Ehh. I don't know! Sorry. My brain is melting. Concierge said I would make it! So. That means... I should try? I think I should try. Right? I don't know. Ehh. Hmm. OK. I don't know. Goodbye? I better go. Running out of time!"

Hugged them both. Left. Them. Bewildered. Scuttled into the elevator. Looked in the mirror. Saw deliria. Concierge waves me over. Stretch hummer limo waiting for me. *What the funk is this*? Just take it! Apparently this is cheaper? And faster? Flat rate. Flat foot. Makes no sense. But. What the sweet funk do I know about sense? Time. Ticking. Jesus Christ. OK. Let's go. Can't be late! Jump in. Pull off. Straight into traffic. Funk! Driver turns around,

"So my friend, the airport?"

"YES! THE AIRPORT PLEASE!!!"

"What airline? What time?"

Rambling back gibberish to him,

"Virgin. Seven o'clock. Think I'll make it?"

"Maybe."

"Maybe?!"

"If not, you can just get a later flight."

"Pardon?
No. Don't say that!
What?
Stop. That's pointless."

"Maybe you could leave tomorrow if there are no later flights tonight. It's OK my friend. Don't worry."

"Huh?
What?
Which?
Wait?
WhatamI-
WhatamIdoing?!
Hang on.
Pull over.
You can't?
You must!
I don't care about traffic.
Pull over.
PLEASE!!!"

Keeps on driving while I reason with myself. Oh sweet Jesus. I'm falling apart. My insides are turning to slush. Why did I just rush off like that? Made sense to go as planned. Right? No. Hang on,

"DRIVER PLEASE PULL OVER!!!"

Driver looking at me. Like I was a nut. Me mumbling at him. Like I was a nut. Incoherent thoughts rambling out. Stay. Go. Don't. Know. Eventually he pulls over. Offers me a drink from the limo bar. Looks like I need it. Cheers, I do. So now I'm sipping champagne. Looking at my surroundings. Plush leather seats. Velvet walls. Nightclub lighting. Bottles of booze. Why am I in a funking hummer limo? Is this real? Why am I not just in a cab? How is this cheaper? How does this make more sense?! Realise I hear a buzzing in my ear. Is that a funking *fly*? Are they back? Have I fully lost it? Buzz. Buzz.

BUZZ. Flying around my head. Start swatting at the fly. Freaking out. Spilling champagne over myself. Grunting like a mad woman,

"What am I doing?!"

Realise the driver is still looking at me. Worried. Disbelief. Fully freaked. All I could do was just look back at him. Feel circuits spark and fry in my head. Silently screaming inside. Floundering. What am I doing - I don't have a funking clue what I'm doing! Mind is running wild!!! Wait. Phone. Check. Text:

'CHOWDER: Mate, what time are you back this evening? The twins want us to play at the Purple Lounge with them.'

Oh Jesus. More money. I need to go back,

"DRIVE ON! Airport is back on. Please!"

Driver shakes his head.
SWERVES back on to the road.
ROARS off again.
RACES around a corner. Less traffic. Puts the foot down. Cheesy chandelier hits off my head,

"Ow."

WHIPS around a corner.
THROWS me to the floor.
What the FUNK is going on?!
Driver's flat foot goes down further. Looks like I'm going to the airport. My shoulders slump. Defeated. Sigh. Look. I made the choice to stay. Somehow ended up going. Seems like my mind has now ran off on me,

"Just deal with it. You sorry heap of a man. Cop on. Try and hold yourself together."

"Look. I'm sorry. Not just any old weekend up here though. Everyone's over from Ireland. In America. At my cousin's wedding. Rare occurrence. Don't want to cut all this short. Might not be another like it again until... God only knows when? Although am I even going to make the flight?"

> "Look. Choice made. Deal with it, I said!"

> "OK. But. Look. Did I even pack everything? Look. Where's my wallet? Here. iPod? Here. Passport? Pass-port? PASSPORT?!"

Frantically ripping my bag apart. Throwing clothes in the air. Not here. Not there. Nowhere?! Fumbling. Passport? No passport,

> "Driver. DRIVER!!! Pull in. Go back. I'm staying. I want to stay. Go back. No. I don't want to go there. Please. Go back. PLEASE."

He continues on.

> "GO BACK! I HAVE NO PASSPORT. STOP THE CAR. LET ME OUT OF THIS FUNKING HUMMER LIMO!!!"

Apologies. Yeah. Game over. Explain I can't leave without it. Driver finally turns the hummer around. And then admits,

> "I wouldn't even have got you there in time anyway."

Good man yourself. Informs me,

> "You must still pay."

> "Yeah, cool. Who needs money. Just take me back to the hotel please while I enjoy this horrific bottle of champagne. Wake me up if I happen to pass out."

Arrive back at the Hilton. Dodge a few relations in the lobby. Elevator. Text:

> 'CHOWDER: Sorry, dates mixed up, gig is next Saturday!'

So that was something. Subtly make my way back up to my room. Stand outside the door for a while. Listen to see if they're there. Hear them all getting ready for the party. Deep breath. Get it together. Knock knock,

> "Hi guys."

Sarah laughs at me,

> "What are *you* doing back?"

> "Ha. Funny story. I, eh, decided to stay! Yeah. I didn't want to miss the party tonight. Only joking when I said I was leaving. Ha ha. Fooled ye all!"

Confused, bewildered looks. Not sure if I fooled anyone. Said nothing. No one said anything back. Unpacked my clothes again before I showered. Discovered my passport was in a side pocket of my bag the whole entire time. Said nothing when I made this discovery. Just chuckled to myself,

> "AH a hahahahah Ha ha ha ha."

Unfortunately it came out like a deranged hyena cackle. Seems like I'm the nutter now. Excused myself. Went out into the hallway. Felt the corridor closing in. Paced up and down. Breathing like a pregnant woman. Took out my phone. And rang Elle,

> "Hiya boyo, it's me, Euro. How are you?
> Yeah, I'm still up here. Going well except I think I'm losing my mind. But enough about me, what are you doing?"

In fairness to Elle, I think she sensed my turmoil. Talked me out of my mental haze. Calmed me down. All in all though, whole incident had me on the ropes. Mumbling. Fumbling. Bumbling. Mess. Thankfully. After all that. Stayed. And my gut let me know that I made the right choice. One last night with everyone. Good laugh at the party. Tried to tell a few people about my day. Didn't make much sense, unsurprise unsurprise. Better off saying nothing. Although I think my Dad knew something was up. Silent support. Bought me a few rounds. Helped me over my hangover. Only one cure really. Few pints brought me back up to a normal level of normality. Just about. Able to have small-talk conversations with people at least. Great work. Able to say proper farewells as well,

> "Until next time. I will miss ye dearly!"

Phew.
Made it.
Barely.
But still.
Intact.

And of course, if you happen to be my parents reading, obviously that was all made up. Not such a mess. Haha. As if. Ha. None of that happened. Obviously. If it had though, from society's angle, let's say it was embarrassing. *If* it had happened. Temporary insanity. Not good. Realised my brain was close to shutting down. Stress. Worry. Panic. Dodge. Although oddly enough, maybe not as dodge as the next day when I ended up being ridden by a couple of taxi men and somehow ended up in South Central. You know, that kind of ghetto place where the notorious Crips and Bloods street gangs hang out/battle each other. Good old hoot. Back to the normal way life in L.A for me...

Chapter 26

CHANCER. DANCER. ROMANCE HER!

I'm guessing a typical Valentine's Day consists of: Bed. Breakfast. Chocolates. Flowers. Wining. Dining. Whining. Drunk. Lingerie? Hip hip hooray! Not too sure. Haven't had a romantic Valentine's since... I don't know if I ever had one actually. At least this year it was similar enough to that. Ish. Kind of. Not at all. Maybe more like a typical Sunday back in the pre-going-down-the-well-writing days.

You know: Handbags. Man bags. Russians. Riding. Chinese. Haggling. Mexicans. Dancing. Carrots. Juice. Flowers. Bouncing. Drag queens. Puff the Magic Dragon. Vaseline. And. An alley. Typical ol' day. Safe to say my mighty plan to regain my sanity in San Fran while out of the insane world of L.A did not really go to plan. Deviated off course really. Almost fully melting down. Meh, plans are flexible. The thing is I'm starting to wonder if I'm the one losing my grip on reality or if reality is just weird? Take the cab ride from the hotel to the airport. Ditched the stretched hummer limos. Shuttle cab with the lay people instead. Simple enough journey. Quite early in the morning. Roads are quiet. I'm feeling slightly more sane. No metaphorical flies appear to be buzzing around my head. Good to go. Surely? Enter Cabman. Our Russian driver who got in three fights along the way. Middle-aged man fights but still.

Fight One: Cabman – vs. - Hotel Concierge:

Cabman overstays his allotted time outside the hotel. Swooping customers from the next driver. Argue commences. Cabman is highly dismissive. Annoyed concierge. Cabman being an idiot. Waves his hand.

Concierge pushes.
Cabman slips. Trips.
Stumbles against his own shuttle.
Tries to push the concierge back. Misses. Slips. Trips. Stumbles over the curb. Starts spitting out incoherent Russian/English/taxi language. Good start.

Fight Two: Cabman (now known as) Cabman #1 – vs. - Cabman #2:

#1 sees a guy running up the street with a suitcase. Tells him to jump in.
#2 next in queue. Not happy. Snaps. Runs over. Shove. Push. Shove. Grapple. Face pushing. Chins moving upwards. Two middle-aged Eastern European men. Both still holding a coffee in one hand. Spilling all over themselves. #2 gives #1 a little SLAP. Stuns #1. Fight over. Backs down. Reverts to verbal. Eventually drives off. Nought for two and everyone in the bus looks a bit concerned.

Fight Three: Cabman – vs. – Suitcase Dude:

En route, cabman starts spitting out Russian on the phone. Married couple in the cab are not happy that he's on the phone while driving. Dodgy. Swerving. Husband, Suitcase Dude, starts giving out to him. Cabman stops talking. Starts texting instead. Suitcase Dude starts freaking out. Driver tells them to,

"Calm down my American friend."

Condescending tone goes down well. Mull over if I should get involved too. Nay. Too tired to speak. Just observe the ridiculousness. Six in the morn. Happy I got up so early. Little hope of engaging. Cabman sends another sneaky text.
Suitcase Dude flips.
Arrive at the airport.
All JUMP out.
Suitcase Dude and Cabman get into a heated argument.
Handbags.
Man bags.
GRAB my bags.
RACE for my gate.
Not before seeing Suitcase Dude PUNCH the Cabman in side of the head. Everyone freaking. Police come over. Take Cabman away. And then, bizarrely, a bird almost flies into my head. What is going on?! All in all, a very sane start to the day. *Right*?

LAX. Arrive. Back. Delighted. Sunny. Hot. Happy. Flag a cab. Chinese guy. Give him directions. Away we go. Heat has me dozing off. Driving rocks me off to sleep. Wake up. Realise we've stopped. Outside my place. Look at the fare. Over $100. What the funk? Usually a $45 ride...,

"Double? How is it double?"

This cabman's English is now not so good,

"What is... doble?"

"I'm not paying double."

Realises I'm not just a tourist who arrived today.
Both get out of the cab.
His English is now perfect.
Speaking to me in an American accent.

"Hey man, you gotta pay the full fare, buddy."

"No hope I'm paying that price - buddy. No."

"Yes. C'mon man, it's Chinese New Year!"

"No. I don't care if it's Chinese New Year. How does that even matter? Should we be pushing faces? I'm sick of cabmen. Look, half is enough. That's all I'm paying. Your move..."

"I'll call the police on you man, give me my money!!!"

Takes out his phone. For funk's sake. No time for this gibber. Took a chance. Called his bluff,

"Call them. In fact, I'll phone them..."

"It's cool. No need to get the police involved."

"Here's half the money so.
Pardon?
You want me to tip you another $10-$15?
That's what you recommend? Ha. That's nice. Thanks for the recommendation. I'll just mull that over while I go inside. Hang on here one second..."

Ridden all morning. At least I was dancing all day. Porsche gig. Mighty. Everyone happy. Sanity levels up. Small talk in full flow,

> "Hey everyone, I'm back!"

At one point a girl came up and handed me a note:

> *'Just thought you should know you're very handsome.'*

> "Why thank you."

Flattering stuff. I *am* back! Also impressed by her balls. (Odd phrase. You know what I mean.) Tasty looking too. In a funky hair, hot body, looks like a professional dancer, lots of tattoos, hot face, kind of way. Smile and a thanks. Comes back up an hour later. Asks,

> "What are you getting me for Valentine's Day?" I really like diamonds..."

> "Oh do you now? I'm not used to that. In Ireland we don't give diamonds as presents. We got mixed up years ago and actually thought *carrots* were the presents. Not diamonds. So a bag of carrots is a great gift to get on Valentine's Day. Ten carrots is usually a good number. Wish I had some carrots myself, now that would make my day."

Manage to confuse her with enough gibberish that she leaves. Didn't want to be slacking on the job and all. Anything beyond small talk is tough when DJing. Half an hour later. Returns with a bag of carrots. Ha. Good work! Mighty present in fairness. Although, if I'd known she was up for buying me something I would've pushed the boat out a bit more. All about the 20 carrots. Before she left, handed me another note with her number:

> *'Would love to meet up. My boyfriend is leaving town in a week for a few days. Call me!'*

Ha. Good woman yourself. At least I got a munch out of it. Happy as Larry driving home. Gig went well. Soul. Bank account. Replenished. Eating my bag of carrots. Brain felt at ease. Until I realised: I have zero clue where I am. Figured my way down to Newport easily enough in the daylight. Nighttime was a different story. Particularly when I took a few shortcuts, seeing as I know my way around despite the fact I've never driven this way before. Well done. Being a man is mighty at times. Although, maybe I am OK. I'll just take this freeway exit. Keep driving. Turn around. Drive a few more blocks. Turn back. Drive twenty or so more blocks over this way. Keep going. Up. Down. Over. Quick carrot. Back again. Yup. That should do it.

Well and truly lost. I am some man.
Actually, according to these signs:
I'm south.
And central.
As in, South Central?
Hmmm. Lost in the hood? Ahh, very good.

That did make my buttocks clench a tad. Is this dodge? Isn't this one of the dodgiest places in the world? Ah no, not to worry. Just rumours. You've kind of met Bloods and Crips before. You'll be grand! Cheers brain, you're right! Until I realised people next to me in traffic weren't just casually glancing left and right into cars next to them.

They're eye-balling me.
Staring.
Seeing who's who?
Or who might be in their neighbourhood that shouldn't here.
Then again they might just be jealous of my carrots?

Being lost got tedious. Being eyeballed got worrying. Pulled into a dodgy-looking petrol station. Fifth dodgy one in a row. Had to be one of them. Took the plunge. Hopefully I won't be mugged. Big stand of flowers and balloons outside. Gang of elderly Mexican ladies. Asked them for directions. No English... Unless I wanted to buy something? Perfect English then.

"Ehhh..."

Hesitation made them have no English again. Tried to buy something. Too late. Go away. Balls. Went inside the shop. No one behind the counter. Waited about six minutes. Wondered what I'd do if someone came in and tried to rob the place. Not sure. Two more minutes. Still no one showed up. Dose. Left with the only other option: Gang of dudes chilling on the wall outside. Some in their twenties. Few in their thirties. One well into his forties. Mixed bunch. All hanging around on a wall. On a Sunday night. At about nine o' clock. Drinking orange juice. Tried to figure out if the majority were wearing blue (Crips) or red (Bloods). Mostly black. Hmmm. Just as I start to make my way towards them, it all got a bit movie like:

They all JUMPED off the wall.
Started towards me.
Oh Jesus. Did I offend one of the Mexican ladies?
Oh Jesús. Angry heads. Stomping towards me.
Should I scream? OhdearJesusGodAlmigh-
They just power-walked past me.

Turned around and saw a car BOUNCING into the petrol station. Hydraulics making it go UP and DOWN. Car almost doing the robot. Radio station BLARING. Although it was only radio ads. Some warehouse clearance. Heard one of them SQUEAL with delight over a DVD player on sale. Maybe these guys aren't so gangster after all? Guy in his forties stops as he walks by me. Asks if I'm OK? Not in a: Hey essa, are you ok? Do you know where you are?! More of a,

> "Hi, are you OK sir? Can I be of assistance?"

Kind of. Just with a gang twang. And yes indeed you can please! So,

> "I'm lost.
> Well I know where I am. Know where I want to be.
> Just trying to figure out how to get there."

Oddly had a life moment with my new buddy. Hooked me up. Gave me directions. Pointed me in the right way. So I gave him a carrot. And then he gave me a look as if to say he knew there was more than this just being a carrot,

> "Ehh, just a carrot, (wink)
> I know you Irish, not just a carrot!
> (Wink nudge wink)"

> "OK?"

Decided not to tell him it was just a carrot. Offered me some juice. I declined,

> "Not just juice, ehh.
> I know you gangsters. (nudge nudge)"

Didn't appreciate my nudges as much as I thought. Nor my winks. I do have a laced wink though. Maybe I just blinked hard at him. Either way. Time for me to escape. Giddy up. And finally got home. Long day. Goosed. Only one thing to do: Sleep on. Until. Got a Text:

> 'ELLE: What do you call a troll who likes to go for a walk?'
>
> "Hmmm..."
>
> 'ME: Trevor?'
>
> 'ELLE: No... Stroll?'
>
> 'ME: Ha. Mighty. Stroll on!'

Met up. Seems she was concerned for my mental wellbeing. That was nice. Strolled around. Got lost in chat. Big fan of Elle. Pity she thinks I'm gay. Tut. I'm either married or gay. Always the way. Curse my Eurosexuality! Somehow ended up down Vaseline Alley, a dubious shortcut in West Hollywood. Very romantic. Only realised this when someone who introduced themself as Puff the Magic Drag Queen asked,

> "Do either of you have a light?"
>
> "Sorry, Puff, not on me. I have a carrot though."

Elle GASPED. Very upset,

> "I had my eye on that."

So I gave her my last carrot. Chancer. Dancer. Romancer! All in all, typical old Valentine's Day. Sanity feels better in L.A. Maybe it was the work. The Elle. Or else I just couldn't hack the normality of San Fran. Whichever way, great to be back amongst the fruits and nuts in L-Heeey!

Chapter 27

MY TIGER TALE

Now. Then. Right. Book. Done. Final. Edit. In. Sooo... What's next? Not sure. Feel like Morgan Freeman. Released out of Shawshank. Take things slowly. People must go mental when they retire. Seriously. Fun at first. Then. Passing time. Just like kidney stones. Should really only retire when you're dead. All I see now is a big black abyss. Land of the unknown. Each thought laced with: Oh Jesus, what to do, nothing to do, what do I do, why did I get up so early?! Decided to have a mental week off. Chilling. Relaxing. Reacclimatizing. Daytime hours. Bear boy emerging from his cave. Hibernation over. Bear boy is back!

First things first:
Hair.
Cut.

Balls. Thought that would take up more time. Although, I barely got anything off. Frightened of hairdressers. Just a trim. And they still butchered me? Moving on. What's next? Ehh, I don't know... Soccer? Fussball it is. Test out the dodgiest of toes. Test out what it's like being back amongst groups of people. Mighty laugh. Good banter with the lads. Rob politely telling me,

> "You look like a bag of s**t. Get out of the cave."

> "Don't worry I'm out."

Cave off. Fussball on! All the while the obligatory photo shoot is going on in the clubhouse behind us. English *X Factor* doing an interview with Rob I think. Not sure really. Too busy getting nutmegged by Jetski. So that was a good hoot. And filled up my Monday nicely. Tuesday was a tremendous success. Cashed a cheque.

And caused a FOUR CAR PILE UP.

People in L.A really can't drive. Also not too good at stopping at zebra crossings that don't have a red light attached. Or a crosswalk, as they call it here. So I'm walking back home from the bank. For some reason I have an onion in one pocket (cooking dinner when I realised the bank was going to close soon) and my remote control in the other pocket (watching TV as I cooked). My mind is also distracted by the clown who wrote out my cheque. Merrick Heiles. Good to know people still can't understand me on the phone. Anyway, between the onion, the remote and the name, I was a tad absent-minded when I approached the zebra crossing. Stuck a foot out. Hey hup, they don't automatically stop here. Quick glance. Oh, mighty. This car is actually stopping. Waving me over. Car comes to a SCREECHING HALT: Full stop. Cross I go. Just as I reach the halfway point of the road, mayhem breaks loose: So the first car stopped fine. Second car stopped behind that. Unfortunately, the clown in the Mini coming up behind them did not stop at all:

SCREECH!
CRASH!
Slide...
BANG!
WALLOP!
SMACK!

Mini ploughs into the back of the second car. Goes up on its two front wheels. Hind legs off the ground, like a little deer lofted into the air. Fourth car behind the Mini follows suit. Ploughs all the cars forward. First car is shoved by the second car which is rammed forward by the Mini which is driven even more by car four. Now all four cars are sliding right past me. Barely a few feet away from me. Holy Jesus. All flashes by so quick. But feels like slow motion. Leaving me glued to the zebra. Unable to move an inch. Staring. Gaping. Shocked. Holding my onion. Gripping the remote. All for dear life. Everyone gets out. No one seems hurt. Clown in the Mini is freaking out. Reveals she was,

> "Just sending one text I didn't see the car stop ohmyGawd!"

Well done. Her friend tells her to,

> "Shut up!
> She wasn't at fault!"

Both then turn on me. I tell them to,

> "Calm down."

Don't think they understand my accent. Try to pawn off the blame onto me somehow,

> "Shouldn't have been crossing the road!
> You did all this.
> Where are you even from?
> The foreigner is at fault!!!"

Police arrive. Question everyone. Then more police arrive. They flock in their hundreds here. Red and blue lights everywhere. Bit over the top. No one was hurt. Only the cars. Front and rears. No tears. Well, besides the crocodile ones the texting clown-girl in the Mini produced. Last-ditch attempt to say she lied about texting. She then points over at me. Ape. Next minute I'm being questioned. Interrogated,

> "What were you doing?!"

> "Crossing the road."

> "Are you on something? Where's that onion from?"

> "No. I was just crossing the road. It's my onion? Is that illegal, officers?"

Clowns. Seemed like angry police folk. Small-man syndrome. Eventually wave me off. Turn to leave. Notice a randumber has been standing next to me on the island. Tall guy. Long hair. Older chap. Demented look in his eyes. Wearing a rolled up white wooly hat. Black jumper. Way too small. And white shorts. Way too short. Asks me,

> "What happened?"

> "Not too sure."

Keeps talking away to me. Or himself. Who knows. Time to go. Nod goodbye to the randumber. Stops me. Asks,

> "Why are you holding an onion?"
>
> "Long story."
>
> "Can I have it?"
>
> "Eh, yeah. Why not?"

Hand it over. Got a bizarre flash-forward. Tingle. Spark. Wince. Did I just give Future Me an onion? Passing on a baton? What's going on here? Thankfully, my brain woke up at this point,

> "Don't be stupid.
> Shut up.
> Leave the Future Me talking to himself."

Or was it myself?

> "Shh. Just go home."

So off I went. And my Tuesday was over. Next day I decided I needed to get a new routine for myself. So far I was just floating about. Randumb. But not productive. Decided to give my old neighbour a call. Fred. Used to live next door to me before when I first arrived in L.A. Writer. Sound as a pound. Big fat gay man, as he liked to describe himself. Always good to give me some advice. Point me on my way! Fred tells me to call over to his apartment. Good to have a chat. Over I go. Tell him about the book. Delighted. Good work,

> "And what else have you been doing? How's the stand-up going? Writing any scripts? Making any videos?"
>
> "Well. The book has kind of what I've been focusing on for the last few months. I wanted to get that sorted. Then I'd do all the rest."
>
> "OK then. When are you starting all the rest? I assume you've started *already*?"
>
> "Well I was going to take this week off. Then I'd go do all that."

Fred shakes his head at me,

> "Do it all.
> Do it *now*!"

Left Fred's pissed off. Purely as he was right. But I didn't want to hear that. I wanted to be *congratulated* on completing a book! And just that. Well maybe also told that I should take a little mental break for myself. Not that I should already be working on new projects! I just finished a big one. You mean to tell me I have more work to do? What about summer holidays?! Ughatha.

How dare he be so straightforward and right. Tried to spend the following day writing stand-up material. Horrible muck. Called around to a few open-mic venues to try it out. No joy. No open-mic on. Went knocking on some doors about DJ gigs instead. None of them opened. Wasteful walking. Woeful writing. Great day. Got frustrated. Called over to Elle. Forgot she was in Vegas for work. Another waste of a walk. Came home. Went boozing with Moe. Just about to go to bed. Email from my publishers:

> *'Hey Mark, we have some book promotion set-up for you. Radio station here in Ireland. Great exposure. Are you available to do an interview in half an hour? It would be nine o'clock our time, one in the morning for you? Let me know.'*

> *'Yes. Sounds good. Give them my phone number. Cheers!'*

Tell Moe. He gives me a shot to get me ready,

> "Who's it for?"

> "Not sure. Probably 2FM? One of the big radio stations in Ireland I'd say!"

> "What's it about?"

> "Well, me and my book. I'll try out some stand-up material on them too.."

Phone rings.

> "Hang on - Hello..."

"Hey Mark! It's Pat Mulcahy here from County Wexford's Best Morning Radio Show, 103FM's Golden Sunshine. How are you today?!"

"Not too bad. Where did you say you're from?"

"103FM. Golden Sunshine!"

(Plays a jingle.)

"Oh right. How's it going? All good here in L.A!"

"That's great Mark. Great to hear. So time is of the essence as we have the local knitting club joining us before the news but we just want to get a reaction from your side of the pond..."

"OK? About..."

"What are people saying about the Tiger scandal over there in America?! Tell us the gossip! Give us some scandal! Are people going crazy there??"

"Huh? Tiger what now?"

"The Tiger scandal! *Come on*, give us what you heard!"

"Tiger scandal? Are they extinct? I don't get it."

"Tiger Woods! Divorce! Celebrity! Scandal! Fill us in!!!"

"What the fu- Huh? Ehh. I don't know. What about my book?"

"Oh yeah, we heard you wrote a book, that's great. So can you give us one more bit of insider info for our listeners: Will Tiger recover from this?"

"Ehhh, yeah, I think so? I don't know. Enough about tigers. How about *horses*? What does a gay horse eat..."

"Thanks a lot Mark! Talk to you again soon! We'll be right back after this commercial break..."

Phone goes dead. I look up at Moe,

"How did it go?"

"Eh.
What the funk was that?"

Chapter 28

Up Next on the Folf Tee... Mr. Williams.

I remember this time back in Cork when I was young, about twelve, I went over to my buddy's house for his birthday party. Slightly apprehensive. Didn't know anyone else going. Different group of primary school friends. My Mum told me not to worry, it'll be fun. OK Mum, whatever you say. Showed up. Front door was open. Walked in with my present. No sign of any other kids. Just strange faces looking at me. Adults wondering: Who is this little kid with the perfectly combed, centre-creased hair? Me silently freaking. Is there actually no party? Did I get it wrong? Was I fooled?? Just about to turn, wail and run. Until I heard my name being called by his Mum,

> "Come in Mark, they're all playing soccer out the back!"

Anyway, I remember this other time too back when I was younger, I think I must've been about twelve as well, when a buddy of mine invited me over to his house for a game of folf.

> "Folf?
> Huh?
> What's that?"
>
> "Folf! It's class. Just come up. You'll see."
>
> "OK. On my way. Folf on!"

Thing was, I was only twelve. And I had no way up to my friend's house. Now usually I'd have asked my Mum but she was probably out with her friends. My Dad probably playing golf. No spin. No lift. No way up. Dose. How about the bus? Nay. Doesn't go that way. Get a cab? Ehh... I suppose. That is the only way. Thing is I'm only twelve and I've just spent a lot of my pocket money on sweets. Expensive sweets I bought at the end of every month. So realising that it was a cab or nothing started to give me cold sweats. There and back could be a bit expensive. Especially after spending so much on those monthly sweets. Still though, would be fun to go to the house. Haven't been up in a while. Ughatha. If only my Mum was here to give me a lift. If only I was old enough to drive. But I'm only twelve. So I can't. In the end I had to bite the bullet and get a cab. I remember the cabman who picked me up. Some plonker. All buddy-buddy. All small talk. All lost. Conniving clown. Started off by going in the complete opposite direction that I asked. When I asked why he was going the wrong way, I remember he told me he didn't know which way was west.

I remember then it took him four streets to do a simple U-turn. Followed by him getting lost again. Missing another turn. Then doing another U-turn out of the blue. And then finally deciding to use his sat-nav, which he had in the taxi the whole time. Some. Prick. I remember getting highly annoyed in the back of the taxi. Asking why he said he knew where he was going when I first got into the taxi. Simply proclaimed his innocence. I remember disliking cabmen even more as a result of that clown. Seeing as he simply stopped answering me. Zero replies. Just a nice chunky cab fare when we arrived at my friend's house. Far more money than I had planned for. Meaning I had spent more than half my budget to get there. So I'd be walking most of the way home as a result. Funking cabman.

I remember then going through the security gates of the estate where my friend lived. By the looks of the security guards, not too many people showed up at the gates asking to walk through. I remember a Bentley and a Porsche were in line behind me waiting to get waved through too. Anyway, got the green light. In I go. I walked through the big gates and see that the views were unreal. Top of the Hollywood Hills. Panoramic all round. My friend lived in a ridiculously savage spot. Down the hill I walked. Not too sure where to go. Following the directions. Got to the house. Rang the doorbell. Mexican lady answered. Asked if my buddy was in. I remember she wasn't able to understand me. I was 12, (wink), after all. I could probably barely speak English properly to adults at that stage.

She was lost. I was confused. I could hear a guitar being played from somewhere in the house. She called out. Guitar music stopped. Out came the owner. Which is when I figured out it was the wrong house. The big top hat ornament outside the front door should've given me a clue,

"Slash?"

"How's it going?"

"Yeah, sorry, wrong house. Across the road? Thank you. Any hope of a Guns & Roses reunion? No. OK. Tell Axel I said howdy anyway. Carry on!"

Over the road I go. Walk up the driveway. Doormat tells me I'm at the right place. Ring the doorbell. No answer. Realised I'm late. By more than just a few minutes. Good work cabbie. Folf must've started already? Whatever folf is. I wonder if no one is indoors? Hmmm. Slight panic. Maybe I should just go around the back? See a builder coming out from the side of the house. He tells me to go around that way if I want. OK so! I will! Great plan, boss! In around I go. Through the side gates. See the back garden. Unreal. Mansion style garden. Big swimming pool. Jacuzzi. Waterfall. Bushes. Deckchairs. Trees. Views. The lot. All that fun stuff. Savage. Pity I'm still clueless. Walking aimlessly around. Where is anyone? Balls. Is this a wind-up? What is folf even meant to be??

Spot the back door. See movement inside. Looks like the kitchen. Take a quick peak in the window. No sign of my buddy. See lots of other people though. Shyly knock on the backdoor. No answer again. Knock knock some more. Still nothing. Balls. What to do? Why can't they hear me? Ah I'll just let myself in. OK, here I go...,

"Ehh, anybody home?"

Big group of people sitting at the kitchen table. All tucking into plates of food. In I waltz. Lost. Confused. Clearing my throat. They all look up. Shared expression lets me know what they're all thinking: Who is this plonk that just strolled in the back door and why is he wearing a Payne Stewart style golf outfit?

"How's it going lads? I'm here for the folf?"

All look up. See me. Confused. Continue eating. I remember that the minute I said the word "folf" I thought the whole thing was definitely a wind-up. There's no such thing as folf! You clown. What have you done?! You dumb!!! Felt like quite a fool. Caught out. Hook, line and sinker. Folf? Gullible twelve year old. How could they wind me up like this though? Should I just turn and run?! If only my Mum had dropped me up. She would've waited outside to make sure I got in all right. Instead I got that dodgy cab man who just took me for an extra-long ride. Balls. Should I just swivel around and leg it? Especially as no one has said anything to me yet. Oh, I'm *some* ape. Just run away. Easiest option. Say nothing. Wind-up off. How could I have been so naive? Will I? Should I? Just play dumb. Turn and run? Do it. Get us out of here! Before anyone recognises you...

Weird that I remembered all that so vividly. Seeing as I was only twelve and all. You know, that time back in Cork when I went over to my friend Rob O'Leary's house for his twelfth birthday party, showed up, didn't know anyone, different friends, walked in, bearing gifts, strange faces looking at me, adults wondering, perfectly combed, centre-creased, my hair, silently freaking, about to turn, wail and run, his Mum, name, called, soccer, back... and you know the rest. Not too bad feeling like a twelve year old when you're twelve I suppose. Don't know any better. Young, dumb, dopey twelve year old. Which is fine, when you're actually twelve.

Maybe not so fine when this all happened last Friday afternoon. And your buddy Rob invites you up to his palace-like abode hidden in the Hollywood Hills. Up to play a game of folf. Although you're not sure what that is exactly. And you're broke enough too. No one around to give you a spin up there. So you either take a cab which is about an eighty to a hundred dollar round trip, depending on what level gimp cabman you get. Or else you stay at home and save the money for next month's rent. Making you mull over whether or not you should go up. Hmm. Play now. Pay later. Folf on.

So that's how I ended up feeling like a twelve year old. Mighty living on the broke line all the time. Cluelessly strolling into the kitchen. Seeing everyone looking at me oddly. About to turn and run. Thinking it was all a wind-up. Until I hear...,

> "Muuurrrrkkkk! Come in!
> We're on a quick break from folf, going back out for another round soon. Here, have a seat.
> Want some food? Everyone, this is Murrrk. Murrk, everyone..."

Phew. Thank Jesus. Howdy everyone. I'm Murk. I'm not twelve. But I do need to use the bathroom. So I'll be right back. Hold those inquisitive looks! Fairly surreal at first. Well-known faces all sitting around the table. Randumb assortment. Ex-England football captain Barry Venison,

"How's it going?"

Celebrity chef Gordon Ramsey,

"Top o' the morn!"

Ex-Arsenal full-back and TV pundit Lee Dixon,

"Howdy."

Sound guy, Martin, who it turned out was the singer from the band Starship, they of *We Built This City* fame. All sorts. Comedians. Actors. Footballer for L.A Galaxy. Some funny Liverpudlian, Chris Dyson. And a twelve year old. Ran. Dumb. On!

Folf was a real thing too. Like golf, just using a football. Instead of a golf club, you just kick the ball. The pin was a rubbish bin. And the course was various different layouts of the estate grounds. For example the first hole involved us going up to Rob's bedroom balcony and kicking down to the bin on the far side of the garden. Other tee boxes included:

The top of the pool.
The other side of the house.
The bottom of the garden.
The middle of the Jacuzzi.

And behind a bush next to the house where I think Paris Hilton lives. All over really. Mighty laugh. Folf could be going global soon! Started off well. Hole in one with my first shot. Lapped up the applause. All went straight to my head. Fluffed the next few holes. Tried to redeem myself on the fourth. Got a bit over-zealous. Went for the glory shot. Power-and-ping over slow-and-steady. Ball zipped off the green. Shot off down the hill behind it. Dose. Chased after it. Down into the slightly woody section of the course. In through the trees and bushes I went. Spotted the ball down the bottom by the fence. Scooped it up. And happened to see into the house across the way, where they were shooting a porn movie. Ha. Something a twelve year old should never see!

Great day up at folf. Actually the first time being in Rob's main house too. About three other smaller mansions. All class. This was a step above all them though. Heaven. Pure bliss. Big huge mansion. Open. Chilled. Inviting. Everyone relaxed. Happy. Smiling. Some atmosphere. Savage day folfing around. Rob is some man to make you feel welcome. I'm always a fan of when someone points me to their fridge and says: Whatever you want, help yourself! Introducing me to everyone in the house. Met the main woman who keeps Rob's abode ticking over, Mairéad. Dancing lady from Dublin. Go on the Irish! Met her husband, Graham, Rob's personal chef. Scottish. Sound. Magician in this massive marble, granite and stainless steel kitchen. I mean *beyond unreal* chef. Even had Gordon Ramsey oohing and ahhing. Whipped me up a ridiculous feast in a matter of minutes. Roast chicken. Quiche. Salad. Roast potatoes. Fruit smoothie. Sweet Jesus. Might just have been the best part of the day.

Although going for a dip in the Greek-God style pool (water slide included) and chilling in the Jacuzzi afterwards surrounded by the Garden of Eden was pretty slick too. Bushes. Trees. Views. Birds. *Betsy*! Throw in a Guinness or two. Banter flowing with everyone. Sun shining down. Mighty. This is the life. Farewell worries and the likes. Hello bliss. All thoughts of my gig hunting, money problems, publisher issues, barely scraping by sailed away. Big to-do list, zero to-done? Who cares! We're folfing. Escape on!

One more quick round of night folf. Just the nine holes. Although that was even slicker with the lit up backdrop of the glistening L.A lights. Few more boozes. About ten o'clock. Time to go home. Swung a lift from Barry Venison. Top man. Pretty cool as well, from a soccer fan's point of view. Only not too long ago I was watching him on TV being a pundit or actually playing in the best league in the world. Now I'm in his car having a laugh about how Americans can't understand a word we say.

Some.
Day.
Hollywood.
Haze.

Reminded me that sometimes being a lost aimless ape with no set schedule isn't so shabby at all. Can't beat a taste of the high life. The only way. All I need now is a budget. Folf. On!

Chapter 29

DANCE, MUNKEY, DANCE!

So what usually happens is that I don't get my hair cut for months. Then I might have a bad day. Blame me hair. Go for a trim. They somehow butcher it. And then I have to get that fixed. Usually that does the trick. Up I go to the Standard Hotel up the road from me. Supposedly a good hairdressers. See if they can sort out the haircut I got not so long ago,

> "Just take a bit off please. Nothing too drastic. Try and fix whatever it was that other crowd did. Just a trim, please."

Sat down. Started reading my book. Let the hairdresser get to work. Not too sure if it was the book that distracted me. Or the fact that the guy in the chopping chair next to me turned out to be Jordan Knight from New Kids On The Block and was constantly getting asked for photos and autographs by randumbers walking by. One or the other. Either way. Didn't pay enough attention to the guy cutting my hair. Diced. Sliced. Chopped. Turned my head into a salad bowl. Finished up. Told me I was done. Took a look in the mirror. Hard to tell with the flattering lighting. Harder still with two girls working there also flattering me with their lies. OK so. Thanks. Off I go. Get outside. Into the honest daylight. See my reflection in a window.

> "Sweet Lord. What has he done? Did he just stab at my hair with a blade or what? *Horrendous.*"

My reflection pondered,

"Unless that's what you're going for again?"

"Eh. No. Funker."

Tut. So off I go to another hairdresser.

"Can you fix this lopsided mess please?
Thank you."

Two haircuts in one day: Mighty! Only took three goes overall to get this one right. At least all this haircutting gibber was for a good cause. Flurry of interviews lined up this week. Radio interviews, but still. Wanted to look sharp. Particularly as so far the radio and I have been mixing like oil and water. After the first interview I did a while back, I emailed my publishers:

'What was with all the gossip questions?'

No reply. Couple of weeks later, I hear back from them. Informing me there are more interviews coming up. Oh, OK, sounds good, book whuring on. Email from a producer of a local radio station in Kerry:

'We will phone at about half two in the afternoon, Irish time.'

Half six in the morning, my time. Fair enough. I'll just stay up or wake up. Cool. Spread the word to people on Facebook and Twitter:

'Big interview everyone! This is the online link, this station, tune in, tune on, hear me here, at this time, listen to me gibber, spreading my word!'

So I decide to stay up as opposed to wake up. Can't really function for a good hour or two speech wise when I wake up. Mostly grunts. Up watching infomercials. Six in the morning, email arrives in the door. Interview pushed back an hour to seven my time. Ah Jesus. Should've slept. Plus. First interview of the bunch, I'm already crying like a wolf:

'Eh, apologies all the folks I bombarded about tuning in. Actually going to be an hour later. Tune in then still though, it'll be mighty. Listen on!'

One hour and ten minutes later, call comes in. Do the interview.

About ten to fifteen minutes of rusty dancing. Gibber jabber. Gibber dish overflowing. Rattled off what I wanted to say.

> "That's great! Cheers for that! We'll edit it down slightly and it'll be played sometime this week on the Morning Show."
>
> "Cool, no worries, wait... what... that wasn't live?"
>
> "No."
>
> "Really?"
>
> "Yes."

Balls.

Magnificent work once more. Seeing as people did actually tune in to listen to me. No joy. Instead just wondered why I was going to be on an afternoon show called *Classic Hits Golden-Oldies*. Mighty stuff. Cue another blanket message:

> *'Sorry everyone, it's on some other time. Recorded. Not sure when. But eh, thanks for tuning in.'*

And with that I lost almost everyone's interest in my radio interviews. Leaving me sobbing in the corner like a little wolf. Wolfaruu, wherrre arrre youuu? At least the next few interviews went well and aired more or less at the time I was told. Except. Got a familiar thread running through each interview,

> "What's the latest Hollywood gossip?"
>
> "Huh? I don't know. Maybe read Perez Hilton's website for that? Let's talk about me and my book! Who cares about gossip?"

Well, it appears that they all cared. Forgot that Ireland - like the rest of the world, in fairness - is obsessed, thrilled and delighted with pointless Hollywood gossip. As opposed to my world-changing stories.

> "Who wore what where?"
>
> "I wore pajamas there?"

Decided to just repeat the questions back to them,

> "Not sure who wore what where but you'll never believe who wore what here! Although you'll have to read my new book to find out."

Quite the master of mystique and promotions. Ahem. Emailed my publishers:

> *'Seriously, why are they all asking me for gossip stories? Please reply. It would make a nice change!!!'*
>
> *'Oh, well, you know, this is less about the book at the moment. More getting your name out there, so we told them all you'd be their inside guy on gossip, what with the Oscars coming up and all. Think of this week as a trial run for when the book comes out. OK?'*

Magnificent. Thanks for that. You want me to be Irish Perez? Paddy Hilton, is it? My ideal funking title. That's exactly why I came to L.A after all. Just to become a gossip monger!!!

After a little artistic huffing and puffing, followed by some mental screaming in the mirror: DO THEY NOT KNOW WHO I AM!?! DO THEY NOT CARE!?! I got my head around it. Two can play conniving games. I'll just twist it all into stories about me. Paddy H off. Nark boy on.

As part of this wonderful week of trial running, I was invited along to the Irish Film Board's Oscar Party. On in a place called Dillons, an Irish pub in Hollywood. Never been. Not sure why. Cheap Guinness. Hot bartenders. Sounds good. Party was to start about eleven-ish. My first phone interview is penciled in for half past ten.

Spent the entire day panned out on the couch. Tired from boozing the night before. Last thing I actually wanted to do was go back out for more. Not like I'm getting paid to report for them. Going to cost me a chunk with cabs and all. Technically not even for the book either. Tut. Well I suppose down the line it's for the book. Come on you clown: Cop on!

OK so, might as well watch the Oscars if I'm going to be reporting on them all night. Put on the start of it while I'm on my couch in a dressing gown. Lose interest pretty quickly. Dull enough. Decide to just Google to see who won what after the show. Oh look at that, an Irish guy won a production Oscar of some sort. Yippee. I can talk about that. Although maybe I should go hunt down some more stories for these interviews. Where are my pants?

About ten o'clock I head down to Barney's for a quick pint to wake me up before the first interview. Pint puts a pep back into my bones. Still early doors though. Yet to hunt down a story. Barney's is more of a local sports bar with a pool table and karaoke and where Jim Morrison used to booze and The Doors used to perform and well-known people go there all the time for a no-frills beverage or three but tonight there is no one of note floating about so no names I can drop to appease the radio heads. And... Balls. My phone is now ringing. Funk this. Sell out. Time to give them what they want. By hook or by crook... Here we go!

Make up complete gibber to them. Deflect their questions so it sounds like what they want to hear. In reality, I'm outside Barney's. In phone land...,

> "Yeah, I'm in Hollywood right now! Oscar. Party. It's amazing! Who's next to me? Eh, Jennifer? Yes, Lopez..."

... might be her second name. Oscar. Party. Stars.

> "I'm touching her hair."

Oscar.

> "Feels like a unicorn's mane."

Party. Amazing stuff. Stars.

> "Yeah, cheers, thanks for having me and don't forget to buy my- "
>
> Beeeeep.
>
> "Bastards."

Off to a start, at least? Next two followed along in a similar vein. Awful horse gibber. Each radio jock repeatedly asking for some "juicy gossip". All sounded oddly sleazy when doing so. Heavy breathing down the phone.

> "C'mon, hmmm, give us something more. Give us an exclusive, hmmmmmmmohyeahbaby."

Go back into Barney's. Another pint. Check my watch. See my reflection in a mirror. Ughatha. Horrendous haircut is growing out too slowly. Look like a state. Why am I even going to this party? Pity no one is around too. Thing is, Oscar parties aren't all that exciting when you live in Hollywood. Well they are and they aren't. Unless I'm going as a nominee or a winner, then they're not appealing to me. If it's your big night out of the year, or you're going out to be seen and your publicist has it lined up for you to be photographed by all the right people, then maybe yes. I was none of the above. As a party, they're less like a Studio 54 kind of buzz and more like the reception before a wedding, kind of feel. And they are always a *pure* delight! So anyway, I wasn't pushed into going along to the Irish party. But seeing as it was set-up, I said might as well. Let's check it out. En route, I get a reply to my invite:

> 'ELLE: I'll come along for an hour if you want?'

Now we're dancing! At least I'll be showing up with a hot dancing blonde! Cab. Scoop up Elle. Fill her in with my radio gibber on the way. Hollywood. Dropped off outside Dillon's. Open the door for Elle. Wave the dude behind me in as well. Stroll in. Whole place erupts. Applause from all angles. Cheers. Whistles. Wuus. Jesus, what's going on? Is my haircut actually amazing??

Elle looks at me, confused. I shrug my shoulders. Maybe they all read early copies of my book? Did my publishers set this up? Who knows? Time to bask! Stand there for a few seconds. Start doing a royal wave to people. Everyone comes to greet me. Delighted looks on their faces. Hands out to congratulate me. This is amazing... Until they all walk past me and instead congratulate the guy who I held the door open for. Realise now that he's been behind me the whole time holding his Oscar up in the air. Victory! Ha. Oh right. Better stop waving, like a royal fool. Crowd has swarmed on the guy. I'm swept up in the middle of it all. Cameras. Flashes. Clicks. Snaps. People taking photos with him. Photos with the Oscar. Group shots. Single photos. Blinded by the lights. I twirl myself free. Elle prods me in the ribs,

> "Go back and get a photo taken. Good PR shot. That's all you want."

"Oh yeah, good call."

Coyly mosey my way back over. Coy as in awkward. Fifteen year old boy at his first school disco about to ask a girl to dance, level of awkwardness,

"Hee... Ahem... Hey. How's it going, sorry there, pardon me, can I just get a quick photo?"

Some older Irish guy named Simon gives me a huge hug,

"Great news for Richie, huh! We knew he'd do it! Say hello to him!"

"Yeah, I just knew Richie would!"

Simon hugs me again. Then just hands me the Oscar. Everyone else is busy hugging Richie. Carry him upstairs in a victorious tidal wave to the party. Crowd moves forward and up. I'm left by the front door holding a freshly won Oscar, being hugged by a strange man who thinks I'm someone I'm not. Elle tells myself and Simon,

"Get in for a photo!"

"Ehh... Cheese!"

Simon takes a fancy to Elle. Introduces himself. Starts to hug Elle instead,

"Where are you from, little lady?"

Elle is taken in by the old man's accent and impromptu jig. Laughs and starts to jig along. Simon puts an arm around her. Waltzes them both up the stairs to the party. So now, somehow, in a mere matter of moments, I'm on my own with Oscar. Look down at him. First thought,

"Not my Oscar. Yet. Might as well be holding a bottle of milk really."

Second thought,

"Imagine if I just took this home. Ha. That'd be some story. Some laugh."

Third thought,

> "Mark, this is your reckless side. Go home with Oscar. Just do it. We'll return him tomorrow. Probably. You can sleep with Oscar tonight and he'll be safe there. No more questions. Just do it. Perfect story for the radio. Give them some good gossip. Stop being a pussy!"
>
> "Huh? What?"

Time suddenly stood still. Thoughts flying,

> "Could I?
> Can I?
> Am I?
> That desperate for a story?
> Would it be worth it?"

Realise I'm still standing right next to the door. Gust of wind blows. The door even opens up for. Route is free.

> "I'm being waved through!"
>
> "You could be out and in a cab home in under 30 seconds!"
>
> "You'd have to sacrifice Elle. Sacrific-elle lamb, so to speak. But she'd understand. I'm sure."
>
> "Good one with the sacrifice-elle lamb."
>
> "Thanks.
> Now.
> Run.
> Go.
> Do it!"

Toes start to move,

> "Am I doing this?
> Are we?
> Here we go."

And now I'm outside. On the street.

"Oh Jesus!"

Middle of Hollywood. Holding up an OSCAR. Arm in the air like I've won the World Cup. In some people's eyes,

"I'VE MADE IT!!!"

Feel a hand on my shoulder,

"Mark?"

Turn around.
Recognise the face.
One of the main guys in the Irish Film Board. Paul. Met before. Sees what I'm holding. Immediate horror on his face.

"Is that yours?"

"Ehh... some guy just handed it to me."

"Well I better take that, just to be safe."

"Yeah, OK, better off."

Hand it over. Voices in my head disappear. Final parting shot,

"Pussy!"

"Shhh - Sorry, no, not you Paul. Eh, how's it going?"

Cue small talk after he saw I was invited,

"I read that you wrote a book; did you? How did you manage to do that?"

Mind now back focused. Realised he was shocked at my ability to do such a thing. Reminded me that there was some weird tension between us when we had first met back when I arrived in L.A originally. Maybe because I'm from Cork and he's a Dub. Maybe because he thinks I'm a chancer while he's too sophisticated to be such a thing. Sorry buddy, you're Irish, you're a chancer. Or else maybe he had actually sensed I was close to leading Oscar down a wild, reckless road. Who knows? I do know that we were both kind of still holding Oscar. (I had my hands on Oscar's head, massaging his scalp.) Although he had kind of edged me back inside the pub.

Funk. I also think that he liked me even less when I replied,

> "I just started writing words until I was finished and that's how I managed to write a book. Have you ever written one yourself?"

Cue a dirty yet polite look,

> "So... still playing soccer?"

> "Yeah."

> "Great. OK then..."

...this is slightly awkward. And now we're back fully in the pub. Balls. Goodbye, story,

> "Well. I'm going upstairs to the party. Great talking to ya. See youse later."

> "OK. I'll be up in a minute."

Grabbed two drinks at the bar. Headed upstairs. Simon comes over, unlit cigar in his mouth,

> "John! John, come over and say hi to Sinead and Susan."

(John?)

> "Hi Sinead, hi Susan."

> "Everyone, this is John!"

> "Hi John."

(Who's John?)

> "Where's Richard's Oscar, John?"

> "Oh, eh, Paul has it. Where is he?"

Looked around. See him by a pool table chatting up Elle. Mighty,

"Hiya Elle! You've met my buddy..."

Put my arm around my Elle. Dub, not happy,

"Oh did you come together?"

"Yes."

BIG SMILE,

"Yes we did!"

Slinks off.
Good duckaduu.
Elle asks,

"What's that weirdness about?"

"Don't really know. I get it from most Irish folk I meet here. Look at me as if I'm cramping their style. Or I'm not Irish enough for their liking. Not sure to be honest."

Party wasn't the greatest, to be true. Full of Irish celebrities, or so I kept getting told. By the people themselves,

"Yeah, I'm big in Ireland, moved here recently, agents want to meet me, put me in movies."

"Oh cool. Any actual movies you're working on?"

"No, not yet. But watch this space."

"OK. Cool. I will stare at it. Best of luck."

No Bono. No Colin Farrell. No Roy Keane. Zero celebrities. Party was useless to me. On the hunt for good stories I say to myself,

"Not awkward small talk with Irish folk...
Should've swooped Oscar when you had the chance!"

Elle and I left after a drink or two. Headed to the SkyBar for a look around. Elle tried to figure out why some people really dislike me straight off the bat. Not sure. Oscar party on for *The Hurt Locker* in there. Just won a load of awards. Ha. Mighty. Mingled with a few winners. Best Director,

"How's it going?"

Party ended early enough though and I asked,

"Time for us to depart, Elle?"

Strolling home. Decided to go for a quick nightcap in the Sunset Marquis. In we go. Order a drink. Find a table. Sit down. See that Alec Baldwin is on the couch next to me. Mighty stuff. All I need. Paddy Hilton's armory of stories is surely plumped up enough at this stage. Dancing! Night over. Hmm. Should I ask Elle back for tea again? Try my luck? Prove it was only my Eurosexuality?! Of course...,

"Well Elle..."

She jumps up,

"I have to go practice."

Balls.

"Ah well. I have these interviews to do too I suppose. OK so, thanks for joining me on the wonderful adventure!"

Elle jumps in a cab. Dose. Practice what actually? What am I doing? Some clown hunting down gossip. Taking my eye off the ball. Cursing myself. Cursing the interviews. Let's just get them done! Arrive home and read my email. Producer of the most popular radio show in Northern Ireland had been sending me bullet points for how the interview with them should go. Rough guide. Should make things smoother:

'We'll start with the book and talking about you, move on to some funny stories, finish off with a quick word about the Oscars'.

Sounds good. Guide on! This one actually sounds like a book interview too. Betsy!

'Can't wait to talk to you on air. Read the blog. Sounds mad. Mad altogether. You're mad. We're mad. Mad for it!'

'OK, sounds fun. Ring on. I'll be up!'

Interview at five in the morning. Decide to stay up. I'll sleep afterwards. About half four I make a sandwich for myself. Quick cup of tea. Waiting for the toast to pop. Phone starts ringing. Dring. Dring. Oh balls. On early,

"Hello...?"

"Hey Mark, this is Sharon from Belfast 101! How the hell are ya?!
MADDDDDD!
We're mad for it!
Mad.
For.
IT!!!
We heard you're mad too! Tell us something mad about the Oscars!"

"Hi, ha, well let me tell you about my mad book- "

"First tell us, right now over in L.A, what are you doing mad that's about the Oscars? Tell us something mad! Any celebrity sightings for us? M-A-D!!!"

"Ha, yeah, I saw a few actually last night. Although I have some funny ones in the book too, I remember there was this time- "
"We'll come back to that. We want MAD! We've heard you're mad and mad craic? What's mad over there now? What are you doing right now? Something mad? What are you doing, what are you doing right now?? MAD!"

"Eh. Right now I'm having a cup of tea.
Pretty mad."

"Cup of tea? What does that mean in L.A?
MAD!"

"It means: I am drinking tea from a cup.
Really mad."

"That's it?
Tell us something proper mad?

Any celebrities?
MAD!"

At this point I got fed up. Were they trying to drive me mad or what was going on? Not one to get mad, I decided to go with my motto: "Don't get even. Just get odder"...,

"Well what's mad is that as of late I've discovered I actually like leaving the teabag in the cup these days whereas before I always used to take it out!
Can you believe that?!
I never thought I'd like that! As in never, I always took it out. Now I leave it in!
Only happened yesterday by accident, pretty mad, right?
L.A is changing me. I've gone mad! Does that work?
Hello?
Sharon?"

...

"Oh my God, are you on something?
Have you just been out all night?
Are you at a party now?
Mad."

"Pardon?
No.
I'm at home drinking tea."

...

"Are you on drugs?
Mad."

"Pardon?
What?
No, why?
Are you?"

Around now I realised I was also hearing a producer saying off-air that she thinks I'm definitely on something, whispers,

"Change the topic..."

"Moving on, so.
Come on, Oscar weekend... L.A... Madness...
We all want to know...
What did you do today that was mad?!

We want MAD!
Give us something
MAD!!!"

"Here, what's with all this madness? Are you mad?
What kind of mad do you want from me? Mad that I got a haircut that makes me look like a mix between a scarecrow and Ellen DeGeneres or which?
Gay horse mad? Orgy mad? We can go down that route if you like? Would you like to hear about the time I nearly had an orgy with a Cat Woman and five guys? Mad enough?
Or no?"

"Jesus, what's wrong with you? We just want to hear some mad stories. You are on drugs..."

Which is when I should've said: No. You funking ape, I'm not on drugs. I'm on a gay horse drinking tea. Should've. Tut. Instead, before I could say anything, the interview was culled. Taken off air mid-sentence. Mighty stuff. Sitting at my dining room table. Cup of tea in hand. Staring at the phone. Finally going MAD. Cherry on top, they didn't fully hang up on me, so I then got to overhear the presenter and her co-presenters take the piss out of me,

"Well that didn't go to plan.
What was up with that guy?
Off on drugs in LALA-land.
Mad. What a spacer!"

Delightful. Ridiculing Paddy Hilton on air.

"Pricks!"

I shouted back. But they couldn't hear me. I could just hear them. Even started a poll, gauging if I was on drugs or not. And then the producer realised my phone was still connected,

"Oh no, he's still on the pho- "

"Beeeeep."

So that was wonderful.
Capped off a very satisfying week.
Dancing around like a dumb little monkey.
Spewing out gossip.

Selling out.
Spoofing on about drivel.
Finished off by being ridiculed on air.
Ahh. Mighty.
Book promo: Off to a flier!

Chapter 30

DANCING WITH LEPERS

Americans are kind of mental. Ah but in a good way. Obviously. They do know how to go all out for an event. Paddy's Day is bigger here than back in Ireland. Even if too many of them celebrate "St. Patty's Day". Which is kind of like me wishing everyone a happy Martina Luther King Day. (Must try that out next year.) Shops here don't just put up an old green balloon or two; they put up hundreds.

Everyone wearing Irish.
Pubs turn into fields of green.
All flooded by seas of Guinness.
People looking to be your Paddy.

Leprechauns dancing.
Shamrockers lurking.
Begoras butchered.
Riverdance blaring.

Just like Ireland. Except, kind of on steroids. Which is better? Well, one would think. Perhaps it's because I didn't get to go to a parade. Maybe I'm just a wee bit of an idiot? Or possibly: Paddy's Day is just ridiculously over-rated? Don't really know. Maybe if I was American and needed to feel more Irish and hide behind my best gene it would be better? Maybe it's because everyone claims to be Irish on Paddy's Day, so one of my two main talents doesn't shine so brightly: I'm in L.A, but now *everyone* claims to be Irish? Oh Jesus. I have no edge! People of all sorts coming up to me the week leading up to it,

"Are you so excited?"
"So great for you."
"Congratulations."
"Well done."
"An Irishman, in L.A, on Paddy's Day, that is *amazing*!!!"

"Yay! You've achieved so much to be here today!
Take a bow.
Have a seat.
Here's a shot.
Get in the photo.
Incredible. Wuu. Wuu for you!"

Hook. Line. Bought. Sold. Dope.

"*Yes!* Yes, this is such a great day for me!
Going to be amazing!
Must get obliterated drunk.
Dance with leprechauns!
Be green.
Go green.
Drink green!
Build her up. Shovel on that hype. Giddy up anticipation. Oh my God this day will rock my sham-socks off! This is it!!!"

And then. Predictably. Over. Ate. It. Hype. Balloon. Burst. Belly. Flop. Oddly enough, I think it was all down to the fact that I forgot to wear a green T-shirt. What a cruel, fickle world we live in. (What was I *thinking*?!) So last week I got a voicemail from a guy who promotes for a club called Ecco, cool house music venue right in the middle of Hollywood. Wants to book me for a gig. Happy days. Phone him back,

"How's it going? Patty's night?
Yeah I'm available. Headline the night?
Ha. Mighty.
You've seen me DJ in the Purple Lounge?
Oh very good-
Pardon? Yeah. I'm fully Irish.
Yeah, that's where I'm from.
100% Irish.
Yeah cool, plaster that all over the fliers and posters if you want.
Pimp me Irish out."

So that's why he booked me to headline the night. Because of my majestic DJigging talents, obviously. Ha. At least one of my main talents was being put to use. Chowder was out of town so I'd be doing the gig on my own. Wednesday night. Not too many folk around or up for clubbing. Down I go Hans Solo. Full club.

"IRISH MARK" plastered on all the posters and banners outside. Mighty mighty. In I go. One DJ on before me. Another on after me. KIIS FM DJ I think. Biggest radio station in L.A. I think he was the real headliner but got bumped promotion wise. At least that's why I think there was a weird buzz off him towards me. Although it might've been my "Where do I plug my mixer wires into?" confusion that made him suspicious of me too. (Chowder usually sets up for us. I'm still pretty clueless about lots of things. I just don't tell people that. Shh.) Besides that though, the place was going nuts. Gig was dancing! Did my hour. Whole room heaving. Happy days. Tip o' the night, top o' the morn. Promoter delighted. Hands me my pay package. Pure pittance. But better than a kick in the balls. Also kindly gives me one drink token. Flashes a fake smile at me,

> "Great job, man! Rocking the Patty!"

Pack up my stuff. Radio dude closes out the event. Only now do I realise I hadn't even had a single booze all night. Money's too tight to mention. Quite a dose. Cab here and back will cost me $50. Needed to keep the earnings for rent. Ah well, at least I have one drink token. Wuu! Can't not have a booze on Paddy's finest day. Tipple on. Up to the bar. People giving me high fives. Great set. Some meathead keeps trying to offer me speed. Please funk off. Order a booze.

> "Bud Light is all I can get with it? Fair enough. Thank you."

Few girls come up to me as I'm propped up at the bar.

> "Are you Irish Mark?"

> "Eh yeah, I am indeed."

> "Are you *really* Irish?"

> "I am."

> "Why aren't you wearing a green T-shirt?"

"Huh?"

"You're not wearing green. You're not Irish! Liar. Fuck you! LOSER!"

Always a delight, meeting these fine drugged up nightclub folk. I like them more and more each time. Hollow shells. Coy, shy, giggling ways quickly turn to drunken/drugger disdain. Reoccurring theme for the rest of my booze,

"Why aren't you wearing green?
You're not Irish!
Liar! Cheat! Whore!!"

"Thanks, lads.
Cheers!"

Sipping on my Bud Light. Looking around. Reminding myself that clubs are really only good when boozing. Same as when I used to do night-club promotions in my university days. Good laugh at the start. And then it became monotonous. Repetitive. Hard to hack unless you were with booze. Fully sober? Horrendous. Although I did just DJ a packed Hollywood club. Headliner! Main attraction! Shouldn't I be happy? I should, right? So why do I feel slightly depressed? Maybe because the place is full of dopes? Probably. Hollywood clubs are filled with the most vapid, soulless people this world has to offer. Even worse, they themselves seem to think they're profound. I've never met more people to quote generic horse manure than in a club,

"The world is my dance floor and we are all just as one. Make the most of it. You know, tonight's the night, so let's do it right. That's *real* talk right there. After-party?"

And then they look at you with their drugged-up, glazed-over, coke-ridden, limey-looking eyes. Expecting a deep response. Clowns. Although why am I up on a pedestal? At least they've the money to pop bottles all over each other, pretend to themselves that they're having fun and then get to drive off home in their big black brand new Escalades. I'm the one barely scraping by. Nursing my one free beer. Freaking out because I have to pay for a cab home. Slowly being surrounded by three robust looking women. Go me. Living the real dream! Decided to call it a night. Finished my booze. Turned down an offer from the three burly barrels, who asked if

I wanted to go to an after-party with them in their hotel room. Looked like they would've dominated and spat me out like there was no tomorrow. Beefy, brash, boisterous women who looked like they had been through the ringer and back again. I'll pass on the potential foursome. Off home I went. Pissed off Patty. Tut. Should've worn my leprechaun outfit. Just sitting in my wardrobe. Wasting away. What a dope. Some leper. Didn't even get a medal for being Irish. Chasing a hyped-up high. Dumb. Done. Dusted. Night over. Early doors. Letting down the Irish, to be whure. Well they can't all be amazing nights, I thought to myself in the cab home while my mouth asked the cabman: Busy night?

Although, oddly enough, I think I now have a manager, for acting and the likes, all down to DJing and the fact I'm Irish. Didn't even have to wear a green T-shirt either. Ha. Who's your Paddy now?!

Chapter 31

The Art of Trolling

I do believe DJing has turned me into a bit of a voyeur. Mmmm. Standing at the DJ booth playing music I like, watching from the shadows; allows me buckets of time to people-watch. The gym is the best for this by far. Mmmhmmm. My vantage point is perfect - halfway up the stairs, underneath the second staircase, kind of like a troll under a bridge, just that I'm under the guise of playing music. Mmmm. Just watching folk do whatever it is they do. And they do do some funny things. Duu.

Take the clown the other day: Dressed up all in white, except for the pink bandana around his head. Kind of like a flamboyant Karate Kid. Physically looked like Ricky Gervais yet somehow as flexible as a gymnast. Bounding around the gym. Warming up. Doing a few quick punches into the punching bag. Followed by running around the room twirling his neck. Pirouetting. Trying to get someone's attention in there, I assume. And he certainly did. Especially when he started to do karate style kicks. One foot planked on the ground, the other kicking straight up in the air. Faster and faster. Getting into a mighty rhythm. Going hell for leather. Until he kicked himself in the head. WACK-CRACK-GUSH. Broke his own nose, with his own foot. Maybe it was his shin. Whichever.

Nose CRUNCHES.
Mouth WAILS.
Blood POURS.
Ruins his nice white outfit. Cleverly uses his pink bandana as a tissue. Stem that flow. Stumbles up against the wall. Panics. Runs downstairs and out the front door Why not the bathroom, I thought. Tremendous viewing for me at least. And, on the upside for him, he

definitely got everybody's attention. Job. Well. Dumb. On the other side of the coin, being a stairway troll allows a lot of people to stop for chats. Sometimes it's the odd girl (very rare). Mostly it's sweaty, flamboyant, prancing men (all the time). High fiving me and asking,

> "Where *else* do you play? Where can we *find* you? I will come find *youuuuu*!"

> "Couple other stairs around town, I like to move around a bit."

All well and good. Although one or two of them do say it with too much of a dead pan tone,

> "Tell me where you DJ or I will hunt you down and find you."

So that's mighty too. Anyway, the other day this one guy came up to me asking if he could buy a mix. Looked pure Hollywood. You could see money had been well spent on making himself look younger than he was. I'm guessing real age about forty-five. Fake tan. Botox head. Big white teeth. Perfectly groomed hair, even after a gym workout. Starts gushing about the music, praise pouring out of his mouth. Enquires about buying a CD. Hey hup, time to turn on my best sales pitch,

> "Yeah well usually they're forty dollars a pop but seeing as you seem like a nice guy I'll sell you one for thirty!"

Tanned face winces slightly. Tut. Too pricey...,

> "Look, what I'll do for you is this: Buy two and we'll call it fifty dollars flat. Deal? Deal! I can go no lower. Jesus, I'm almost giving them away!!"

Done. He's in. Sucker born every minute. Ahem. While he's giving me his number so I can let them know when they're ready, he asks where I'm from,

> "Ohhh, Irish is *very* in right now. You have a great look too. Very... Hmmm... *Wild.* Have you ever acted before?"

Ha. A likely chancer. DJing at a gym full of mostly gay men leads to me shrugging off most conversations with umms, ahhs and hubbullas. Tell him I'm umm writing at the moment, hubbulla, although I do stand-up as well when I get a chance, ahh. His surgery enhanced eyes light up.

"Are you represented by anyone?"

"No, I'm managing myself at the moment. Going well, look at me here under the stairs. Why's that?"

"How rude, I never introduced myself... Dick Goldstein, I'm a talent manager. My specialty is discovering new talent."

Hmmm. Interesting. Although, isn't that why Orgy Joe also said? Let's see if this dude is a spoof too,

"Oh yeah. So, who have discovered?"

"Have you ever heard of Ger*ard* Butler? I discovered him right here in this exact same gym! Unfortunately he was already signed elsewhere, but I helped him on his way."

Nice name drop. Fools a fool. Hmmm. Might I be discovered in the gym? We all have to start somewhere!

"So then, Dick, tell me more..."

"Well here's what we'll do. You get the CDs ready. Give me a call. We'll meet this Saturday for coffee. I think you could be big, you have the whole package."

"Ah Jesus, *Dick*, you're making me blush. Go on away you, get out of here you scamp. I'll get those CDs sorted and be in touch."

Ruffle his hair. Wave him away. Off he goes. Pack up my stuff. And then gleefully run home like Charlie in the Chocolate Factory. Ran like the wind, so I did. Must get Dick's CDs ready as fast as I can! A talent manager wants to meet with *me*! Coffee - with me! I'm going to be a talent and managed! About to become a fully-fledged star now, surely? GRANDAD: I'm going to make it!!! Saturday comes. Meeting at Starbucks up by the gym. Roasting hot day. Shirt on. Hair combed. Palms sweaty. On time. Happy days. See Dick at the counter ordering. In I go. Dick's gay eyes twinkle brightly,

> "Heeey!"

Orders me a coffee,

> "Milk?"

> "No thanks Dick, I'm trying to show you how easy I am to manage, so I'm fine. Huh-ha."

Awkward laugh. Great one by me! Outside we go for the meeting. Starts off with weird silence. Dick making sure he's comfortable in his seat. Sipping his coffee for two to three minutes. Smacking his lips with the taste. Looking at me oddly. Well then, this is fun. Is he trying to play a game of some sort? Well, two can play that weird role. I sit back in my chair. Close my eyes. Soak in the sun.

Dick breaks. Begins to give me his talent manager spiel. Who he's managed, is managing, almost managed,

> "Wow. You've almost managed some of the BIGGEST stars!"

Does enough to impress me with his current list of clients. Not full-on A-listers or anything but some of them have their own TV shows where they are the main star. Other folk are in movies I've seen (*Wedding Crashers*, for example) and there are even a few actors from *The Sopranos* who I know of. All sounds legit. Although I had Googled all this beforehand already. Just wanted to hear it from the Dick's mouth. Now. Time for me to impress back. Dick asks me to tell him about myself. Sure thing Dick, hang on, I'll just whet my pallet first before I answer. One. Big. Dumb. GULP.

Roasting.
Hot.
Coffee.
Sweet Jesus.
Me mouth! Holy FUNK!
Tongue on fire. Throat on hold.
Eyes watering. Oh God. Too hot to swallow.
I can't keep it in either.
My tongue!

Lips start to break open like a dam. Mouth now dribbling. Roasting coffee starts running down my chin. Foaming at the mouth. Trying to hold it in. Give up. Too hot.

"BLAAGHH!"

Spit the mouthful out. Sprays. Thankfully most of it into a bush next to me.

"Jesus Christ. My poor tongue. I need a bib. Apologies Dick. Sweet Mother of..."

Ends with me sitting there blowing on my own tongue for a minute or two while I recover. Dick just sits and waits. *Highly* impressive start. Quite the talent. Come one. Come all. Come manage me!

"So, eh, where was I?"

Oh yeah... Hubulla. In the end I was dancing. Dick seemed very eager. He was going to set up a few things. See if they suited me. Let's take it from there. Mighty. Few minor actors from *The Sopranos* interrupt our meeting to say hi to Dick. One girl in particular gives me a very dirty look – calm down, we won't be going for the same role. So that was nice. Wrap up the meeting. Dick heads off to the gym (I was wondering why he was dressed so casually while I'm in my Sunday best). Off home I go. Anyway, me shall see. Lesson learnt at least: No more coffee at coffee meetings. Cold drinks only. Dribble off. Meet on!

Speaking of which, I'm on a meeting roll. Another one yesterday. Writing agent looking for new clients. Elle set it up. Mighty work. Lunch in Beverly Hills, the three of us. Wake up. Throw on some clothes. Elle swoops me up in her slick BMW. (Go on the Elle bird!) Head off to the meeting. Get down to Beverly Hills. Remembered how classy the whole area is. Swank everywhere. Marble streets. Diamonds sparkling. Chandelier style lampposts. And then there was casual me. Shorts. T-shirt. And just-out-of-bed-Big-Bird-Ellen-bob hair. Oh, and flip-flops. All I needed was a cup and a sign for my homeless man look to be fully complete. Could've sat down on the curb with ease. Please give me money. Free shrugs for food. Hi-diddy-ho, I am ho-diddy-bo. Tut. Did well making the effort. Looking the part of a successful writer!

Elle face indicates she's thinking the exact same thing. Balls. Should really go home and change? Too late now. You've been spotted... How's it going?! Here for the meeting. Hubulla, homeless, hobo, head up on me? Hubulla! Thankfully, somehow, besides the fact I was asked what is it I'm wearing, that meeting also went quite well. In fact, very promising. Buzz words flung at me. Stand-up, headshots, spec, scripts, book, brand. Giddy up. Hobo off. Mate on! Although between the coffee and the clothing, it was almost like I was trying to sabotage myself twice. Thankfully I dodged my efforts. My biggest saboteur is something else it seems. Need to sort it out. Easy enough. Not a big deal or anything. Just my inability to clearly speak the English language. That's all.

I speak it. They speak it. Apparently we just don't speak the same brand. I used to think that people didn't get every fourth or fifth word out of my mouth,

"Howdy. My name is Mark. I am from Ireland."

"Merrick? From Maryland? Heeeey!"

That kind of thing. Now, I see that I'm lucky if people fully understand one sentence in every four. My version of English appears to sound more like grunting noises to people. Gist, appears to be the highest level of understanding I can get. Beginning to think that if I was to change topic mid-stream, people would be none the wiser. Might start throwing in the word 'carrots' at random intervals from now on to test that theory out. As it is, I just get a lot of confused nodding in my direction when I open my – carrots - mouth. Seemingly interested in what I have to say. Just missing their cue to speak when I ask a question. Nodding along while I wait for a – carrot - answer. Realising they've no clue what I just said. So I pick up the baton myself once more and answer my own question... Hubulla hubulla hubulla. Finally they realise it must be their turn to speak. Eyes widening. All asking the same question,

"Sooo... Can you do an American accent?"

Presuming this is just their polite way of asking if I am, in fact, able to speak English. So I white lie,

"Yup, my American accent is down to a tee."

Respond with a few Yee-haws. Brings a smile back to their faces. Look at me once more like I have the potential to be a cash cow. Smile on! All of which is why I've been wondering and pondering out loud the past couple of days. Various sentences. Any sentence. Bucket of accents. Walking around. Talking to myself. Almost shouting. Trying to fine-tune my American twang. I'm actually good enough at accents too. My problem is consistency. I seem to enjoy jumping around the world while saying one sentence. Start in America. Jump to Ireland for a word. Over to Boston. Down to Australia. End in gibber,

> "Yee-haw (Texas), like (Cork), where's the ba' (Boston), mate (Australia), boss (Irish traveler), duu (Gibber)?"

Work needed, perhaps. Might be time to bite the bullet. Something which Fred has actually been saying to me ever since I first met him: Voice lessons. Learning how to talk. Tried to avoid. (Because I can speaks I tells you!) Time to cave. Voice coach now lined up. Recommended by my potential new manager Dick, who also has a few more things already set up by the sounds of it. All of which is making me think that Dick might be legit after all. Maybe he's not a con artist. Or an Orgy Joe. Perhaps. Go on the Dick! I mean... You know what I mean. Come on. Cop on. Dick's nice. Huh. What? Hopefully these voice lessons will include the ability for me to make sense too. As quite clearly what I'm trying to say is: Dick on? *Dick on!*

Chapter 32

FREEDUMB!

Routines can be a dose. Trudging through drudgery. Recycling days. Waiting until they just run out. Groundhogging to a halt. Slowly but inevitably. Work. Dinner. TV. Sleep. On repeat. Unless of course you like your work, I imagine it's a bit of a dose, to be true. Just watching a life pass you by. On the other hand, having no routine whatsoever can also be a bit of a riddle. Too much free time. Too much to do. Too much freedom. All of which seems to be making me quite dumb. Err. Making me highly interested in innocuous events. Such as: New type of soap I bought. Not sure which brand. Just some plain soap. Or so I thought. Seems to omit a weird fragrance. Now every time I walk into my bathroom my eyes water up as if I've been pepper sprayed. Making me fall to my knees. And puke. Only stopping when I eventually manage to crawl back out the bathroom door. Leaving the soap behind. Well, maybe only one of those things happen. Still though, the very fact that this scenario has played out in my head has made me realise that my mind might have too much freedumb at the moment.

So this week my publishers sent me the almost final draft of my book, laid out in a PDF. As in it actually looks like a book would look, as opposed to just my gibberish bundled into a Word document. I won't lie: It is pretty, pretty, *pre-tty* savage seeing my gibberish in a book form. Actually looks like a *book*? Giddy up! On the other side of savage, they also sent me a draft of the cover. Sweet Lord. Literally made me fall off the toilet. That bad. And yes, I do read my email sitting down sometimes. Originally the publishers told me they'd send three potential covers, then I give them feedback and we'd go from there. What they actually did was hire a three year old, filled her up full of booze, handed over a few bizarre looking photos and a font which was popular in the eighties, suggested the theme "papier-mâché?" and then the baby worked her magic.

Or at least that's what it looked like to me. It. Was. *Bruuutal.* Seriously, beyond laughable. Looked like a home-made VHS video cover. Full-on fall off the toilet seat, kind of a laugh. Thrashed out an email back. Almost sobbing in anger:

> *'WHAT IS THIS? Some sort of JOKE? Are you trying to RUIN me? Can you not see I'm ruined ALREADY? What is WRONG with you people? What happened to the THREE different covers to choose from? How can ye actually WANT to use this cover?!! Who is the three year old??! TELL ME HER NAME!!!'*

So, cover design and tweaks have been ongoing all week. That has been... Fun. I think the eight hour time difference makes communication flow a tad poorly. Never too sure if they're asleep or just ignoring me. Making me sit and stew in disgust until they eventually reply. They were sleeping. OK then. I forgive ye. On the upside, apparently the book is almost good to go. Which is mighty. Although I think the black abyss has actually kicked in more than I thought. Seeing as I can't let the editing go. I am an ediot. Told to read over the PDF. *Final* comb over. See if there are any minor tweaks to be made. Minor. Shouldn't be many, I'm told. Oh yeah? And then I manage about thirty pages of changes. Some are blatant typos. How are they reluctant to change that kind of thing? Others are only slight. Word change. Word order. Order word. That kind of thing. Miniscule. Actually. No. Minute - That kind of thing. Still. The devil is in the detail. So that war was waged all week as well. Battles all over the place. Finally agreed on a mid-point. Also agreed on a major overhaul of the cover. Publishers are tiring work. I imagine they say the same about me. Anyway, no longer am I finishing off the book. It is:

Done. And. Dumb.
Finito.
No more.
Now I am walking book free.
Crutch-less. World is my oyster.
Time to plough on. Time to get going on the next step.
I know what I must do. Don't I? Oh yeah, stand-up, scripts - all that.
So.
Then.

Go?
Eh, where?

Well, stay away from the black abyss of nothing. Run free into the other one - The white abyss of endless possibilities! So many routes of where to go next. Here I come! Here I dumb... Oh Jesus. Drifting. Floundering. Flapping. Don't know. Where. What. To. Do. No Wikipedia page showing me the way!
White.
Black.
Pot.
Tom.
Ate.
Toe.
Lost.
Woke up the next day. Determined to get a productive buzz going. Bouncing into the twenty-six items on my to-do list. Productive on! First thing penciled in to do: Nope. Not happening. Meeting with Dick just got pushed back a week. OK. No worries. Still twenty-five more things to go. Next big thing on the list: Stand-up. OK. Let's do it! Try a few open-mics. And... No joy. No stage time. Tut. Ughatha. Not to worry though. Plenty more on this list. White abyss. Endless. Bountiful. So much to do.

First. I'll just watch some of this soccer match online. The one involving a team I don't like. And I'm watching it with Japanese commentary. Well worth watching this first though. I'll get my plough on after. So much to do, so I'll do nothing! Great work. Productivity levels soaring! Let's see what's next... Shoot my head. Emm. Seems I do need headshots. Few people asking for a photo of my head. Balls. Must wrangle some of them. Preferably for free. Not looking likely today. Let's come back to that. Next: Write a spec script. Emm. I do need to write a spec script. Again, a few people asking to see one. My head is a bit empty today though. Drained. Not sure if I can churn one out so quickly after being an ediot. I'll come back to that too. Excuses, how are ye cutting?

I suppose I did see a girl get thrown into my pool in the evening time. Fully clothed. So that was fun, to be true. And by see, I mean throw. Wasn't really on my to-do list though. So that was just a side bonus. Not *really* productive. And apologies Elle. Although in my defence, she did throw the first push. At least one good thing happened soon after: Day was killed. Turned into night. I can fool myself far easier at night that I'm being productive. Something about the feel of night. Watching a match in Japanese wasn't the most productive thing after all. Gym, let's dance! Article for an Irish magazine, let's scribble! Managed to do those two things. Worked out. Ish. And wrote. Gibberish. Fooling a fool. Keeping myself busy. Well done me. What else? There's that - No, need something more solid than that. Next... No, a bit too far down the to-do list to do today. Next... Balls.

All speculative. Anything definite on the list I can do? Anything involving the influx of cash? Need to try and balance the outflow. Trying to hopefully avoid the impending dread of my monthly man-period for a change. End of the month. Worst time. Only time I really care about money. Only concern: Rent. Boy. Not a fan. Although, besides landlords, who is? Even worse, I'm now throwing away money. Yesterday being Easter Sunday, I went to mass. Head down. No sign of Orgy Joe. No priest getting me drunk. Just very high-brow. And by that, I mean high eyebrows. Church was mostly filled with plastic-looking cougars, faces and eyebrows injected to the max. Along with guys who had the thinnest of highly arched waxed eyebrows. High-brow all round. Not too many interactions really. Although one Freddie Cougar took a shine. By cougar I mean an older, older, *older* lady. Although, to be fair, 70 is the new 60 these days. Oddly, when she came up to me afterwards, she knew I was Irish without me saying a word. Bizarre. It is L.A though. Bizarre a dozen.

Anyway. Back to being in mass. Time came for the first of three collections. Notes in my pocket. Exactly five notes. Assumed they were all the same. Basket thrust under my nose. Randomly took a note out. Horsed it into the basket. Took no notice. Until it glanced back at me. Corner of my eye. Caught. Balls. All those notes weren't the same amount. One chunky one. Fifty dollars. Which obviously would have to be the one I horsed in. Checked my other notes. All only one dollars bills. Clown. I actually kind of need that money for food and the likes. I haven't shaved all week because I ran out of gel. I *need* that bill. Thought hits me. Predicament. Should I? Could I? Just take it back? Swap it for the one I meant to put in. Or. No? Is it possible to maybe take change from the basket? I'll just take forty back?

Looked up and saw the grumpy dude who was collecting the money. Gave me a fake smile. Then started prodding the girl next to me with the money basket. Eventually she gave in. Donated the amount I had intended to give. Gutted. Had to grab my hand. Hold it back. *Restrain* from refunding myself. Easter Sunday. Couldn't do it. Unintentionally throwing money down the church drain. Surely that'll buy me some karma at least,

> "Jesus, you better be watching!"

Rambles are kicking in. I wonder if it's the extra few notches of heat that has me rambling beyond belief past few days. L.A is getting hotter. Might just be the heat. At least I can edit these gibber rambles. Unlike the recent voice mails I've left people over the past few days. Distracted. Rambling. Answering machines. Not a good mix. I blame that odd looking bird out the window. Swaying and floating mid-air, in a drunk-looking fashion. Kind of odd. Brutal voice-mail. Think I mentioned the bird in the voicemail. And that I was making a cup of tea. Horrific. Barely knew the photographer I left the voice-mail for. I'm sure he'd love to give me free headshots.

Although I think the one I left later that day where I was heavy breathing and panting like a pedophile might have been worse. Like a man in heat. Walking up a steep hill. Hot climate. Returning a missed call from Dick. Phoned back. No answer. Voice-mail. Rambles donkey-kick in...

> "How's it going Dick! Mighty. Phew. Agh. Jeekers. Some heat. Some hill. So anyway, what was I saying, are you still on the phone, oh yeah, forgot this was your answering machine, *Jesus*, this hill, like climbing a ladder, sweating like a whure, and I'm wearing jeans - What am I doing?! Anyway..."

And so on. For far too long. Still waiting for that call to be returned. Pants off. Pants on. Back to my original point: Too much freedom? Trying to find a routine of some sort? Free the dumb? Maybe it's that instead of me embracing this freedumb, I'm too busy just being dumb. Need to sort that out. So. Eh. Focus on!

Chapter 33

Wrestle Mania

Weird week. Lots of walking. And far too many naked men for my liking. Oddly enough, I think it all started with the mysterious sparks flying out of my phone. Not sure what happened. Just that it almost went on fire when I plugged in the charger. So a pint of water was hurriedly thrown over that. And another phone was gone. Thankfully Charlotte had a spare. Herself and Chowder are some pair! Out with the old. In with the BlackBerry. Just meant I had to relearn some phone basics. Texting. New style Qwerty keyboard. Typing in slow motion. Attempting to text and walk. Near impossible. Two-handed typing. Like a senile dog begrudgingly learning a new trick. Now I know how Dads must feel. Confused. Lost. Stuck. Head buried in the phone. Walking aimlessly along. Surprised I didn't walk into a pole. More surprised when I did walk into that bush. Yelping. Ahhh. Leaves in my face. Looking around. Coast clear. All good. Few scrapes. Not too bad. Lesson learnt. Until the next day. Going up my street. Slowly texting. Quickly walking. Saw a pole in front of me. Made sure to dodge around it. Well, actually, just let me look down and type this highly important text right now as I do that. Swivel. Thrust that body weight. Completely misjudge. And crack my shoulder into the sign on the pole. Bang. Oww. Hmm. No pain? Delayed. Now. Arrrggghhh. Funk me pink. Sweet Jesus. Grasping my shoulder. Trickles of blood. The berries. What am I doing? I tried my best to avoid that. What's *wrong* with me? Oh, and look: Right next to the sign, parked car full of women. Looking at me. Howdy. Ugh. My shoulder. No time to almost keel over on the path in pain. Let's just walk away as cool as can be. Strut. Shoulder. Strut. Smooth. See ye girls. We must do this again. I meant to do that by the way. Sure. Same trip. Keeping on. Strutting along. Responding once again to texts. (I try to avoid speaking on the phone as much as possible. The frustrations of being misunderstood every second word drive me up the wall.) Fingers tapping. Funny reply. Laughing. Absentminded. Waiting to cross the road. See some dude at his front door across the way. Standing there in a dressing gown. Sees me. Eye contact. Balls. Give him an awkward nod hello. Wince a smile. Before I know it, he just whips open his dressing gown. Nada underneath. Waving. Laughing. Helicoptering. Rotating his waist around. Then scuttles back inside his house. Ehh. What the funk just happened? My eyes! Did I just get a Weho Wave? Particularly nice of him to wave "it" to and fro. Keep it in the pants boss! Unfortunately, not an isolated incident. Way home. Head buried. Thumbs frantic. Texting gibberish. Walking along. Wondering how far I had gone. Where am I? Look up. See a ground-level apartment balcony in front of me and a naked guy running out of the sliding doors straight at me. Giggling. Screaming. Scurrying. Followed by two more naked guys behind him. One with a camera. The other with something in his hand. Something making a whirling noise. Is that a dild- Oh God, why did I look up? Look down. LOOK DOWN! Too late. See the apparatus being waved around while naked guy #1 exclaims,

"I am not doing *that* again on camera!"

Guy with camera. Looks up. Sees me. Looking like a startled clown. Standing there holding up a Blackberry.

"Heeey!"

"Huh?"

"Wave to the camera!"

"Wave?"

Wave. Oh Jesus. Why is my hand waving? Get me out of here! Off I RAN. One last flurry of places to call into down the road from me. In I stroll to one bar. Not really realising what kind of bar it is. Still early evening. Just opened. Wander in. Ask for the manager. Waiting. Assessing. Wondering. Hmmm. Kind of odd. Why is that guy on a table at the other side of the bar? Bit early to be dancing on tables at this hour, isn't it? Wearing a police hat and sunglasses too? Wearing only a police hat and sunglasses. Ehh. What's that that he's holding in his hand? Oh. Right. It's his... Oh Jesus. Eyes. Bruised. Brain. Burned. Giddy up. Get out. What am I doing? Although in hindsight, the name really should've given me a hint:

Mickey's. In my defence, I was kind of weary at this stage. All my walking all week has been me going from bar to club to shop to anywhere, hunting down and following up on possible DJ leads. Money possibilities. All well and good thinking this, that or the other might happen down the line, but my main concern right now is the right now. And right now I need money. So writing, stand-up and horsing around are on hold. Walking boots on. And my trudging commenced. Far too many naked men seen along the way. But at least after five days of that, I finally saw some fruit. Although oddly enough, none of it came from anywhere I walked to. I'm sure it's all interlinked somehow - put the effort in here, something besides my phone sparks over there. Forgot that the huge music festival Coachella was on this weekend over in Palm Springs. Meaning most people were going to be out of town. All the cool folk anyway. Meaning a lot of DJs and clubbing heads were gone. Me being a chump, stayed put. Lucky chump it turns out. Seeing as the Purple Lounge asked me to cover three nights in a row. Oh. Yes. Betsy! DJig. On. Chalk. Me. Down!

Good for the soul. White abyss momentarily filled up. Friday night. Bottles popping. People dancing. Club heaving. Filled to the brim full of hype, which I now realise is the main currency passed around clubs. Funny enough. I think people want to build you up so much purely for their own benefit as opposed to yours. They can tell all their friends about their amazing trip to L.A and how the DJ was amazing and it was the best night ever and all their friends should be jealous and sick to the stomach as they weren't there. So HA! Can't really see why they would get so carried away otherwise. Not like I'm up there playing my own music or anything. And I'm not saying that they're having a Beatles-mania meltdown over me. Just that they do like to jump way over the top. Randumbers screaming at me,

> "YOU'RE KILLING IT!!! YOU'RE MAKING THIS THE GREATEST NIGHT OF MY LIFE!!! WANT SOME SHOTS/DRUGS/ORGIES???"

Well I'd prefer if you just ate some mints or freshened up your breath somehow but thanks for the compliments nonetheless! Anyway, one group in particular seemed to be big fans. Kept coming up. Kept giving me high fives. Kept giving me drinks. Asking where was good to go afterwards? Not sure really. Most places close. You could go down to Avalon. Too far?

> "Well. Actually. I do know of one place just around

the corner. Open late. Club. Kind of. No booze. But they do sell apple juice. More a place where girls dance on tables."

"What's it called?"

"Eh, The Body Shop."

So I used to go to The Body Shop maybe the odd night or three when I first arrived in L.A. Most clubs finish up by about two o'clock here. My body clock is for some reason set to only really get going at about one. So I'm in flying mode when the clubs close. Which is a dose. Until The Body Shop reopened after been shut for months because of renovations. Meaning I did not even realize this place existed at the top of my street until I saw the lit-up lights coming home one night. Stumbled out of a cab. Hey hup! What's going on in there...? Since coming back this time around though, I haven't really gone too often. No longer do I live on the same street. Novelty wore off. Also kind of a dive. Unless of course you have the right amount of booze in you. Thanks to this group ploughing booze into me all night, I must have - All right so, I'll come along! Ye seem like a laugh. Off in we go. Dark. Mank. Neon blue lights. Creepy MC voice describing,

"Scintillating Sandy's hobbies include horse riding, shopping and keeping fit. Ooooh yeaaah. *Scintillating.*"

Busy enough. Too many guys. Barely see a girl. Find some seats. Order some apple juice. Gibbering talking to a girl and two guys from the group. Quickly copped on that the girl was pretty keen on the Irish accent. Not too keen in return though. Backing off when she tried to get closer. Not the fairest flower in the pot, to be true. Also noticed that I was getting dodgy looks from the two guys. Really dirty looks. Asked her,

"Why they suddenly turned sour towards me? Are you going out with one of them?"

"No."

"Why are you laughing so much - Pardon?"

"Oh that one is my son."

"Jesus. How old are you?"

"Fifty-six."

"Fifty- how many? No way."

"How old is he?"

"About your age."

"I just thought you were about thirty. Your fake..."

Fake everything hid that well. There's more...

"We don't really go out together too often. First night out in a while. Because he has kids."

"Oh."

"Don't worry, I'm a divorcee."

"I see what you mean...
Wait.
Your son has kids?
So that makes you a Gran- "

"Yeah."

Sweet Lord. I'm in a strip club drinking apple juice with a granny? All right. Well then. That's my cue if ever I've seen one. My night just reached its pinnacle. Time for me to go,

"Pleasure meeting ye all. I'll be off. Giddy up!"

Hmm. Yeah. So as I said: Weird week of walking. Far too many naked men. But at least it didn't end up a naked gran. I swear... It actually ended with some odd wrestling. Tut. Me and my Eurosexual ways. On the Saturday night Elle called in to see me DJing. Couldn't really talk too much though. Dose. Sunday. Get a text:

'ELLE: What time are you finished DJing?'

'ME: Hopefully early, maybe one?'

'ELLE: Want to call over to my place if you're finished then?'

'ME: I certainly do. Duu!'

So Sunday comes. Quiet enough compared to the other nights. Finish up DJing early. I scuttle off to Elle's,

"How's it going? Tip o' the- "

"Come in. Shh. Shawnie is sleeping on the couch."

"Oh, my bad, don't want to wake your sister. Yeah cool, we can hang out in your room if you insist!"

Elle introduces me to her two cats. Magic and Lady. Mighty little felines. Sees I'm kind of clueless with animals. Not sure how to pet them. Laughing at me. Doctor Duulittle, I might not be. Spot that Elle has a piano in her room,

"No way, so this is what you meant by practicing! Can you play me something?"

Elle tries to resist. I give her a poke,

"Come on, just one!"

Poke poke. Elle gives in,

"Just the one."

Sit down on her bed. Elle opens the piano. Tells me,

"I only know my own songs."

Mighty!

"I only want to hear one of your songs. I can't believe you haven't played for me before!"

Elle shushes my drunk bellowing whispers. Starts to quietly play. Softly starts singing. Fully blows my mind away. Holy. Funk. This is unreal,

"You're really good. Don't stop. Play on!"

Elle is delighted. Keeps playing. Ethereal kind of music. Reminds me of Sigur Ros in a way. I *knew* she would like them! I just sit on Elle's bed in silence.

Soak it in.
Drift away.
She.
Is.
Savage.
Elle is this good and that hot? Betsy! Quite the dancer. After three more songs, Elle says,

"I better stop. Getting late."

"Nooo."

I start bouncing up and down on her bed,

"One more tune. One more tune. One more tune!"

Laughs,

"Hush. You loud drunken Irishman."

I start poking her to play one more. She pokes back,

"I can't."

I poke again,

"Come on. One more!"

She pokes back,

"No. No more!"

Both now sitting on the bed. Half laughing. Fully poking,

"Truce. No more pokes."

She looks at me. OK so. I go for one last sneaky poke. Elle blocks. Holds onto my finger. Bends it back. It's hurting. But I'm laughing. Our eyes lock. We move closer. And then...

We wrestle.
And wrestle.

And WRESTLE.

On the bed. Against the wall. On the floor. Rolling around. Neither giving in. Glint of a chancer in both our eyes. Poking. Wrestling. For a really long time. Hulk Hogan vs. Andre the Giant. Brett "The Hitman Hart" vs. Shawn Michaels. Tricks Hayes vs. Wres-Elle! Battle of wits. Wills. Titans!

Clothes Line.
Pile Driver.
Sleeper.
Half Nelson.
Back Breaker.
Boston Crab.
Sharpshooter.
Neck Foot - Elle's foot. My poor neck.
Pillow Pendulum - Me sitting on top of Elle using a pillow as a pendulum whacking off her head.

(On a quick side-note, did you know, much to my Mum and Dad's dislike, I was a fan of wrestling growing up. So I like to wrestle around, make up moves and submissions and the likes. I enjoy wrestling. I also think that Elle and I are the both middle siblings. Maybe we're competitive. I don't really know. What I do know is that...) We kind of got to the point where any sexual buzz going on was completely taken over by a "I'm not losing this wrestling match" buzz. You know the one, right? Ahem. Neither going to quit. Not until the other was in bits. As if I was back in my sitting room in Cork wrestling one of my buddies while WrestleMania is on TV behind us. Only when Magic and Lady jump on me and claw into my skin, did we both kind of stop. I then learnt that I might be allergic to cats. Couldn't stop sneezing for twenty minutes. Eyes went puffy. Could barely see. And eventually just had to go home because of it all. It. Was. Odd? Next day. Woke up. Copious amount of pain. Groggy. Felt like I had whiplash. Text:

> 'ELLE: So... Weird night?'
>
> 'Yeah. Very weird.'
>
> 'ELLE: I feel like I've been in a car accident from all the wrestling.'
>
> 'Not sure if I'm allergic to your cats as well or what happened. Was that a plan to ambush me?'

'ELLE: No, you just lost to me.'

'Ha. Nay. Quite clearly *I* won. But anyway, odd night. Good laugh though. Ha. Wasn't it?'

'ELLE: Yeah... Sure. OK, don't get mad but I must ask again...'

Here we go:

'Go on...'

'ELLE: Are you gay?'

'Ha. Again? No! Just Irish. Or weird. One of the two. Next time, I'll show you. Rematch! I mean I'll... Well, you'll see. I didn't mean that in a weird way. I just meant... Eh. OK better go. Bye!'

So yeah. Weird week. Lots of walking. Naked men. Apple juice. A granny. *And.* Wrestling. At least I know I'm still as smooth as ever - Smooth as a funking razor sharp cucumber. Go. Me. Some champ. Wrestle. On!

Chapter 34

Double Oh Heaven

Technically, you might say I'm Bond, James Bond. Double oh. In heaven. Hmm. Kind of. Didn't JB live a double life? Secret agent but no one knew? Yeah? See. I am *exactly* like that. Well, the double life living part. On the one hand, I am a struggling, disillusioned, broke writer currently living on the breadline. Tremendous fun. And then, in another world completely, I'm doing all these kind of things... Dodging, which all good spies do. Out Friday night with Chowder in Barney's. Busy. Full. Brimming. Up at the bar,

"I'll have a pint of water please."

Look around. Wait for my pint. Brunette in the bar stool next to me stands up. Thought she was leaving for the bathroom. Gave her a let-me-get-out-of-your-way nod and a smile. Almost spits in my face with disgust. OK?

"Can you leave?"

"Excuse me?"

"You're in my way. Get out of my space."

"Huh?"

"What's your problem? Do you not understand? Get out of my area. Go away. You. Fucking. Loser!"

"Have we met?
My presence is that bad?"

"If you don't back away and leave now, I'm going to hurt you."

"OK, who are you and what's your buzz? Also, why are you clenching your fists like you're about to punch me? And finally, what's the protocol for fighting a girl again?"

"You better leave right now."

Hmmm. This is odd. But I don't want her to win. What to do? Let me mull. I know...,

"Pardon?"

"Are you deaf? Get out of my area, I can't see the rest of the bar."

"Pardon?"

"Are you dumb too? Do you not speak English? Get away from this area! You're blocking my view."

"Pardon?"

"Can you not say anything else? I'm warning you. Leave! You're so ugly."

So I said... Nothing. Just drank my pint of water. And smiled at her with the *dumbest* face I could muster. Wasn't too hard to pull out of the bag. And then she left for the bathroom. Pushing her way past me. Shouldering me and my pint. Nicely done, female ape head. Only when she vacated her stool, did I notice who the two blondes were sitting next to her at the bar: The Nutter. Along with a blonde clone. In fairness to them, they were looking well. In that obvious American good-looking way. Eye-catching. Ape-herding. Nutter swivels her head towards me in that all now too familiar Chuckie-the-psycho-puppet way. I salute a hello. Nutter gives me the middle finger. Her friend follows suit. Ah, this is nice. Nice quiet pint at the local. Pleasant all round. I turn my attention back to my pint of water. Feel my phone buzzing in my pocket. Text:

'NUTTER: You're dead.'

Oh Jesus. Am I going to be beaten up by a gang of girls? How do I defend myself? Just blocking? What *is* the protocol when a girl starts properly throwing punches?! Can you wrestle at least? Someone fill me. The whole time Chowder has been on the phone outside. Arrives back looking all happy,

> "Want to go to the Hudson Bar instead? Charlotte is up there."
>
> "Eh. Yeah. Safer bet. I'll explain outside."

Giddy up. Away we went. While on the ten minute walk to the Hudson, I think I got about twenty different texts:

> 'NUTTER: You're going to be sorry you ever met me. There are guys looking for you now. You're dead!'
>
> 'NUTTER: Did you leave? Why did you leave? Why didn't you say goodbye? HOW RUDE!!!'
>
> 'NUTTER: I was only joking. Come back. Sorry about my friend. She's just drunk. Come back. You know I love you!'
>
> 'NUTTER: Tell me you love me too! Are you coming back? Want some whiskey?'
>
> 'NUTTER: We should get married. I'll marry you so you can get a visa. Come back??'

And so on. Followed by a flurry of missed calls. Dodge on. Voicemails:

> "Heeey you, what are you up to?"
> "Where should we meet?"
> "Come back. Please."
> "I saw you today by your house."
> "Green looks good on you."
> "I really liked that T-shirt."
> "Where did you buy it?"
> "OK, call me back."
> "Tell me where to meet. Love you!"

While I played these to Chowder, another text buzzed in:

> 'NUTTER: FUCK YOU SO YOUR JUST A FAGGOT!!!'

This was the toughest not to reply to, purely as I just wanted to say: It's spelt "you're". But I decided not to add fuel to her flammable fires. Started to wonder if I was maybe going to have to change my number. (But then the terrorist wins!) Eventually the madness stopped. Thank. Funk. Proof for my theory: Be wise about rejecting the best looking women. They're not used to it. Drives them clinically insane. Dodge off. Move on. Went for a spot of folf the following day. Some way to chill out. Rob has his abode down to a tee. Like a slice of heaven. Just like chilling in any of your buddies' abodes. Banter. Stories. Gibber. Plus the big heated swimming pool, Jacuzzi, personal chef and views of Hollywood. It's unreal. You'd think it might be kind of strange up there with all the folk coming and going plus the fact it's surreal from one point of view, but in reality, it's strangely weirdly really normal.

Take after the first round of folf we played. Some people headed home. Group of us stayed on. Pool time. Muggins Molloy here tries a few fancy dives. All obviously end up being full-on belly flops. Got a few too many ahhs and ohhs from the watching crowd. All in all, good fun. Besides that suspected cracked rib I gave myself. Banter on. Chilling on a Lilo. Sipping on a Guinness. Floating off to the deep end of the pool. Mairéad (the mighty Dub) calls out to Rob that he has a visitor on the way out to the pool.

> "Hiya Rob!"
>
> "Hey Tom, how are you? How about this weather?!"
>
> "Same as yesterday! It's not unusual..."
>
> "Coming for a dip?"
>
> "I'm all right, thanks, just popping in quickly to say hello."
>
> "Tom, this is everyone. Everyone this is Tom."

My inflatable bed turns around fully to say howdy to Tom.

> "It's not unusual to be loved by anyone, da da da dung..."

Instantly starts singing in my head. No way. Tom Jones?? The Welsh superstar singer?! That's Tom? Howdy Tom! Tom salutes. Tells Rob he'll pop in again soon. And away he goes. Pretty surreal. Yet strangely normal. If you know what I mean. Just like your buddy Jimmy calling in to say hi, as he was passing by your house back in Cork. Except that up here, it's just one of the world's most famous singers. Come to the think of it, the whole weekend was a bit like that. Surreal. Normal. Same night, Charlotte had a work event on in the W Hotel in Hollywood. Fancy new place that just opened up. New hot spot. Chowder was going. I was asked along too. Free bar? Betsy. Nightclub in the hotel called Drais. Cool looking club. Big fancy red velvet covered elevator up to the top floor of the hotel. Opens out to plush leather couches and black marble tables. Dance floor in the middle. Bar to my left. Opened out to the outside club area to my right. Lit up swimming pool. Another DJ. Another bar. All that fine malarkey. All on the rooftop of the hotel. Right in the heart of Hollywood. They do design well, in fairness to them. Bouncers were pretty cool in fairness to them too. As in "I am cool" kind of cool. Frustrated actors putting on head-wrecking performances for someone or another. Overacting everything. Eyebrow cocking. I will do everything in the slowest of slow motions in order to make this process longer, and more drawn out, and heighten my power, that I have, for being a small man, in a suit, who's behind a velvet rope, and there we go, you can go in actually, no wait, first let me chew this chewing gum extra slow and shrug my shoulders like I own the place, even though I am actually just a bouncer, OK so, I allow you in - that kind of cool. Macho Man Randy Savage didn't draw out a process for so long. Charlotte did well to skip us through after all that. Wingaduu on!

Club: Rammed. Looked like a stylish zoo. Packed with pretty. Models. Actors. Athletes. Talent. Beautiful. Boars. *Everywhere.* Littered with celebrities of all kind. Everyone acting fun. Posing. Just like how they act on TV. Looking the part. At one stage a Ludacris song came on and then Ludacris stood up on his table and started MC'ing along. Like a scene from the TV show *Entourage*, I remember thinking, while I stood at the bar, trying to pose along. Wasn't feeling the part though. Went outside for a look instead. Bumped into Craig Robinson again,

"Howdy boss!"

"Hey Irish, tip o' the morn to ye me laddie."

"Booze on?"

"Boo-ooze on lad!"

So we boozed on for a good while. Apparently this was also a premiere party for his new movie *Hot Tub Time Machine*. Happy days. He/I insisted again that I write him a role in my sitcom. You know, the one I shall be making. Soon. If. When. Part. Plan,

"If you insist boss!"

Verbal contract: On! Good old hoot all round really. Free bar probably helped a lot. Sunday was mighty too. Chowder and myself DJigged for the day in the SkyBar. Six hours of poolside dancing. Rotating the shifts. Drinks being served to us. Surrounded by pleasant-looking women. All in all, not a bad way to earn money. Feed me that green honey. Monday was a bit odd. Dick had a meeting set up for me. L.A Models. L.A Talent. Same company. Interested in signing me. Apparently. Model? Talent? Are you *sure* Dick? Have you ever seen me pose for a photo? OK. If you say so. Up I go. Sitting around the waiting room. Two girls with striking cheekbones and dull faces waiting along with me.
Some dude walks in off the street.
Says nothing.
Steps in the doors.
Strips down.
Middle of the room.
Clothes off.
Calvin Klein's left on.

Standing there with his hands on his hips. White Y fronts. No one says anything. Bizarre. Receptionist then sees him. Puts her phone to her ear. Presumably the police. Nay. Some dude in the back office comes running out. Whips out a camera. Takes photos of Y Front Man. Ten clicks later. Y Fronts puts back on his clothes. Turns. And leaves. What was that all about? Oh right - He's a model. Portfolio photos of some kind. OK. Still odd.

"Do I have to do that?"

What boxers do I have on? Do I have any on? Receptionist laughs,

"Not today. Maybe if you're signed."

Ha. Something to look forward to, I suppose. Then I went into my meeting. Met two girls who worked at the agency. Irish gibbered all the way. Seemed like fans of the accent. Told them about my book. Signed some papers. Shook their hands. Off I went. Got home. Read my email. And now I do believe I have an agent? Wuu huu! Although, I did still need proper headshots. Made a few calls. Got a favour from a friend of a friend. He'd do headshots for me if in return I would be in his commercial? Sounds good. Flex my acting chops! Arranged to come over to my apartment the following morning. Early doors,

> "Eight in the morning?
> OK. See you then."

On the couch that night watching TV. Saw something with Cindy Crawford flash up. Reminded me of that time I was in the doctor's office when I was young. Flicking through a woman's magazine waiting for my turn. Catch up on my gossip, it'd be rude not to. Flick on through, as you do. Article about Cindy Crawfoot, as I mistakenly called her. Hot lady. 'What is your secret?' she was asked. Sleep. Buckets of sleep. Or at least eight hours. Keeps her young. Keeps her hot. Particularly leading up to a fashion shoot. Tip from the top. Beauty sleep. Must remember that, I probably thought. Store it up. Never know when I may need that again.

Anyway, that flashback must've lasted ages or else I'm a complete idiot. Either way, before I knew it, I see it's almost five in the morning. Why am I not asleep?! Some clown. Barely scrape three hours in before the shoot. Not a good start. Even worse, I really don't like photos. Taking a camera. Aiming it at my head. Pressing the trigger. Not a fan. Churning out a smile part. Smile... Cheese! Did it work? No, smile again... Cheese! Sorry, flash didn't work! Again... Cheese... Camera shuts down. One more... Cheese... Smile... Sugar, didn't get your head in. Last one... Smile... Cheddar! OK, stop. That will do. Maybe it's the person taking photos? Maybe it's fake smiles, faces twitches and cracks. All are pitiful excuses really. Then again, I can be quite the pity. It's all me. Thankfully the first thing that came out of the photographer's mouth,

> "You know you don't have to smile? You don't even
> have to look at the camera. Just do whatever."

Hip hop hooray! Let's stare blankly at the wall! Let's just look up. Let's just look like an ape! Plain. Pose. On. Pale. Puffy. Eyes. No doubt they are looking dandy. Ha. Haw. Photo shop me up. All about the editing! Photos taken. Finally, after avoiding getting them for so long, headshots finally sorted. That night I went along to my first commercial shoot. Is that even the right term? Not too sure. Easy enough really. Besides the standing around in the freezing cold for really long intervals. Should've brought a jacket. Schoolboy. Although I was expecting my own trailer. Tut. Do they not know who I am?! Anyway, it was a five minute commercial for a lawyer's website. My segment was going to be about thirty seconds maximum. Director went through what he wanted me to do,

> "You've just been caught speeding. A police officer has pulled you over. You are very worried. You roll down the window, look at the camera and say: Is there a problem officer? Or something to that effect. Sound good?"
>
> "Yeah."

Although my acting skills might be a tad rusty. On-screen debut and all. So, emm, let me pretend like I know what I'm doing and talking about,

> "What's my character's motivation? Why was he speeding, mmmkay?"
>
> "I don't know. Make one up."
>
> "OK so. I'm a guy who just pillaged a town. Murderer. On the run. Nun like. Maybe a rogue spy actually! Speeding away from the scene of the crime. Pulled over by a cop. I look to the camera. Then he asks me to step out of the car. And I just know he's going to handcuff me and beat me up, so I *very* looked worried. Does that work for you director?"
>
> "Whatever. OK... ACTION!"

Eventually we got the take. I think. Hopefully the editor can work some magic. Rusty nail mixed with a bit of ad-libbing. Might have mentioned a goat at one point. Hopefully that gibber will get chopped. Hopefully. Not. Sweet Lord. Never know, could come back to haunt me. Have to start somewhere and all that. I'll look back at it and laugh. Ha ha. Ha haw. Harking back to my first small acting role. Laughing along as part of a *This Is Your Life* type show. Laughing, as I hold my Oscar. I can see it now. Back-story. Future-story. Same difference. All about the edit, as I have discovered. So eh, yeah. That's the kind of life I am currently living at the moment. Double life. Triple life even? Step up from James B. - James Beyond, they don't call me. Hard to tell at the moment what's going on? Bit all over the place. Is this heaven or is this hell? Good laugh, to be true.

Although the monkeys did show up a couple of times to remind me that I only worked one day out of a lot and I actually don't have anything else definite lined up for the foreseeable future either. Which is why I spent the past five days knocking on more potential work doors. No room at the inn. Time and time again. But let's not dwell on that. For the flying gin monkeys' sake. Especially as they did swarm in droves last night. Lying in bed. Still the quietest place ever created. No cats outside my window either to help lull me off. Too quiet to sleep. Pillow screaming at me. Thoughts wouldn't shut up. Magnified with nothing to fill the gap. Freaking out. Into the bathroom. Washed my face. Looked in the mirror. Saw I needed a shave. Blades are expensive though. Saving money. Which is when it hit me like a ton of bricks. Into the knees. Flopped down on the toilet. Tried to stand up. Dizzy head. Swift kick. Cramps. Sick feeling. Deep in my bowels.

Rocking.
Reeling.
Wobbling.
Wadding.
Waddling.

How could I forget my cycle? Four weeks have gone by *already*?! Time of the month, *again*?! Pea. Emm. Yes. Kicking in. Coming up. Nooo. You whure... Rent! Not now! Particularly when my funds are out of fashion. Not the in thing. Gushing out. Dose. Balls. Funk! Rent... You whure!

Floundered. Rattled. Literally making me go numb from the waist down. Although I soon realised that was down to me sitting on the toilet for too long. Few waddles around the bathroom; Fine again. Physically. Mentally, tad dodge. Enough for this month. Just cut back on some stuff I suppose. Who needs food anyway? Ha-ha... Ughatha. Why did I buy all those T-shirts growing up?! All now sitting in my wardrobe back in Ireland. Clown! Some ape. OK. Calm down, no point in worrying about the future. You'll find enough gigs to keep you dancing. Don't forget about going back to Ireland in a few weeks too though - Shhh. I know. Just think of the now. Focus on the positives. Like... When was the last time you felt bored? See! Exactly. Plus your days are kind of free so you get to do all those fun things? So that's good too. And. Also. Ehh- Oh, hang on. Another text from the Nutter. Just let me read this...

She's going to hunt me down if I don't take her on a date tonight? And she still despises my fictional German wife Gertrude and wants me to end it with her now? See! That's great news. A good-looking psychopath is losing her grip on reality over you. That really is *wonderful*. Everything's fine. Nothing to worry about!!!

Oh yeah?

Oh Jesus.

Door. Knocking. On.

Chapter 35

The Circle of Strife

Great news: I found a new place to do it! You know... It. So I used to be a big fan of doing it in the shower. Just me and myself. No one else around. Bit of alone time. Work away. Happy days. Until I found it can get too hot at times in the shower, particularly if I do it for too long. Almost passing out by the end. Doing it in my bed is a good place as well, of course. Thing is I don't last as long there. Fatigue is an issue. But if I manage to get a quick burst, I do at least have a nice deep slumber afterwards. Pass out. Happy. Content. Anyway, this week I stumbled upon a *mighty* new place to do it... My bathroom! Specifically, on the toilet itself. True, it can be a bit awkward. However if you just leave the lid down, it's actually more comfortable than you think - Presuming you've never tried doing it there before yourself. I am, of course, referring to: Pondering. Thinking. Mulling. Obviously. What *else* would I be on about? Quite the thinker.

So in a few weeks I must head back to Ireland for book promotions et al. Instead of being fully pumped about going back to Ireland - for the release of my first book! - my mind is pondering all the smaller stuff. Which aren't really that small at all. Like the cost of return flights home. Paying rent while I'm gone. Spending-money while I'm home. Travel costs for going around Ireland. Money. Money. Money. Grumble. Cough. Splutter. Spit. Dumb and pointless to worry, I know. But it is getting to me. Likewise is the constant battling with my publishers. Past two weeks has been non-stop over the cover. Wearing me down. For far too long they had a girl on the cover who looked like she had been shipped around the world in a crate, walked out looking fragile and close to death, and then someone snapped a photo. That was their idea of the "Hollywood look".

They also had a black guy on the cover who I'm still to this day unsure of why he's there. Not in a racist way. Just in a "What relevance to the story does he have?" kind of a way. Unless, of course, they haven't actually read the book and are just bluffing of what they think it's about. Either way, in the end we compromised. Found the right girl here who had the proper Hollywood look. Swapped her in. Fitted in nicely with the black guy and the dodgy looking photo of me that they decided to use. But at least that got sorted. And the book has gone to print. So thanks to them for that.

On the downside, they then kindly told me that all the travel expenses for coming back are all my own. Nothing to do with them. Must cough up myself. Here's a few pennies. And I must come back. Says so in my contract. So cheers as well for that. Apes. All of which has made me almost definitely not want to go back. More than almost: I don't want to go home for my book launch. It's freaking me out. Going home is going to bankrupt me. Unless I somehow make three thousand dollars in the next two weeks, I'm goosed. Slim picking. Even worse, despite my best efforts, I've slipped. Fallen. Flopped into a routine. Appears all I do now is just whittle. Every day feels the same. Wake up, get out of bed, right side, walk around, over to my laptop, turn it on, open the blinds, open the window, make my bed, pick up my laptop, go to the bathroom, sit down, surf, Gmail, BBC, Trickaduu, Facebook, Twitter, flush, wash, kitchen, bowl, porridge, protein, microwave, drink some water, drink some more, hear a ding, eat the thing, chug some coffee, one more pint of water, brush my teeth, clothes on, hair ruffled, and away I go. Off to whittle away my day. Gibber around. Follow up on DJigs. Fruitless. Walk around. Knock on doors. Closed on my face. Literally, at times. Hours later. Walk home. Weary. Dejected. Kill. Fill. Whittle some more. Eat a meal. Write a few emails. Check Craigslist. Knock on some online doors. Head back out. Try some stand-up venues nearby. Open-mics. Lucky if I get on. If not, I just go to the gym. Come home. Whittle one last time. Write some gibberish in my blog. Sigh. Check my online banking. See my balance. Shake my head. Exhale. And go to bed. Well done. Mighty day. Whittled that down nicely. Ground. Hogging. Even my productive days are really just me fooling myself. Take Thursday. Meeting with Dick, the manager. Went well, except it was more or less the exact same as the first one. He's going to wait to set up various meetings until I'm back from Ireland after the book launch. Voice lessons and all that on hold too. Everything seems to be on hold until I come back from Ireland, now that I think of it. At least he got very giddy when he realised that the book was a legit thing. Not just Hollywood hype from Hollywood Hayes. So that was good. Invited me over to his abode for some celebratory champagne that night. Him and his two buddies, Ralph and Gregory. For some reason my blink said it had the feel of a gay orgy written all over it. Sorry, Dick, I'm busy whittling. Cheers though. So that was grand. Good meeting. However, getting there and back took about an hour and a half because I walked. If I drove, fifteen minutes tops. No bobs these days for frivolous things like a taxi. Bus wasn't going that route. Par for the course. Got home and took a twenty minute break because walking in the heat back to my apartment "took it out of me". Basically my whole day revolved around that thirty minute meeting, where nothing really was achieved. Just stuff on hold. Not really right. Bluffing. Something's amiss. Killing. Filling. Time. Whittling on. Just running down the clock until I have to go home. Almost feels like when I first arrived in L.A. No clue what I was doing. Whittling. Running. Circling. Busy? Ish. Foolish? Completely. Time to giddy up out of it. Badly need more tangibles. Tangibles that bring me money. Meeting with managers. Modeling agencies (ha, I know). Literary agents as well. All of that is great. But still a country mile from even being close to the chance of me making money out of any of that.

Quite clearly money is my issue. My mind is going mental. Zero coming in. All going out. Not good for the brain. No clue how guys who lose their jobs and have a family to support manage to cope. Can barely look after myself. Struggling to survive! Which makes me feel like a funking chump. Dope. Idiot. Seriously. Which in turn does not help your own motivation. Self-belief wavers. And it's all your own fault. Ughatha. Circle of strife. Feeling useless all the time because you're kind of failing is not that much fun. Unless you're a fan of punching yourself in your own face. Perhaps I've been trying too hard. Or pushing people too much. Those folk who express interest in things I've been chasing. Couple of bars might be interested in me DJing regularly for them over the summer. Which would be mighty. Just that people seem to move in slow motion. Well, slower than I'd like. Lacking patience. Lacking tact. Ye seem interested in doing this so? Good stuff! When should we start, now?! No? In a few weeks, perhaps? Funk. Ehh, what about right NOW? As in tomorrow? C'mon, we're on the same page, let's do this sooner! Commit. Confirm. *Please*!

Chasing.
Hounding.
Desperate.
Reeking.
Like a clingy woman on the hunt for a husband. (I've never seen

a man hunt down a wife, but I presume this analogy works both ways.) Eventually being told it might be better just to wait a while. Here's some free drink. And maybe in a couple of weeks we can get that going. Until then, let's just be friends. Pardon? No green honey? Noooo! Feed me!!! I really can't afford to go home. It's kind of like taking a holiday to the other side of the world when you have no money. Little sense. Close to making a few drastic calls. Even going as far as typing out the emails:

> *'Sorry everyone, I'm not coming home for the book launch. I know. I'm a failure. Ye were right: I wouldn't last out here. Well done for doubting me.'*

About to press send. Second thoughts.
Followed by third, fourth, fifth and sixth.

Should I stay or go?
What did I come here to do again?
Am I doing it?
Should I just give up?
Chopping.
Changing.
Confused.
Wheels spinning.
Over and over.
Highly tiring.

Feeling goosed all week. The surreal surface of L.A can make you forget about reality bubbling below. Small things have being wobbling this bubble to the fore. Went to Trader Joe's the other night. Buy a few essentials. Minimal. Potato. Chicken. Carrots. Who do I see: Good old Orgy Joe. For funk's sake. Well, I didn't see him. He spotted me. Started queuing up behind me,

> "Heeey, I know you.
> Irish guy, right?
> You never called me?"
>
> "Oh Jesus. Not now Joe."
>
> "Are you OK? Did I do something wrong? You don't look so good."
>
> "I'm fine Joe, thanks. Lot on my mind."

"Well you know I'm always here to help. You just let me know if you ever need someone to talk to."

"Ah well, that's nice of you to say, cheers."

"By the way, I meant to ask last time... (whispers) Have you ever thought of doing pornography? Tasteful, of course."

"Funk me pink. Get away from me you sleazy old man!"

Scuttled away home. Started to make my dinner. Mind drifted from my chicken breasts. Pondering how much porn stars get paid. Hmmm. I wonder. Although I remember that documentary on Channel 4 that I saw before said that male porn stars make far less than the women. Which is why so many of the guys go into gay porn. I wonder how much you'd make from one movie? And why am I thinking these fabulous thoughts again? All right, enough of that. Time for my dinner. And then I sat down at the table, reached for my glass and accidentally spilt a pint of water all over my dinner. Covered the plate. Mighty. Can't beat some watery chicken breasts and potatoes. I ate the wet lumps anyway. Just as I was finishing, Moe came home from work. Chit. Chat. As you do, starts telling me he just found out his buddy donates sperm all the time. Jokingly suggested I should give it a go. Ha-ha. I laughed along. Then gave it some thought. Hmmm. How hard could it be– No. Nay. Being a nark and all,

"I value my knowledge too much for that. *Far* too sacred. Unless a girl was just looking to throw a cup in her face? Then. Maybe."

Moe laughed. But thought it was doubtful. Tut. Dose. Decided to go to the gym. Badly needed to clear my head. Walking along. Listening to my iPod. My mind replaying the image of my bank balance. Being broke is draining. Fatigue is a killer. Worrying about rent. Food. Shaving utensils. Booze! Being creative has taken a backseat. No spark. No joy. No dancing.

"No no, not until we get some money for ourselves."

Says the inner me to the outer me.

"Thanks, inner me."

My mental enemy. Stupid innemy. Realised I had stopped walking. Shoulders slumped. Chips down. Hope gone. Felt like I had been on the run. Fugitive. Hiding from money issues. Chasing me for months and months. Since before I started the book. Just held it off. Constantly not knowing how I'll manage. Scraped by. Skin of my teeth. Ignore reality and it'll go away. Bury those thoughts. Worry. The Fear. Deep down. Until it all caught up on me. Innemy won the war. Ambushed on the way to the gym. Floored. Floundered. Funked. Sat down on the curb on the side of road. Needed a rest. Why was I even bothering going to the gym? After that I was just going to go home, go to bed, sleep, then I just wake up and realise once again who I am and how I've no job. Lie there and wonder if I should even bother getting up? Yeah. Might as well. Then go look for a job. Spend the rest of the day wondering about money. Then go to the gym to release the worry. And the circle would start over. Tired. Weary. Goosed. Ape. Felt like crying. Didn't even have the energy for that. After a good few songs and a long sitting spell, I phoned Elle,

"Can I call over?"

We had been going for a good few strolls together recently. I had kind of been telling Elle about my indecision to go home and maybe hinting as to why so. Not something to boast about really. Not something you want to even tell people about. Embarrassing. Makes you feel trapped. At least when we went for strolls, Elle settled my brain. Took it somewhere else. Somewhere better. But that was another dose about not having any money. Besides the pointless overwhelming despair, I couldn't ask Elle out anywhere. Strolls were all I had, seeing as they were free. Cinema? Nay. Dinner? Ha. Pub? Barely. Unless we were just going to split a pint? Quite the gentleman. Anyway, Elle invited me over. Played me some mighty songs on the piano. No poking or wrestling after. Although, I did fall asleep there. Lulled me off. Goosed. And I woke up dancing! Well, at least with a bit more pep in my step. Decided I need to get out of this purple patch. Not really sure what that actually meant, but it sounded about right. Purple patch off. Too much time banging my head against a wall. Half the time, missing the wall. No more! Time to create something from nothing. Needs to be done. I shall rise again. Phoenix style!!

My neighbour might have shown me the way. Arrived back at my building. Walked out of my lift. Went down the hallway towards my apartment. Fork. Turned left. Glanced right. Happened to see a guy panned out on the ground. Face down. Hands sprawled out.

Grocery bags around him. Lying there. Down. Out. Motionless. Stopped going left. Stood. Looked. Wondered. Waited for him to move. Finally he shifted. Muttered something to himself. Asked if he was OK? Stopped shifting. Took a step closer to him. Asked again. Heard him say he was,

"OK. OK. OK."

Got the feeling he didn't want me to help. Proud fool. Made sure one last time,

"Are you sure you're OK?"

Didn't respond this time. Shifted his hands as if he was about to push himself up. Not much I could do. Except just leave him be. Headed off to my apartment. Subtly looking back, of course. Watching as the proud fool lifted himself up. PHOENIX, rising from the floor! Didn't need my help. Hauled himself back up on his own! Well, he actually just rolled over. Half sat up. Cursed his shoe. And tied his shoelace. Which is when I realised it was my deaf neighbour. Who then saw me just standing down the hallway. Looking at him. Probably wondering why I didn't offer to help him up. Proud fool. No wonder my neighbours are such big fans of me.

Well, at least he showed me how. Time to haul myself back up after a useless few weeks. Not done yet. Chips might be down. But the spirits shall remain high! Battle through.

Or as a wise old owl might say: Porn off. Plough. *On*!

Chapter 36

Calm Before the Norm

Did you know that in Ireland the first thing people do when something bad happens is... Have a cup of tea! Tea - Quite the magic potion, to be true. Like any Irish: man, woman, child, ape, leprechaun or dancing clown, I do enjoy the odd cup. About eight times a day. Can't beat it. Step one to get over any incident.

Wife's cheated on you? Cup of tea!
Car broke down? Have a cup of tea!
Hungover? Here's a teacup full of whiskey!
Tea. On.

Unfortunately as an Irishman now living in America, tea bags are not as readily available as back home. Proper ones, at least. Which is why sacks of these little tea filled bags are smuggled over the border by little green men on a daily basis. Irish gold. All of which makes offering tea to anyone in my abode, whenever I go to make a cup, mostly a polite gesture. Willing, hoping, *prompting* them to say no,

"So, eh, would you like a cup of tea, *no*?"

I do this now as I know what will invariably happen... Most American folk like to try new things. So being asked by an Irish Mark if they want an Irish cup of tea means that they will, more often than not, say yes! As if it is a little treat. If crystal meth was seen as a jovial Irish thing, I am pretty sure people would say yes just as easily. Seriously. Try it. Just one hit. You'll see little green men in no time. The thing is most Americans will accept a cup of tea without having a clue what it tastes like. Acceptance purely and probably based on the fact they themselves are 1/13th Irish, which they usually tell you at this point. Now embracing their diluted heritage with exuberant enthusiasm,

> "Tea, you say?
> I would love a cup.
> Made by a leper-*chaun*! Oh my *Gawd... I'm* Irish!
> This is *awe*some!"

They then look on with amazement as you go through the whole magical leper-chaun-like process of making a masterful cup of tea.

Kettle. Water. Boil.
Cup. Tea bag.
Pour.
Do that secret magic thing only Irish folk know.
Wait two minutes.
Tea's ready. Drink on.
As you go to pour milk into your cup of tea, a look of disappointment will appear on their face,

> "Just milk? That's not very Irish! I'm going to make it even better!!!"

And then they go and ruin your masterful work. Pouring in honey, pepper, salt, hazelnut, swirls, red-pepper flakes, vinegar, cold water or anything else they can get their hands on, all to add their own personal twist. Eyes gleeful. Giddy. Proud. Take one sip. Sour. Wince. Regret. Put the cup down. And that's it. First and only mouthful. Feigning slurps. Mmmm. Nodding politely along. While you subtly *urge* them to at least drink half the cup. Can't waste a teabag! And then they dump the full cup down the drain. Mighty stuff. You dirty whu- Ah it's just one teabag, I hear you say. I know. But to all the teabaggers who live in limited supply... What a waste! Should really just buy a pot for myself. Seeing as the next time, oddly, they will still accept a cup. Not sure why. Although maybe I'm just odd for offering once again. At least there is always the one out of ten who actually enjoys the full cup. My roommate Moe now starts his day with a cup of tea. And a potato, cooked in the microwave. Ha. Poor soul. Fully converted. Crusade on! Not too sure where this tea ramble came from. Oh yeah: I think I had my most expensive cup of tea ever the other day. Quite the pretty penny. Hundreds and thousands of pennies, to be more vaguely precise. Have you ever been playing a game of chicken with booking flights online? Find a cheapish one. Wavers in price. Dips slightly cheaper. Might this go even lower? Wait. Nope. Missed your chance. Jumps slightly back up. Balls. Although... Might dip one more time. Wait. Just wait. Sit. Wait. Watch. Chicken. Head. Wait. Dip... Dip... *C'mon* Dip! Then a rocket sails over the sky. And the price shoots up. Sky high. You lose, Dip Hayes. Chicken. During the week this happened. Cheap flight. Did its little dip. Dip again? Nay. Jumped back to what it was. All thirty five euros jump back up. Big difference. Ploughed on with that price. Went through the motions. Filled out the forms. Name. Address. Payment. All that gibber. Time to press "Purchase". Just about to click. Until I heard the kettle boil - Ping! So I decided, quite obviously, to have a quick cup of tea first. Not sure why. Perhaps I just like to pick the most ill-timed moments to have cups of tea. Perhaps I thought the cup of tea was my reward for doing such an arduous task as booking a flight back to Ireland, all on my own! Perhaps I just have mental issues. Probably all of the above. Anyway, cup of tea in hand, back to the computer I go: Clickity click. Now processing this transaction. May take a minute. I'll just enjoy this tea while I wait. Ahh, nice cup of tea. Tea bag in the cup, still amazed with that. Taking longer than a minute. Page loading. Unexpected message starts screaming out from the screen:

> THE PRICE OF YOUR FLIGHT HAS INCREASED TO €2496.38
>
> "What the whating what?! What what?! Oh Jesus, did I just book that?"

Head gets dizzy, knees flutter, tea sloshes around. Struggle to stay on my feet, almost fall like a floosy, grabbing hold of the wall. Until I remembered: Bob Hope my Irish credit card has that limit left on it. Wuu. And. Phew. Missed out on the lowly priced flight. Sky rocketing up. Balls. Expensive cup of magic. Can't blame the tea really though. Never the tea. Mostly me. Although, in my defence, a certain website (starts with Ex, ends with pediatrician) has been advertising that low price ever since. Keeps shooting rockets into the sky whenever I click to proceed. Either way, and here is my mighty linkage point, it did remind me of how I have just been sitting around, waiting, sitting, waiting, OK time to take action, actually I'll just have a cup of tea first and then I end up not doing what I had planned. Putting stuff off. Life on hold until I have to go back to Ireland. Back to the norm. Well, no more. Time to get what I can dumb!

First thing to do: Book my flight home. And... Done. Despite the fact I've actually DJed three times this week, I am still a tad off my three thousand dollar mark. Meaning I could only afford a one-way ticket. Which is a balls. But I will sort something out. At least that was taken care of. Next on my list... Free clothes! My publishers have told me I have lots of interviews lined up. Even some TV ones. Apparently. Looks like I shall be exposed when I go home. Which is mighty. Charlotte's friend Patti also works for Ted Baker as their PR/Publicist guru, a mighty Welsh dancer who actually looks more like Dolly Parton than Patti Smith, despite being named after the latter. Her job is to dress celebrities in Ted outfits and make sure they get photographed in those clothes. Exposure? Me? About to be exposed? Two plus duu equals: Free the clothes! I shall be looking dapper for the book promotions at least. Go on the Charlotte and Patti! Mighty clothes as well. Discovered two new things during my fitting:

1. Skinnier jeans are actually not that bad. (How I've changed!)
2. Trying on clothes that are skinnier and tighter than ones you usually wear after you walked to the shop when it is absolutely *roasting* outside, can be dodge. Let's just say I should've stayed away from trying on the tight baby blue shirt.

Oh, I also discovered that the last person to get clothes from Ted Baker was Ricky Gervais for his recent stint at the Oscars. So I'm in good company. Although he had to give his back. Mine are mine. I think. Say nothing. I bribed Patti with wads of chocolate bars - as suggested by Charlotte - so I think that sweetened the deal further for me. Also led to me christening Patti as Chocolate Face, which I now realise might sound a *tad* racist if heard out of context. Moving on. I've also been getting back up on the stand-up horse. So far my return has been... Patchy. Getting stage time is tough enough at times. Competitive fecks here. All about sucking people's lollipops it seems, if you know what I blatantly mean. Anyway, I have obviously not been sucking the right lollipop. So my stage time has been limited. However, I did manage to flirt with the girl in charge of the open-mic last Sunday night in the Comedy Store. Giddy up. Got on. Stood up. Danced on! (My act is mostly built around a gay horse joke – Heeeeey! – and my accent.) Came off stage. And was approached by a woman named Cindy, a promoter who worked there, asking if I'd be interested in being in her show next month. Some proper stage time at the world famous Comedy Store on Sunset Boulevard, home of Jim Carrey, Jerry Seinfeld and Richard Pryor? Sounds mighty! Count me in! As long as I'm somehow here, of course.

The Man swung back into town on Monday. En route to the Caribbean. Few days in L.A. Some life. Some man. Mighty calming influence too. Seemed to sense my inner me battling my outer me. All about highlighting the good stuff. Too true. Positive on. His enthusiasm for my book got me back dancing as well. Who cares about the ongoing battles with the publisher - Book on!

Group of us went along to Mr. Chow's for dinner on the Monday. Heard a fair bit about the place. Might be the best restaurant in L.A. Kind of looks like a really good restaurant you'd see in a mafia movie like Casino, if that makes any sense. Rows of circular tables. Very tight. Everyone packed in. Mirrors on the walls. Abundance of waiters in their white shirts and black waistcoats scuttling around like precise penguins. Wall to wall cleavage. Diamonds dripping everywhere. Plates and plates of ridiculously good food. Fresh scallops. Chicken satay. Crispy duck. Squid ink noodles. Wild black sea bass. Velvet chicken. Lamb shank. And of course: Chicken Joanna, whoever she may be. *Savage*! For any name-dropping folk this place is a good spot to go. Brimming. Bumped into Mr. Plow in the bathroom. Mr. Plow in Mr. Chow! Poetic. And by Mr. Plow, I mean Homer. And by that, I mean the guy who does the voice of Homer Simpson! Pretty sure it was him anyway. He did have half a beard. I'm also a bit wary of giving guys third or fourth long glances, especially in the bathroom. Long and longing are a thin line here. Our brief chat involved him recommending a dish to me,

"Very good duck."

Unfortunately ended with Homer walking out the bathroom door just before I got to finish my great joke... I do enjoy a good duc- Gone. G'duck! Ah, telling brutal jokes to myself in the bathroom. Always a hoot! Headed back to our table. About to rattle off my bathroom story as I sat down, until I bumped elbows with the guy at the table next to us. Swiveled to my right to apologise - Instantly started humming *Grease Lightning*... Go Grease Lightning! Followed by a few Bee Gees songs. Filling up my head. Sudden urge to start disco dancing. Before my hands could get their *Saturday Night Fever* on, I sat down, on them. And instead just gave Mr. John Travolta a nod hello. How's it going, John? Give me some el-bow. Cue a strange look. Only then did I notice the person two seats down. No way. Is that *Forrest Gump*? *Big*? Is that [insert a ridiculously long, long, long list of other names]? Indeed it is! Mr. Tom Hanks, looking sharp – Where's Wilson tonight? Actually, lads, just a quick heads up: I hear the duck is mighty. To which Tom coyly replied,

"I do enjoy a good..."

"Wahey!"

And then a birthday cake showed up for someone at their table, they all started singing "Happy Birthday", I obviously joined in, arm in arm around the bewildered lads until our fun was ruined by *somebody* accidentally smashing a glass on the ground. Cheers, Chowder. Mighty night all round really. Savage spot. Wining. Dining. Top quality. All about the banter though. Rubbing shoulders, bumping elbows and singing songs were just an added bonus to be true. Porridge and nagon of vodka will do me if needed. (In Ireland we call what Americans describe as a shoulder of vodka, a nagon. Some Irish folk spell it nagan, naggin or nagin. I spell it: Nagon. Nag on.) Still, the high life is quite fun, to be true! If this was to be my Last Supper, nay too shabby. All I was missing was Elle. Unfortunately in New York getting her model on. Although at least she was still wielding her mighty influence on me from afar. Told her about my flight mess-up. She told me I need to cop on...

> "Stop being a weirdo who doesn't brush his hair and dwells in caves. Stop sabotaging yourself."

Wise words from the Miss Elle! No more Sabotage Hayes. Time to get back dancing. Need to be in flying form for when I go back to Ireland in a few days. Even if my lack of money and return flight do give my bowels slight wobbles. Although oddly enough, the tea incident might've worked out for the best. Received a pretty mighty offer from Rob to go to England on the day I originally hoped to fly back to L.A. He's going back as well for a charity event. Invited me along as his VIP guest. So it looks like I'll be going to that, seeing as I have not yet committed to a return flight. Go on the cup of tea! Woke up this morning to an email from my publishers:

> *'Hi Mark, just to let you know your book is out today. Available to buy. Tell your friends. Bye.'*

> *'Seriously? Just like that? What about fanfare? Build up? Drama? No?'*

No reply. So that was wonderful. In a way. Don't get me wrong - Absolutely mighty that it's out. And despite a HUGE chunk of "buddies" asking: "Where's my free copy?" ... Sales went global! Tom Holohan back in Cork ordering the first copy. Just pipped Barbara in Germany who did the same. Graza in Poland. Snoops in Barcelona. Yu in Japan. Aisling in Hong Kong. Debbie in Santa Barbara. All rounded off by my buddy Buddy Shaw up in San Fran ordering two. Global on! So that was mighty. It was just that I did think the way the publishers told me was slightly odd. Felt like it limped out the gate. I was expecting a flock of pigeons to be released in every country around the world to commemorate such a glorious event. Nay. Which put a dent in my big dumb ego. Kind of got me thinking about why I'm going home for the launch if they've just released it already? I don't really know. Not much of what they do makes sense. Must just be me. I'm sure the publishers know what they're doing, right? Publishing world is smart. Right? Definitely me.

Speaking of which, invited to a barbeque with Chowder and Charlotte that afternoon. Not that big a fan of barbeques, but seeing as it was my last day before I had to go home for the launch of my already released book (have I mentioned this before?), I said I would be *delighted* to come along! I'll tell them all my book news, I thought. Never know, maybe someone has a pigeon for me. Wuu huu. Off we went to their friend's house. Birthday. Chilling. Grilling. American fun and games. No one had a pigeon. But someone did bring a water slide. Took ages to set up. Kind of a letdown. In the photo on the packaging the models seemed to be having way more fun. Not to worry. Food's ready. Here's a booze. BBQ on. Evening time came. Slightly restless. Still to pack. Can't just eat and leave, can I? Apparently not. Just have a kip for myself to pass the time. Lay down on a reclining chair. Eyes closed. Drifted off. Half asleep. Felt something on my arm. Heard people yelping. Looked up. Oh hello there Baxter, the dog- Oh Jesus what are you doing, dog?! Baxter. Urinating on me. All over my elbow. That's weird, I thought. Didn't even know dogs did that? Purely thought it was humping only. Anyway, kind of odd. Waved Baxter away. People at the barbeque freaking out. Found it very strange. Calm down folks. *Wee* bit bizarre, I suppose. Being honest, I didn't find it overly odd. What the funk, I guess? Innocuous. Random. Dumb. Happens all the time. Not that strange. Joys of living in L.A. Or maybe I've just lost all concept of what strange is anymore. Who knows? Who cares? Because tomorrow, I'm going home for a reason – Yay! Book launch! Even though it's already out! Wuu! - which to me, personally, seems far stranger...

Chapter 37

Release the Dumb!

"Mark *Hayes*. Where do *you* think you're going?"

Oh no. The Nutter. Why is she outside my house?

"Did you just happen to be parked here or were you waiting for me?"

"Are you leaving?"

"Yeah. Gotta go."

"Where to?!"

"Ireland."

"When are you coming back?"

"I don't know. One way flight. I'll miss your nutterness."

"You can't leave – Let me take you the airport!"

Hmmm. I could save on cab fare. But then again I could also end up in a *Misery* style situation – you know the movie where Kathy Bates keeps James Caan prisoner in her remote home and then breaks his legs with a sledgehammer when he tries to leave. Hmmm. What to do...,

"No I'm OK, thanks, leave my legs alone. Must bounce!"

At which point the Nutter burst into hysterical crocodile tears. Pounding the steering wheel of her convertible. Making quite a scene outside on my street.

"I'll wait for you—no! I'm going with you!"

"Ha-ha. Good one. Must run. Stay dumb. G'duckaduu!"

Misery bullet: Dodged. Nutter off. Taxi on.

Flight home. Upgraded by Virgin. Wuu. Get to the gate. About to board. Hear my name being called. Aw yeh, first class all the way...,

"Pardon?"

Girl at the gate,

"$500 please."

"Pardon?
What?
Why?
For you upgrading me?
What what?!
No way?"

"Yes way."

"No way."

"Yes. Pay?"

No. Tut. Degraded. Back to my original seat. Making me slum it. Whures. Board the plane. Sit down. Armenian guy and his wife next to me. Before I even manage to buckle the seatbelt, he offers to sell me an iPhone. Then a laptop? And then...,

"You buy my wife? Very good deal my friend!"

Oh dear Jesus. Orders a round of drinks for us in broken English. Vodka Red Bull. Doubles. One for him. One for me. And one for his seven months pregnant wife,

"You will drink it! I don't care if you're pregnant..."

Swivels in his chair,

"You want my wife? You want her. And an iPhone? Good deal my friend!"

Sweet Lord. Going to be a long flight. Another round please, Virgin hostess! Next five minutes I'm told all about Armenia. Sounds like a lovely place. I think. Couldn't understand what he was saying besides,

"... Armenia is good, yes?"

Asked me what I was going to Ireland for?

"Book tour."

Eyes light up.

"Are you a celebrity?!"

"Ha. Nay. Calm down."

Didn't care. Wife is instructed to take photos of us on his iPhone. Cheers. Yay. This is fun!

"So tell me my friend, what do you do on a book tour? Are you going on TV? What are you going to do...?"

Before I could answer, he checks his phone, then turns to freak at his wife,

"You take the shit photo!"

They then get in another yelling match. And I decide enough is enough. Time to rectify Virgin degrading me. Get up. Peek my head through the VIP curtain. Half empty class. Say nothing. Slip in. Sit down. Blanket over the head. Kip on! Self-upgrade. Only way to go. Virgin, I owe you 500 bones. It's in the post, I swear. My Armenian friend did get me thinking at least. While I was busy keeping a low profile in business class, I realised I didn't really have an answer to his question: What are you going to do on a book tour? My publishers had basically told me very little. Making me question what I was actually going back for again, particularly now I've spent all my money on doing so? Slightly worrying. But I just went with the "Ah, calm down, they know what they're doing, trust them" approach. Everything will be sorted by the time I get back to Ireland, I told myself,

"But what if it's not?!"

My innemy quickly and annoyingly answered with another question. Oh Jesus. Stomach. Dropped. Bowels. Plop. Dread washes over. No money to get back. What am I *doing*? Why am I leaving? Is this *it*?! Grabbed the inflight magazine. Flicked quickly to distract myself. Land on an ad for a bag. Hmm. Nice bag. Page opposite, spot a quote down the corner...

"I will find a way or make one."
~ Hannibal

Ha. Mighty. Perfect. Not sure if it's Hannibal Lecter or that military guy I read about in my Roman history books, but it does the trick,

"I will find a way!" I proudly mutter a bit too loudly.

Shh. Head down. Sleep on! Twelve hour flight. Eight hour connection in London. Funny chat about Japanese comics with a Japanese guy who doesn't speak English. Keeps me occupied.. And then I'm back in Cork. My Mum, Dad and sister greet me at the airport. Mighty to see them! Once I got there, delighted to be home. Felt slightly weird at first though. Walking into the kitchen. In the sitting room. Flicking through channels on the TV again. Everything felt smaller but better than I imagined, for some reason. If that makes any sense. Quickly settled in. Bowl of porridge and a cup of tea: Flying!

Parents pumped to hear what's going on with the book tour. Ha, yeah... Me too. Let me just check my email. Publishers said they'd be emailing me the book promo itinerary. Time to hit the ground running! Hmmm. Any updates? Bare. Boneless. Nothing? What the - Oh no, there's one interview arranged for twenty minutes time. But that's all that's confirmed? One thing? Loads of maybes. Waiting to hear back from people. That's it? Publishers then inform me they'll start the promotion push now that I'm physically back. What?! Why weren't ye doing that beforehand? You told me to be back this week? Clowns!

Checked my other emails. Gibber. Gibber. Gibber. Hey hup! Offer from Porsche in Beverly Hills. Want me to DJ. Three days. Bucket of money. No way. Would cover all of my rent for the next three months. Oh Jesus. That's my lifeline! When... This coming weekend?! FUNK!!! Why did I come back?! For one phone interview? I could've done that from L.A! Some shower of apes.

Told my Mum and Dad what was going on. Then checked out flights back to L.A for the next day. Found a cheap one. Ehh, I think I'm going to book this. I know it's weird if I leave again so soon, but the publishers have nothing setup and I really need to work. Seriously. Money talks. Keeps my sanity intact. Parents told me to chill. Do the interview tonight. Sleep on it then. OK. Fair enough. Phone rings. Interview time. Thankfully, that was a complete flyer. Dublin radio station. Both hosts loving my stories and tales. Couldn't have went any better. Gibber flowing. All in a good way. Danced a merry dance to my own tune. Happy days. Now. Time to sit. Wait. See. What will the publishers say tomorrow? Stew until they do. Woke up. Phoned the publishers. Still nothing confirmed. All maybes. Working on it. Well then, I'm off. Actually- email from Porsche arrived:

> *'Sorry, got a bit confused, the gigs aren't on this weekend. We'll be in touch!'*

OK. All right. Fair enough. Not going back to L.A straightaway after all. Although come to think of it, how was I going to book the flight back as it was? Hmm. Forgot about that. Maybe I could get my credit card limit increased? Good call,

> "Mum, Dad, I'm off to the bank. Back in a while!"

At least I had transport while I was at home. Once again, the mighty Eddie Murphy (CEO of Ford Ireland) hooked me up with a slick, complimentary executive Ford car of some sort for my stay. (Eddie used to be one of my soccer coaches in university. Some man. Everyone: Buy Ford!) Off I go to the AIB bank up by my old university, U.C.C. Try to set up a meeting with a loan manager. No one around today, I'm told. Meeting arranged for the Monday morning. Well, looks like I'll be here until at least the weekend, providing I can get the credit push. Last chance saloon time. Decided to go into the city for a stroll. Also on a little mission. Friends were all at work (although most now live in Dublin, London, Australia or anywhere but here) so I would be flying solo once again. The mission: Go see my book in a bookstore for the first time!

Even though *RanDumb* was released into the open a while back and was now running free like a demented headless chicken, I had yet to see or hold a copy. Publishers told me to go check it out. In all the bookstores. Mighty. At least that's one dancing plus! Particularly since as far back as I can remember - about nine months - it has always been a dream of mine to be a published author. Ever since my buddy Dave Buckley asked me one day on Facebook chat:

> *'You're obviously going to turn your blog into a book, are ya?'*

Hmm. Now there's an idea... Finally, after *all* that time, I was now going to see my first ever book on the bookshelves of a real-life bookstore! Mighty. Also a bit strange, I imagine. Speaking of, being back in Cork felt a tad alien but still the same I suppose. Sting's "I'm an alien, I'm a legal alien, I'm a Cork man in Corrrkk..." on repeat in my head while I drove around. Still as cold as ever, despite the fact it was summer. Everywhere looked grey. People striding along. Wrapped in jackets. Tracksuits. At least the streets were busy. More bustle here than on the streets of L.A, oddly enough. Anyway, I parked up in the middle of the city. Went off to complete my mission. First shop I try: Waterstones. Favourite bookstore growing up. Seriously never imagined that I'd have a book in here one day. This is going to be kind of cool! I wonder where it might be? Mosey around by the front window. New releases - No sign of it. Tut. Disappointing. Check in memoirs - Nothing. Hmmm. Comedy? No. What the funk? Alphabetical order? No sign of me? Where the sweet Jesus is it? Publishers said it was definitely out!

By now my ideal situation - me walking into the shop, seeing my book all over the shelves everywhere, posters on the windows, the whole place just plastered in *RanDumb* - was clearly not happening. At least I wouldn't have to deal with the horde of people freaking out when they realised that it was *me* on all those posters. So at least that was avoided. My scenario was at the other end of the scale: No sign whatsoever that my book even existed. Only one thing to do. Time to be chump. Queue up in line with everyone else. And ask if they have it...,

> "Hi, just wondering if you have a book called *RanDumb* in stock? New book. Just out. I hear it's mighty. Ha ha." (wink)

Cashier checks her computer. Looks at the screen. Looks at me. Squints at the screen. Back to me,

"Is that you?"

"Ha, yeah. It's my book. That's me on the cover."

For some reason saying this brought weird embarrassment. As if I needed to be on the cover so people would believe it's me? Not too sure.

"You wrote a book?"

"Yeah. Managed to pop one out of me. Do ye have it in store?"

"No, not meant to be in for another month or so it says here. Who told you it was out?"

"My publishers. Sweet Jesus, they're brutal. That's why I'm back in Ireland. Book tour, book launch, you know yourself, all *terribly* exciting. Kind of."

"I'll pass on the message that it's out now so, if you like?"

"Yeah that'd be grea- "

Shouts to another cashier across the room,

"GERALDINE! This guy says he wrote a book. Claims it's out now but we're not meant to get in until next month. Should I order it sooner or will I bother?"

Sounds like I'm shopping for a new brand of tampons. Mighty. Either way, Geraldine doesn't care. Shrugs her shoulder.

"I'll order it sooner so. Should be here next week maybe. Come back then. Congratulations too. Must be very exciting to be a new author. Well done!"

"Yeah. Thanks. It's better than I ever dreamed. Well I never really dreamt about being an author growing up but I suppose I would've imagined it that you'd be treated the same as a Greek God or a Roman

> Emperor – like Zeus or Augustus Caeasar, that kind of thing. You know, people would serve you grapes and fan you with palm leaves and you just stroll around in your toga, half naked bodies everywhere, all because you're now a published author and your book's on shelves. That's how I imagine I *would've* imagined it I suppose. Living the wonderful life of an author. Amazing! Although my book is quite clearly not yet on the shelves, so maybe that's why all that hasn't happened *yet*. Ha ha, I think I'm rambling, what did you say your name was - Fionnuala. OK so Fionnuala. I'll be off. I'll call in again next week. You should read it as well. In fact, EVERYONE HERE SHOULD!"

Long.
Silent.
Pause.

Big hand gesture to the room. And then I got the funk out of there. Left feeling a tad chumpish. Walking aimlessly down the main street in Cork. Yearning for some grapes. That went well. Bloody publishers. Cluelessness grows by the day it seems. Imagining people having a right old laugh at me as they walk by me on the street. Ah funk ye all! All right, cop on. Not to be deterred: I'll try Eason's up the road. Subtly make my way in. Head down, collar up kind of approach this time. Nothing in the window. Nothing at the front. Nothing in the middle. Tut. Wander down the back. Past the pens and school supplies. Irish section. Scan the shelves. Nada. Should I ask this girl who works here if they have it in stock? Probably not. Funk it, just ask her,

> "Sorry, just wondering if ye have- Oh you don't work here? My bad, apolog- "

And then I saw.

It.

Third row of a double sided shelf in the middle of the aisle, opposite side of the shelf facing out. My face. My book. A part of my soul! On a bookshelf. Available to buy. In a real life bookstore! A day I've dreamt about for a full nine months. A moment I imagined would be pretty *mighty* ever since I first started writing the book. It's my book! I'm on the cover! Oh Betsy! Success!!! Picked it up. Jesus.

Feels beautiful. Hand vortex that almost drove me fully mental. You little dancer. Opened a page. Flicked through. Smelt the book. Unreal. Took a longer one. Even better. (New book smell is *savage*!) Looked at the cover again. Then the back. Another smell. Face buried between the pages. Hmm. What should I do now? Actually, no - I know. Time to take a photo of me and my book. Proof! Out with my camera. Subtle self-portrait snap. Horrendous photo. Who cares?! OhsweetLord: Thisisamazing! Duu!

Look around. Chuffed. See who I could share my joy with. Few old people staring at bookshelves. One really old guy just looking at the wall,

> "High five lads! Look, my book! Although actually, how come it's on the third shelf down. One away from the bottom shelf. Almost on the floor. That's not so amazing now is it?"

Interrupted by a girl who actually works in the shop,

> "Are you OK?"
>
> "Oh yeah, I'm OK, not lost, thanks. Just came in to see a book. Ha-ha, yeah, that's my book. Just out. You should definitely read it. Oh you're busy, no worries, cheers, thanks."

My brief minute of joy came plummeting back down to earth. Makes me very self-aware. Next set of emotions are weird. Back away from the book. Fear of being caught out - Fraud! Fear of people not liking it - Whures! I wonder if anyone here has read it already? What if they didn't like it? I know: If people like it, I'll take full credit. If not, dodge on. Deny I know anything about it. Call me Peter. Hmm. How about I just lurk here and listen? See if anyone says anything about it. OH MY GOD WHY DID I WRITE A BOOK!?! I silently scream while nodding at the old man now slowly shuffling past me. Next emotion is pure annoyance. Inner me and outer me start to go at it,

> "Brand new release!"
>
> "How come it's not up the front?"
>
> "Why is it back here in the... Travel Section?"

"Never happy."

"Can you not just be happy?!"

"Although in fairness, you're right, it is hidden down the back here."

"Well then grow some balls and get it moved up the front!"

Find a different girl who works in the shop. Slightly older lady this time. Far more excited about the fact that it's my book and I'm now in the shop,

"How can I help you, Mr. Hayes?"

"Well, just wondering if you could maybe move *RanDumb* up to the front of the store? Window display perhaps?"

"Of course we can, Mr. Hayes!"

Sound-Lady grabs a basket. Throws every copy of *RanDumb* into it.

"Follow me!
Let's just move this Dan Brown one over here.
Sorry Russell Brand, you've got to go too.
This Corkonian needs his room to shine."

Makes my book the most prominent of all. Turns to me,

"How does that look now for you Mr. Hayes?"

"Looks mighty!
Upper middle row of the front shelf in the store.
Eye line territory. Golden grail. You're too kind!"

"Could I have a photo with you next to the book? Can I call you Mark?"

"Ha. Of course. I insist!"

Strolled out feeling a lot more pumped up than Waterstones. Wave goodbye to everyone. Sound-Lady waves back. Chest puffed out like a rooster. Start getting my cock-a-doodle-duu strut on. Stevie

Wonder's *Superstition* starts playing in my head. Slight twirl as I walk down the street. Fingers clicking along. What a mighty day! Feel someone tapping me on the arm,

"Hello."

Some randumb younger girl holding out my book,

"Here, is this you?"

Maybe not so bad being on the cover after all.

"Yeah, it is! Da-da dung-dung da-da-diddle-dung, da-dung dung dung duu- Pardon?"

"Will you sign it for me?"

"Ehh..."

Thought it was a wind-up. Surely. Don't think I've signed an autograph before. Checked. Looked around. Any candid cameras? No. OK. Seems legit. Took out my lucky pen. Wonder what I should write? Well, my name, of course. Signed that. Rambled out some more gibberish as a personal message:

"What a mighty dayaduuu for you! Book on!!! - Mark Hayes"

Could've done with tipex. Fun times though. Book groupies. Or broupies, as I now call them. They exist! Finish my gibberish message. Hand the book back to the girl. Corner of my eye I see the Sound-Lady from Eason's running down the street. Shouting out,

"You have to pay for that!"

Girl runs off. Book in hand. Gone. Leaves me standing dumb.

"Why didn't you stop her?"

"Pardon? What do you mean?"

"She just *stole* your book. What were you doing, you had it in your hands?!"

"I was, eh, signing it for her. Sorry. I didn't know."

Now-Not-So-Sound-Lady rolls her eyes. Walks away, shaking her head. Final thing I hear her mutter...,

“Fecking eejit.”

So I go back and pay for the stolen book. Wuu. More of a muted walk out of me now. *Superstition* only being hummed quietly. Checked a few more bookstores on the way back to my car. Some had it. Others weren't getting it in until next month. Good work by the publishers it seems. Confusing people is a great way to sell the book! Not to worry though. I'm sure it's going to get mightier from here on in. Come Monday I'll be on my book tour. Ha. Time to tell everyone about the world's newest literary classic. Pretty soon I'll be selling millions. People clamouring to read it. All in awe of my unique writing style. Betsy! Can't wait. Finally. Delighted. Now everything's going to be absolutely perfect! I've made it - Haven't I? Right? Yeah? Wuu!

Ran.
Dumb.
On!

Chapter 38

EUREKA!

Saturday: Day-off, on my otherwise *hectic* book promotion calendar. HECTIC! Ahem. Time to beat off the jet lag. Sleep on. Doubles as a mighty way to save money. Forgot how expensive everything is in Ireland. Except the air. That's cheap. And pleasant. No boozing or gallivanting for me though. Tie up those shoelaces tight, as they say. Not sure which they. Anyway...

My brother Darren flew down from Dublin for the weekend. Woke me up when he arrived. Few buddies called over to my abode throughout the evening. Rob "Bob Hoff" Heffernan. Shane "Wanchope" Hennessy. Richie "Dicksy" Arnopp. Graham "The Buddah" Wilshaw. Barry "The Lump" Leahy. The Brothers Bambury: Kevin "Chisel" and Mark "Blueballs". Brian "Leonard" Lenihan. Brendan "Morty" Kelly. Kieran "Krin" O'Kane. Derek "Dino Patsy" Peyton. And last but not least, Aonghus "*Jimmy B*" Bolster. Randumb collection. Good old hoot. Swapped stories. Exchanged tales. All asked if they were mentioned in the book. All very upset when I said nay. Apologies lads, I'll make it up to ye in my next book, I swear. Spoof on! And then we all laughed about that,

"As if you'll manage a second book!"

"Ha, yeah I know. Ahem."

My Dad joined us for a while. Sport talk all the way. My Mum gleefully whipped up some food and drinks for all of us. (Did I mention she's delighted to have me home?) In fairness to my family, they are mighty. Take my Dad. Whenever I have a buddy over, they all say the same thing when they leave my house,

"Your Dad is as cool as they come. Some man for the chats!"

Not in a leather jacket and jeans way. He's not the Fonz. In a chilled, interesting way. Big fan of soccer. Big fan of golf. Easy to talk to. Always asking me before I leave the house,

"Do you have enough money now? Here, take this."

Some man. Mighty Dad! Whenever a girl meets my mighty Mum, they too echo similar sentiments,

"Your Mum is the best! I could talk to her all day."

Always making sure I have everything ready, organized, together, fed, washed, clothed, prepared, cleaned, tidied, sorted - Good to go? OK then. Now go off and have fun! Just make sure to be safe. Whenever I come home, my Mum asks,

"Are you hungry? I've food on for you already."

Again: Mighty Mum! My sister Sarah is highly chilled and some might also say highly sarcastic. Not me though. I would not say or agree with that. I. Swear. Myself and Darren get on well too. He's only a year older. But we don't look like each other at all. We've always more or less had the same core group of friends. Even though we're not *really* alike, compared to other brothers I know. In fact, our university soccer teammates used to call us Mario and Wario after the characters in the Mario Bros computer game. I was Wario, the eviler of the two. Harsh enough. Funny though. Anyway... Family on! Sunday: Chilled. Relaxed. Read the Sunday newspapers. Enjoyed my Mum's mighty roast dinner. (Two Sunday traditions which I must say are lacking in L.A, although pool parties are a fair substitute.) Watched TV. Drove around where I once lived. It's been a while. Soaked in all the familiar places. Shopping centre. Church. Little village. Now full of super-pubs. (New thing in Ireland. The bigger the pub the better, appears to be the new logic.)

Called down to my grandparents. Mighty chat and cup of tea with them. My Grandad is some chancer. Always a glint in his eye. Laughed at my tales while my Gran – who is *some* Gran and I actually call her Nana - tried to force-feed me some cakes. Not happy with my new healthy eating regime. (Most Irish folk are highly suspicious of it actually. Look at me as if this means I must be on heroine. Why is he not eating seven potatoes for dinner anymore – *Drugs!*) Anyway, headed back home after that. Sat around for the rest of the evening. Tapped my fingers off the table. Waited for the phone to ring. Emails to arrive. Waited. Waited. No sign. Ughatha.

Monday: Woke up. Checked. Phone. No. Emails. Nada. Pigeon mail. Nothing. What. The. Funk?! Publishers!? Patience running dry. Time for me to get in touch again. Email:

> *'Hi Publishers,*
>
> *How are you today? That's great.*
>
> *Just wondering WHAT'S GOING ON WITH ALL THE BOOK PROMOTION STUFF I FLEW HOME FOR? WHY DID YE TELL ME TO COME BACK IF NOTHING WAS LINED UP?*
>
> *Cheers,*
>
> *Mrs. Mark Hayes'*

Then they:

> *'Ah shur, how long are you back? A month is it? Or for good? We'll get going now.'*
>
> *'No, clowns, I'm not home for good. I just want to be here two weeks max. I told you this. You said come home on this date specifically, as promotions would be underway in full force for these two weeks.'*
>
> *'We'll get going now so properly. Sit tight. Let's hope for something later in the week.'*

Often left baffled after these conversations. You'd imagine you were meant to feel like your publishers were working *with* you, not against you. Well - You'd imagine wrong. On the upside, I did get a phone call from my buddy "Choo-Choo", or Steve Dinan as his parents might call him. Reporter for the Evening Echo, the main newspaper in Cork,

> "Marky! Read the book. Fantastic work. Loved it. Up for an interview? Get a spread in the paper this week?"

"Ehh.
Yes.
Please."

And thank you. Let that ball start rolling. So I met with the mighty man. Gibbered on. Signed his book. Rambled out some more tales. Wrapped it up. Choo-Choo mentions he's already spread the word to other reporters he knows. He'll let them know I don't think I'll be back in Ireland for too long. Expect to get a few phone calls soon. Go on the Choo-Choo train! Next stop: Bank on! Met with the loan manager. Very nice lady, Catherine, who at first laughed and then very nicely told me that the chances of me getting a loan were...,

"In this economy?
With your current fixed income?
Emmm..."

Or as I understood it: Not a chance, boss. However, I did manage to get a slight increase on my credit card limit. Not much by a country mile. But. Hopefully. Enough. Providing I can miraculously find the cheapest Cork to LAX flight ever known to mankind, of course. Cross those fingers. Just as long as I can get back. I'll figure out what to do if I end up homeless and starving, if and when I come to that bridge. (Orgy Joe could be getting a phone call!) Headed home after the bank. Walked in. Saw my Dad in the sitting room reading *RanDumb*. Looked up,

"Popped into Eason's on my way home from work and bought a copy. Told all the teachers at school to buy one too. I'm enjoying it so far."

(My Dad's a principal.)

"Me too."

Hummed my Mum. (My Mum's a teacher. I come from such a stable background. Where did I go so wrong, right?)

"Oh that's great, thanks for that. Although I was going to give ye copies when I collected a box from the publishers. Small token of my thanks for all ye do for me!"

"Don't be silly, of course we were going to buy your book!"

"Ha, cheers, ehh...

Have ye read much?"

So my plan had been to give both my parents a copy of the book literally moments before I left Cork again for L.A, whenever that may be. That way, when they read it, particularly any iffy parts, I would be in a land so far away. Now. Plan. Out. Window. Dose. Cautiously threw an eye to see what part of the book they might be reading whenever I walked by. Gave the old "By the way ye do know I made it all up, right?" glance if I thought they were reading something a tad dodge. They nodded along... Knowingly? Hmm.

Tuesday: Emails. Publishers? Nothing. Well that's more delight. On the uppity, Choo-Choo had worked his magic. My phone was peppered. Three national newspaper interviews. Betsy! Spent the whole morning on the phone to them. Weekend and Sunday newspapers wanting to do a page or two spread on me and my book. Wuu. Even had photographers call over to do a shoot of me at my house. On my street. Little green area at the bottom of my road. Down by the trees where twelve-year-old me used to run around and play soccer. Now posing up against them trying to look casual in my quite slick Ted Baker clothes. Expose on!

Funny thing about phone interviews is they have no clue where you are when they call. Naked in my bedroom. On the toilet in my bathroom. Lodging money in the bank. (Odd looks from people in the bank while I'm trying to be all animated and non-monotone on the phone. You know, sell my book by selling myself.) Sitting in my car on the side of the road. Wandering the streets of a tiny village on the way to Tipperary, lost and bursting for the bathroom.

Decided to visit my Gran's farmhouse in Tipperary for the day. Far too empty now both my Nana and Grandad on my Mum's side have passed away but I still like the house a lot. Mighty memories coming to visit here. Ridiculously quiet. Always full of life. Surrounded by bushes heavy with blackberries, bright wet emerald fields and mooing herds of cows. If I could, I would come here at least once a month, flying over on my private jet from L.A, landing in the field out the back, and go make jam and marmalade for myself. Just eat scones and brown bread. Give me five years. Private jet all the way! (Guinness and the internet included, obviously.)

So I was off strolling down a pastoral lane by the house when my phone started ringing. Reporter. Dublin magazine. Quick interview? Of course. Although I could barely understand a word he said to me. Flickering bar of phone reception. Just started answering what

I assumed he might've asked. Texted me after saying he only got every second word of what I said too, he'd just make up the rest? Ehh - Yeah, cool, whatever. Article came out. Headline read:

> 'Hot Weather - Hot Women – HOTTYWOOD! Why Wouldn't I Want to Live Here?!'

So that one turned out very well. His term, I swear. Wednesday: Choo-Choo's article ran in the Echo. Nice spread. Delivering the goods big time! Another buddy from soccer, Mark "Hopicano" Hopkins read it. Phoned me up. Told me I should've got in touch with him before the book launched,

> "Could've got you sponsorship, bud, all you would've had to do was hold two bottles of Corona on the cover. Missed out!"

Oh yeah. Forgot you ran a PR company. Balls. Then asked if I'd be interested in some national radio or TV stuff? Knows a guy in Today FM (second biggest radio station in Ireland, probably the most popular for my age group). Publishers had been unable to hook me up. Hopicano to the rescue! Two hours later - Producer from Today FM phones me,

> "Want to come on the KC Show tonight?"

> "More national exposure? Yes. Please. Dance. On!"

Some whure. Book on. Thursday: Thanks to my Irish agent (my Mum) I was asked to do a few different book signings at local shopping centers. Still feel like I'm "caught" when someone sees me looking at my book. As if it is the ultimate sign of narcissism. Perhaps it's because I'm taking deep whiffs of new book smell from each book when I get asked if I'm OK?

> "Just making sure it's real... Yeah, that's me in the yellow. Howdy. OK. Emm. Where do I sign?"

My aunts and friends of my agent were my main book signing entourage.

> "Hi Margaret, Jean, Marie, Maura, Ber, Mary, Regina, Liz, Celene, Maureen and Ms. Hennessy! Ye're back again? Ha. Thanks for buying another copy of the book. Read on!"

Randumbers then shuffled over to see what was going on - Why such a flock of women over here, kind of thing. Salesman Hayes would duly step forward,

> "Ah go on, why not buy a copy or four? It's amazing!"

Finishing off by signing the biggest load of gibberish in each book. Collectors' items, I keep telling them. Oddly enough, while out and about (as in not just in a bookstore!), a few randumbers stopped me on the street to say hi. One girl even asked me to sign her... Hands. Obviously. Tut. Friday: Eyes. Open. Check. Phone. Email. Post. No. Nothing. Nada. Politely knock on the publishers electronic door again:

> *'Anything lined up yet?'*

> *'Not yet. Let's hope for next week. Ah shur not to worry, you must be having great craic being home!'*

At that moment I wondered if this is what Roy Keane must've felt like back in Saipan. Bit presumptuous to compare myself to such a mighty man, but bear with me... In case you're unaware Roy Keane is probably Ireland's best ever soccer player. Fellow Corkonian. Just before the 2002 World Cup in South Korea and Japan was about to start, he walked out on the Irish team because the Irish FA's organization of the whole thing was a complete shambles. Unprofessional. Lackadaisical. Joke. Team had to train on a pitch covered with stones - That kind of thing. Probably smiled off with a 'Ah but that doesn't matter because we're Irish and shur we're just here to have a laugh and a bit o' the craic!'

Roy Keane wanted to win. Got fed up with the whole thing. So he left the camp. Went home to walk his dog only a few days before the first game. Whether or not he should've stayed is still a decisive topic in Ireland. Anyway, I always felt that my publishers were a bit like the Irish Football Association,

> "Ah it'll be alright, we'll get that sorted for you perhaps, if not, shur you're having the craic... Right?"

Perhaps the publishers and I were just not the greatest fit. Most of their books were written by Irish politicians, university professors and even the Irish president. Odd mix really. In music terms, let's just say they were like a country music label and I was like an experimental rapper who sung in Japanese. Although they did take a chance on an unknown writer and published *RanDumb*, so giddy up and thanks for that! Catch 22. But now I was done. Making me come home. For... What? Nothing. I spent all my money to come back. All I have now is my student credit card. And they think I'm here for a bit of the- Hang on a sec. Just got an email from Porsche. Please Jesus John Lennon, let it be... Scan scan scan:

> *'Are you available to DJ... these five dates... so that would be that Sunday and Monday in Newport as well as the Saturday, Sunday and Monday after that in Beverly Hills?'*

My. Sweet. Lord. What Sunday is that... Sunday after this one. All right. Calm down. Figure this out. When's that? One day, two days, three days, four days... OK. THAT'S SUNDAY WEEK. I CAN DO THAT. I'M GOING BACK. OHMYGODIMSAVED! My sister Sarah pops her sarcastic head in my bedroom door,

> "Is everything OK? Are you doing a phone interview? Did they kick you off... *Again*?"

> "No Sarah, yes Sarah, I mean everything's MIGHTY SARAH! I think. Just got offered a load of gigs so I need to get back to L.A SO I CAN DO THEM AND SURVIVE AND YEESSSS!!! APOLOGIES FOR ALL THE shouting."

> "OK I'll let you get back to the interview, best of luck now."

> "Thanks Sarah."

Furiously type my reply:

> *'Yes. I can. I'll be there! Thank you. See you then. You mighty dancers!'*

About to press send... Oh balls. I need to find a cheap flight. Furiously scour the internet. All the usual websites. Orbitz. Expedia. Kayak. All telling me a one-way ticket to L.A is about one thousand dollars? Credit card still can't handle that. How so dear?! Returns are almost cheaper. Ye whures! Actually why don't I just book a return- *Funk.* Twelve hundred dollars. Balls Malone,

> "Think quick think quick.

ThisisyourlifelinebacktoL.A.
Lifelinelifelinelifeline. Think. Come on.
Lifelinelifelinewifewinewifewinewhyfine...
Why fine? Wife wine? Wife. Wine? Huh? What?
Actually - Cureka! I never tried GoHop."

How could I forget this beautiful little Irish dancer of a website?! Input. Date. Destination. Search. Flights. First choice: One-way. Saturday. Virgin Atlantic. *The* most ideal flight. Gets me back the night before the gig. Price. Price. PRICE??! Oh Betsy: Dirt cheap! And I mean *DIRT* cheap. My credit card can actually pay for this flight and still have change left over, kind of cheap. I mean my first suit, kind of cheap. How, I don't know. Don't care. Just. Funking. Buy.

"Betsy. This is glorious. Just book it. Book it now!"

"Wait, what *if* there's book promotions and stuff?"

"Shut up. Book it. They had their chance. Don't mess us up again. Remember that time you messed up the cheap flight home to Ireland because you decided to make a cup of tea while booking and the flight jumped up by over $2000? Remember that?"

"OK."

"Now don't be an ape. You know what to do."

"I. Duu!"

Flight. Booked. Cheap. Sorted. Done. Dumb. *Dancing*! Eureka: I'm going back! Duu! And. Phew. Some relief. The adventure continues. Giddy. UP!

(Cherry on top, it also seems my Mum and Dad's copies of *RanDumb* have mysteriously disappeared too. Ha. Weird. Ahem. Someday!)

Chapter 39

What Would Woody Do?

So a few weeks ago, I'm in a Jacuzzi, top of the Hollywood Hills, eating a sandwich, drinking a fruit smoothie and relaxing after a tough day of folf. To my left, Chris Dyson. To my right, Robert Williams.

Chilling. Gibbering. Blabbering on. This. That. Our mothers. Rob asks,

"When's the book out?"

"Few weeks I think."

"Are you having a launch party and all that?"

"Yeah, back in Ireland. Must go back and do promo!"

"I think I'll be back in England at the same time. Maybe I'll come over for it, that'd be a laugh. What date is it on?"

"Ehh, don't know. Publishers haven't really told me anything specific. They're good like that."

"Oh. Well, that's good of them. You should come over to Manchester so instead. Come to Soccer Aid as my guest of honour?"

"Soccer Aid?"

"Charity match where football legends play against celebrities and the likes. Raises a load of money."

"Oh yeah. Sounds good."

"Cool, I'll set it up. I'll email you all the details."

"Cheers boss! Mighty. I think I'll have a little dip in the pool after hearing that good news. Soccer Aid all the wayyyygeronimoooooo..."

And then I kind of did a belly flop and think I may have broken a rib when I splattered on the water. Collective,

"GASP!"

Ow. Say nothing. Played it cool. Chris Dyson almost choked on his sandwich laughing. Fun times! Anyway, now here we are a few weeks later and despite the fact I am as tight as a fish's ass money-wise, I did have three aces up my sleeve. One: Early birthday money. Two: Knowing I was going back to five DJ gigs has settled my worries. And three: All taken care of. Frugal trip. All of which means: I'm now in Manchester. Adventure on!

Perfect timing too. On my way back from mass that morning in Cork, I stopped off at my local shop to buy the Sunday papers. Flicking through one of them. Sunday tabloid. Check for the sports gossip. Flick. Flick. Middle page. Hang on - What the funk?! That's me. My name. My book. Two-page spread. Photos of Brad Pitt, George Clooney, Rob and... Ahem? Ha. Looked around the petrol station to see if anyone had recognized me. Nope. Texted few buddies in my phone to buy the paper. Then read the article. "EXCLUSIVE INTERVIEW" ran across the two pages. That's odd, I thought. Don't remember ever speaking to that reporter or paper. Everything in the article pumped up to the max:

Sex.
Fuelled.
Drugs.
Naked.
Women.
Gay orgies.
Debauchery.
Sleaze.
Hollywood.

Corruption.
9-11.
TERROR!
George Clooney.
Brad Pitt.
Jesus Christ.

None of it really made any sense. Made-up quotes. All completely fabricated. That's strange.

> "Huh. I never said that. Or that. In fact, I never did an interview with this reporter?"

Some amount of spoof. Why would they make all that up? Just to sell papers? Surely not.

> "And come to think of it, why are Brad Pitt and George Clooney's photos even used?"

Names are never mentioned. And why would they be? About as relevant to the article as the black guy is on my book cover. Kind of odd. Thought nothing more of it. Until I got home. Forgot my parents might read it. Balls. My sister had seen it too and brought one home before me. *Sarah*!

Sense that they're upset. Slight state of shock. Tried to put them at ease,

> "Mum... Dad... It was all made up. Don't worry, I'm not the ring leader of a gay terrorist orgy group. All spoof. The other interviews I did will show the true light. And, if we are to put a positive spin on it, it is still a two-page spread in the biggest tabloid in Ireland. All publicity is good?"

Nay. My parents didn't really care about the last bit. So that little incident was a dose. Felt bad. Over exposed. Awkward buzz. Thankfully. Escape route sorted. Soccer Aid. To my aid. Manchester. On! Flew over for the night. Just myself, Andy and Colin Todd. As in me, myself and Eileen. You know, I went on my own. (In Ireland "on your tod" means on your own. I think it's actually a cockney term. Andy Todd and Colin Todd used to play soccer in England. So for some reason the phrase "just myself, Andy and Colin Todd" is now used by my brain. Well dumb me.)

Arrived in the afternoon. Checked in to my hotel in the middle of Manchester. Quick shower. Changed my clothes. Ted Baker once again. Different combination this time. Spruce it up. Still have time to kill. Hmmm. Go for a pint? Or just chill in my small but quaint hotel room... And booze on here? Quaint on. High five with make-believe Andy and Colin. Pour us some vodka. Cheers. Good to go. Old Trafford: Giddy up! Everything I needed had been posted to me in Ireland by Rob's mighty manager, Josie. Ticket for the Directors' Box: Check. VIP wristband: Mighty. Hotel concierge told me the bus was the best way to get to Old Trafford, Manchester United's 75,000 seater stadium where the match was being played. Bus it is. On I hop. Place is buzzing. Everyone seems to be going to the game. Overhear people going on about the match. The event. Rob. L.A. Everyone on the bus seems to love Rob. Wondering,

"What's he like?"

"Heard he's off in L.A living the life."

"Shur why wouldn't he?!"

"Wonder what it's like over there?"

Sat there pondering. Hmm. Wonder if I should tell them all about my book? Life in L.A and all that? Ha. Nay. Head down. Get to Old Trafford. Packed. Throngs of people. No clue where I'm going. Go up to a group of stewards outside the stadium. All look at me like I'm a messy piece of chewing gum they just sat on,

"What do you want?"

"Just wondering where I go for this sea- "

"Let me see the ticket."

Yanks my ticket out of my hands. Seeing the look on his face when he read where I was sitting was pre-tty priceless. Almost took a knee and bowed down to me.

"Lads, this guy here's a VIP. Directors' Box."

"Which is the quickest way?

"Follow us!"

SWAT team of luminous yellow jacket wearing stewards part the sea of people in front of us. Almost carry me on their shoulders to the entrance. Clap me off as I waltz through the pearly golden doors. Few asking to themselves, "Who's that, I wonder?" If only ye knew... For some reason as I climbed the stairs to the Directors' Box, a slight wave of apprehension washed over me. Mild trepidation. I've no clue who else is going to be here. Rob invited me (some man!). But he's playing. God only knows who I'm going to be sitting with. Slowly enter through the big wooden doors. Ahh. Mighty. Bar in front of me. Entrance to the seats to my left. Quick pit stop. Vodka-anything. Cheers boss. Horse. Chug. Wash that trepidation away. Good to go. Make my way up the hallowed steps. Out into the Old Trafford Directors' Box... First thing I see:
FLASH
FLASH
FLASH!
Swarms of people facing me taking photos. Normal cameras. TV cameras. Camera phones. All going off. Obstructing my view of the savage looking pitch behind them. Try to get a better look. I think it looks unreal. But they're blurring my vision. No clue who I am. But I'm in the box. Looking sharp in Ted Baker. Let's take a few photos just in case! Next minute I hear,

"MUUUUUUUUURRRRKKKK!"

I know that voice: Betsy! Someone I know...,

"AYYYYYDAAAA!"

Miss Ayda Field. Ridiculously cool chancer. Sound as a regal pound! Actress. Engaged to Rob. Mighty lady! Oh, and...,

"INDIIIIAAAAA."

Miss India Standing. Delightful lady. Fashionista to the stars. Met once or twice up in Rob's. Last but not least...,

"SUSSSIIIEEE!"

Miss Susie Amy. Mighty dancer. Actress. Also met up in Rob's before. Thank funk. Familiar faces. Dancing. Girls' night out. Yay! Next fifteen minutes were spent boozing, watching the players warm up, and having our photos taken by various photographers and punters from all different angles. Odd. But a good hoot. Sitting in the VIP, flanked by three beauties, not looking too shabby in my slick Ted Baker clothes - I wasn't doing too bad for myself, now was I?! Game was good to watch as well. Featured some of my favourite soccer players to some of the funniest comedic actors. Likes of Zinedine Zidane (French *genius* with a sublime first touch who is one of only three players to have won the FIFA World Player of the Year three times) to Mike Myers (*Shrek*, *Wayne's World*, *Austin Powers*!), Luis Figo (Portuguese footballer, 2001 FIFA World Player of the Year) to Woody Harrelson (*Natural Born Killers* and *Kingpin* all the way!). Wide range. Match went to penalties. Score. Miss. Score. Miss. Score. Score. Score. Miss. Miss. Score. Sudden death. Miss. Woody Harrelson steps up,

"This to win."

Slips. But.

"Scores!"

Everyone trundles back to a hotel nearby afterwards for a post-game shindig. Really fancy expensive-looking hotel. Big glass doors. Huge spiraling staircase. Dripping in chandeliers. White marble. All that jazz. I arrive with the group of girls. Appears we're early. Champagne and caviar come our way. Tuck in. Party starts to fill up. Celebs from A-Z. India takes the reins. (Like all good book whures, I had a copy in my back pocket.) Starts introducing me and my book to everyone,

"Jamie..." (Redknapp - former England soccer player and TV pundit) " ...meet Murk."

"Bryan..." (Robson - former captain of the English soccer team) " ...have you met Murk?"

"Hey Jimmy," (Carr - voted one of the funniest stand-up comedian in England) "...Murk."

"Henrik..." (Larson - former Celtic and Swedish soccer player, OK you don't want to meet Murk. Just give him a dirty look. That's OK.)

"Kenny!" (Dalglish - former Scottish and Liverpool football player and league winning manager) "You must meet Murk."

"How's it going Kenny?"

Kenny mumbles something to me in a thicker accent than mine could ever be.

"Eh. Yeah? It is a good book. Check it out."

"Ahublalaheysupportha?"

"Hmmm. Who do I... Support? Everton actually."

Did not go down well. Everton and Liverpool being bitter football rivals and all. Cue Kenny not saying another word to me. Just another dirty look. Thankfully I'm interrupted by the legend that is Phil Taylor, probably the greatest darts player ever, who that very night, had won another World Champion Crown. Just arrived straight from the venue. Trophy in hand. Go on the Power! Phil says,

"Rob's buddy? I'm a friend of his Dad's, Pete. How can I get a copy of this book of yours then?"

Look around to see where my book is... Eh... See Jamie Redknapp flicking through it. Woody Harrelson is next to him, takes the book for a look. Turn back to Phil...,

"Give me two minutes, I'll get it for you."

Turn back around: Woody's gone. Small talk with Jamie Redknapp, sound dude. Where did Woody go? Not sure. Booze? Booze. Bryan Robson now asking me,

"So what do you do? Why weren't you playing?"

"Should've brought my boots alright. Next time!"

The Irish band "Westlife" come along by the bar. Everyone is being sound as a pound. Handing me boozes. Telling me jokes. Not sure if it's because the girls have told people I'm Rob's guest from L.A or what, happy days. Unfortunately no sign of Zidane. Dose. Rob had to depart as well. Party was filling up and I think his star attraction was getting even the celebs worked up. Couple of boozes later my bladder tapped me on the leg. Ahem. Need the bathroom. On the way, I spot Woody Harrelson sitting on a big white couch. Wearing an Armani suit. No shoes. Reading my book. Ha. That's pretty randumb right there. Started laughing out loud to my now drunken self. Woody looks up at me,

"What's so funny man? You sound like a donkey."

"Ah nothing really. Just that's my book you're reading."

"You're wrong man, it's my book now. Can I keep it? Thanks."

"My pleasure. Let me know what you think. Oh yeah, where are your shoes?"

"Lost them. Let me know if you see them anywhere."

"Will. Duu."

Come back out of the bathroom. India is outside. Tells me that herself and Susie have to get going. Must drive back to London. Hands me a hotel room key,

"Rob said to take his room upstairs if you want to spend the night. Presidential suite."

Oddly enough indecision kicks in. Not sure why. Maybe because once the girls left, I'd be on my own. And I was also a bit worried about getting goosed and not waking up in time. Cue the mutters kicking in,

"No way. Hmmm. Actually. Not fully sure. Don't want to miss my flight back in the morning and this hotel is a bit out of the way. Don't know if I'd get back in time. Let me mull. What should I do?"

India shrugs her shoulders. She's gotta go,

"Bye Murk!"

See that Woody is still on the couch reading,

"Woody, what do you think? Stay the night in the suite or go back to my own hotel? What would you do?"

"Stay man. Live it up!"

Ha. Go on the Woody. President Hayes on! Headed back to the bar for a while. Few more boozes. Then a bucket more. High-five

Woody a goodbye. Tried to make peace with Kenny. No joy. Off to bed. Mighty night. Woke up the next day by room service, banging on the door. Heavy head. Answered. Told me I had asked for the wakeup call. Hadn't been answering the phone.

"Oh yeah. Cheers."

Balls. I'm late. Lay back down on the bed for a minute. Barely even saw the room last night. Looked around. Half-asleep. Looks unreal. I think. Couches? King-size bed? Posters. Few flat screens? Pool table? More than one room in the hotel room? Mighty? I think. Can barely open my eyes and see. Goosed. Half dozed off again. Woke up half an hour later when the cleaning lady shook me.

"Huh? Oh. Hi. What time is it?"

Balls. Now I am late.

"Taxi!"

Car service took me back to my hotel. Driver was impressed when I told him this was my other hotel. Ha. Presidential. Changed. Packed. Thought: One night and I brought a big huge bag? Some clown. Chanced my arm with the car service. Mind if we swing by the airport as well? Dancing! Kipped in the car on the way. Checked my texts just before I boarded the plane. One from my brother:

'DARREN: By the looks of it, RanDumb has sold out on Amazon.'

Mighty. Sell out or sell out! Sweet ear music. Pumped. Boarded the flight home. Sat next to a mighty lady. Gave me a mint to suck on for ear-popping. Asked if I had a nice weekend?

"Hmmm. You know what. I did. You probably won't believe me if I told you..."

So I did and by the expressions on her face, she didn't. Popped my iPod on. Fell asleep. Wondered if everything going on was a dream? Is this the new way of life? Everything all down to the book? Not too sure. I do know I've got a few more days in Cork. Then back to the normality of L.A. Ha. Mighty. Should have a sequel in the making going by the past week alone. Seven-part trilogy all the way!!!

Chapter 40

And We're Back...

BUZZ! BUZZ! BUZZ! Hmm. Private number. Dodge on. Or. Funk it...,

"Hello?"

"Murk!"

"Nutter?"

"Who? No – It's me!"

"Oh. *Howdy boss*!"

"You made it back to L.A."

"I did."

"*Mighty*. Was it good?"

"Which now – Being back in Ireland? Yeah, good enough alright."

"Did the book go well?"

"I think so. I know it sold out on Amazon twice alright but not sure what that means really."

"Do any TV stuff?"

"No, publishers are clowns. Even though they told me to come back when I did, they messed up the dates and the TV chat shows were all just finished for the summer. I was a week too late. Although a buddy almost got me on a daytime TV talk show at the very end but I was asked on the same day as my flight back so no joy boss!"

"Did you get much publicity?"

"Ehh, I suppose so, yeah. My buddies hooked most of it up. Publishers are idiots. Got me a few regional radio interviews before I left. That was about it. Could've done them from here on the phone. Did a reading and gave a talk up in Dublin as well, so that was good. Besides that, they were useless. One guy gave an interview on my behalf to a Sunday tabloid. Made out me to be a bit of a drug-head-sex-maniac-terrorist. Most of the other weekend papers I did interviews with then didn't run their articles on me because it would've been a week after the tabloid stuff. Old news. Publishers are clowns."

"I didn't understand a word of that except: Your publishers are clowns?"

"Correct. Boss."

"Were the Irish people happy you were there at least?"

"Yeah, went well. Big book launch party in Cork. Mighty hoot. Got some free clothes off a suit company. One girl asked me to sign her hands. Another girl robbed my book. All dancing really!"

"All I got there was "dancing really" - Are you drunk?"

"No! Just rambling from coffee. Haven't boozed since I got back. DJigging. Head down. No more reckless gallivanting. Sensible on!"

"Are you still on for tomorrow?"

"Pardon? Tomorrow?"

"Coming on a yacht with us for Ayda's birthday?"

"Oh yeah. Ehh..."

Duu!

Chapter 41

Yacht. Police. Punch In The Face.

"Wahey man! Where are ya?"

"Huh? Pardon?"

"Wake up, man! I'm outside. Let's go!"

"Heh... Who is this?"

Check my phone. Oh balls. Early doors. But I've overslept.

"Hurry up man. Don't want to be late!"

"Hang on BV, I'll be down in two!"

Jump up. Out of bed. Grab some clothes. My best sailor boy outfit. Actually. Might get chilly. Need a jacket. Where's my leather one? Haven't worn it in a while - Oh for funk's sake. Notice there's a hole in the sleeve. How did that get there? My favourite jacket! Want to cry. No time to cry. Grab my yellow hoodie. Run out the door. Hurtle down the lift. Sheepish wave to everyone waiting for me in the car. How's it going lads? Jump in the white Beamer. Tired smile around the car. And away we go.

Time to go have a hoot on a boot!

So a group of us had been invited out for a day on a boat by the once again ridiculously generous Rob. Surprise birthday celebrations for his soon-to-be-bride, Ayda. Plan was to meet down at Newport Beach somewhere. Not sure who was going. All I knew was that

Barry Venison had kindly offered me a lift down. And that his son Max was invited along too (sound as a pound, around my age).

Drive down was mighty. Not so many years ago I was on my couch back in Ireland watching Barry on TV, either playing in the English Premiership for Newcastle United or as a funny soccer pundit on the English TV station ITV after he retired. Dodgy style at the time. Mullets and bright sports jackets. Changed man since. Stylish. Smooth. Serene. Big into the yoga now. California ways had gripped him too.

Now here I was listening to Barry (or BV as I called him) tell me stories about those glorious Newcastle years. Tales from playing in Turkey. This one time he was on a yacht here. Perks of being a footballer there. How it used to be boozing wise. Good old days. Insider tales. I was riveted. Some banter. All of which made the hour or so drive down to Newport Beach pass by in no time. The man knows how to tell a story. And his Geordie accent makes them all even better. I'll say no more!

Anyway, we arrive down at a posh yachting club. Pull up outside. The lovely Mrs. Venison has kindly agreed to drive the car back. Waves us off. Look around. Fancy folk everywhere. Forgot this was Moneysville. My yellow hoodie is making us blend in nicely. Now then: Where are we meant to go? All we know is the name of the boat: Tulip. Stroll down the pier. Weather is pretty cloudy. The one day we go on a boat... Tut. Out of the corner of my ear, I hear an,

"Arrr... "

Turn around. See who's waving. Oh Betsy. Is that our boat?! Being honest, I was expecting a fisherman type of boat. Old reliable. One level. Few chairs. Captain twirling the wheel. Look at the water. Sail along. Get a bit of sun. Regular old boot. I was wrong. This was no boot. In my uneducated seaman opinion, this was more of a yacht. Although I have technically worked for the Irish Navy before. So actually, this was a funking yacht and a half. How many feet? I'm guessing one hundred plus? How many levels? One level, two level, three levels, four. Jesus, it's class!

Rob greets us with open arms. Ushers us in. Gives us a quick tour. Bottom deck. Dinghies. Crew. TV room. Bedrooms. Mahogany. Red carpet. Plush. Lush. Top level. Captain. Vice-captain? Computers. Wheel. Steering. Main area. Banqueting room. Wining. Dining. Looks like a room fit for a King and Queen. Royal blue carpet.

Waitresses scurrying around. People handing out goblets! Full on yacht. Mighty altogether. Quick headcount. About 20 of us going on the trip. Know a good few from soccer and folf. Jetski. Jaymoe. Dyson. India. Susie. Others I know to see. Everyone looks pumped. Seems like a fun group. Singers. Songwriters. Designers. Actors. Stylists. DJs. Producers. Trainers. Ex-soccer pros. And. Ahem, me. Boot on! We all get hushed quiet. Go hide. Surprise time! Ayda is brought on board. We all jump out from behind bush coloured cushions,

"SURPRISE! HAPPY BIRTHDAY!"

Here's the present I got you from CVS last night at about midnight, your favourite: Romance novels! Someone turns on some music. Party buzz gets going. Cel-e-brate, good times, come on! (On a quick side-note, is it a waitress or a stewardess? Not a servant? Nay sure.) A crew member hands me a goblet,

"Champagne, sir?"

Jesus, what time is it? Barely even eleven o'clock in the morning. Don't want to be the only one. Look over at BV,

"Is it a bit early for booze?"

"Wahey man! What are ya on aboot?! Never too early. Get it inta ya!"

That's what I was politely waiting to hear. Goblet filled. Smile on. Toast the boot. And we're off. Sailing the high seas. Living the life! Plan is to sail out to a secluded island for the day, Catalina. On the way out it's all very mellow. Small talk. Everyone is chilling. Eating the fresh fruit. Tuting about the weather. Myself, BV and Max are tucking into the champagne. Arrive at the island. Captain parks the boat. (Park is the right terminology, isn't it?) All sorts of water activities lined up. Everyone strips down to swimwear attire. Rob takes the lead,

"OK then... Who wants to jump on this rubber raft that's attached to that dinghy and that guy will drive the dinghy around as fast as he can and try to make us fly off?"

Wait for it...,

“Murk?”

“Eh. Yeah. Sure thing.”

Rob lies down on it first. I stumble on behind him. Lying face down. Side by side. Holding on to small handles.

“Hang on tight!”

I’m told,

“This will burn your arms.”

Ah yeah, no worries. Hang on… Finish my champagne. Thumbs up to the driver.

“Good to gooooooooohhhhBETSYNOOOOOOO!!!”

Dinghy whips off. Gripping on for dear life. Arms burning. Teeth gritting. Driver putting the foot down. Speeding up. Rob yelling at me…,

“Hold On!”

“I AM!!! I AMM!!!!”

Water whipping into my face. Hanging on for dear life. Capt’n is going at least 7000 miles an hour. Whipping it! Salty water punching me in the face. Raft flying up and down over bumps.

“Don’t let go! We must stay on!”

“I AM!!! I AMMM!!!”

About now I realise: Oh balls. My shorts are coming loose. Never tied them fully.

“ROB!! MY SHORTS!!! THEY’RE COMING OFFF!!!!”

“Don’t let go!!!”

“OK!! I AM. I MEAN I’M NOT!!!”

Flew over another bump. Raft takes off. Up in the air. Slow motion style. Rob flies off. I’m still holding on. My shorts beg to differ.

Abandon ship. Off they go. Leaving me naked on the raft, clenched for dear life. Looking around. Slow motion style,

"NOOOOAAHHHOOOOOO."

Land with a BUMP. Driver almost capsizes his speedboat from laughing too much. Slows down. Gives me a clap. My hands are red raw. Stand up on the raft. Delighted. Half naked. Only wearing a life jacket. Who cares. Victory is mine! Wuu huu! Everyone on the boat is cheering me on. Why,

"Thank you, thank you."

Take a bow. As I do. Driver takes off again. And I back flop into the water,

"Ow. You prick. My ass!"

Swim over to the boat. Collect my shorts en route. Ask the girls,

"Don't have a sneaky peek."

Jump out. Dress myself. And politely enquire...,

"Can we do that again please?
Some hoot!"

Dinghy dancing continues on for another hour or so. Can barely feel my hands by the end of it from holding on so tight. Mighty rush. Epic battle with BV at one point. Trying to get the other person to fly off. (I was going to say trying to get each other off, but that sounds a tad odd.) In the end we both flew off mid-air again, grappling, taking some hopper. Time to retire. Go for a gentle kayak instead. Myself, Max and a few others go off towards the island.

"Isn't this lovely?"

"Yeah, just very quaint."

VRRROOOOOOM VROOM!

"What's that?"

Jetski shows up on a jet ski,

"Lads, jet skis are out. Grab one now!"

Kayak off. Jetski on. They're another level again. Ripping through waves. Belting along. Jetting it up. Tiring ourselves out. Some laugh. The motorbikes of the sea world, I imagine. Now then: Time for a feast! Banquet waiting onboard. Servants showering us yacht royalty with food and beverages. Rob asks a few of us to join him on the top level. Six of us, around a round table,

"Lads, I want to know if ye want to set up a soccer club? I tried before and it didn't work. I have a better feeling with this group of lads though. Are ye in?"

"Yes. Like Flynn."

And with that Gypsy FC was born. One of the six founding fathers. Rules and decrees all laid out. Someone took a mighty photo of us to document the occasion. (Still waiting for my copy of that, lads!) Most of us celebrate with glasses of red wine. Sun is setting. Clouds coming in. Day almost done. On cue, word comes up from the captain that we should head back to the mainland. Weather might start to get a bit rough soon. Dose. Actually, no dose. On the way back, the party really kicked off. Champagne flowing. Music pumping. Yacht suddenly turns in a disco boot. Dancers. Prancers. Chancers. All popping off! Trying to battle with Rob and Max over iPod duties,

"Come on lads, I know ye both sing and that, but I DJ in a gay gym - I got this."

Dancing circle forms. Jetski starts doing the worm in the middle. Ridiculously well. Someone else does it even better. Dance off is on it seems! Two people start dancing in sync. Have ye rehearsed?! Someone does the robot. Shoulders popping. People jiving. Dancing through two lines of people. Everyone having a go.

"What what, my turn?! Wuu. Champers. Let's dance!"

Off I go down the lines of people. Boats hits a wave. iPod jumps out of the speaker. Music goes dead. I'm halfway down the runway of people. And they all stop clapping. So now I'm just standing. Head bopping. Walking on the spot. Clicking my fingers. Yeah! Waiting for the music to reload. Oh yeah, I got this. Put the music back on... And there we go! Off I went back again. Choruses of,

"Murk! Murk! Murk!"

showering over me. Merrick has evolved! I remember at one point D:Ream's mighty song *Things Can Only Get Better* was blasting out over the speakers. Everyone arm in arm. Singing along. Big happy smiling faces. Rob to my left. BV to my right. Funk, this is surreal enough,

> "THINGS, CAN ONLY GET BETTEEERRR, they can only get BETTTTERRR... (If and when they do... Funk me pink!) THEY CAN ONLY GET, THEY CAN ONLY GET BETTTERRRR!!"

Unfortunately BV then informed me that we had drank the boot dry. Not a drop left in the house. Dose. Thankfully, we had also just landed at the dock. Everyone saying their goodbyes. Hugs all round. Cheers Rob, some day, some dancer! Yeah, definitely must do it again! Mighty day in fairness. Sound group of people. Not an agenda in sight. Refreshing change from the L.A norm. Everyone just out for a laugh. Hoot. On. The Boot! So then, great day... But is that it? Call it a day? Ehh, nay. Night is still young. What should we do? Actually, how do we get back to L.A from here? Balls. Myself. BV. Max. Half drunk. Fully wondering. Cab? Nay. Too far. Let's try and blag a spin with one of the others instead. Max chats up a Swedish girl that was on the boat,

> "Just wondering, who are you getting a lift back with... Bryan! Any chance of a..."

> "Ask the wife."

> "Bryan's wife, any chance of a spin back in your mini-bus please? Jump out in Hollywood as you're passing through? We can? Mighty. Cheers!"

All pile into the minibus. Head back home. Stop off at a garage to get gas. And maybe a few cans of beer for the drive back.

Three of us sitting in the back of the bus. Booze flowing. BV gets back to telling some savage stories. Newcastle era.

Lords of the Land by the sounds of it:
Asprilla this.
Ginola that.
Albert.

Andy Cole.
Gillespie.
Peter Beardsley man! Beardsley!

Once again, I'm soaking in the tales, particularly as a soccer fan. Got up to all sorts of antics. Some boozers by the sounds of it. Train all morning. Booze all day. Repeat. Always professional though. Never missed a day training. Real pros, like.

Anyway, while we're reveling in the back, I think domestics are ongoing up the front. Wifey doesn't want Bryan to booze with us. He has to sit up front. But he wants to go in the back for one. Back and forth. On and on. Awkward at first. Forgot about it after a can. Mid-slurping though, the mini bus yanks to a halt. Gas, again?

"Why are we stopped here?"

"Sorry, you all have to get out!"

"Pardon? Is there something wrong?"

"GET OUT!!!"

"Bryan?"

"Sorry guys. This is as far as she'll take you. Is that cool?"

"Eh, all right, OK so, of course."

Three of us bundle out. Clueless.
Mini bus SHOOTS OFF.
Max, BV and I left wondering why the funk we were just discarded in the middle of nowhere.

"Seriously, any idea where this is?"

"No."

Crossroads of somewhere. Starbucks. Chevron. Mobil. McDonald's. One of those places. While the two Vensions head into McDonald's for some food, I stay outside and phone a cab.

"Beverly Hills Cab Company..."

"Hi could I order a cab please?"

"Yes sir. Where are you?"

"Ehh. Not sure. Hang on."

Look up to see what cross streets we're on. Eventually figure it out.

"That's a bit far, about forty five minutes to an hour away from here. Let me just check... Oh you're in luck. One car is about ten minutes away."

"*Mighty*. See you in ten."

BV and Max finish up their food. Cab pulls into the car park. Beverly Hills on the side. Dancing. All jump in. Tell him the address. Cabman starts up the engine. Presses a load of buttons. Price on the meter shoots up to $30 and we haven't even moved.

"How come that price is on already?"

BV sees this too. Asks,

"Why did that happen?"

"Call out charge. Just deal with it."

"Just deal with it? Why are you charging that much and we haven't even moved? Is this a joke?"

Cabman takes off. Turns out of the car park. Presses more buttons. Price shoots up again.

"What are you doing man?! We can see you!"

Cabman goes right. And right again. Turns back into the car park. Stops the car. Shouts at BV,

"GET OUT!"

And we all end up piling out. Cheers buddy.

"Prick!"

Cabman shoots off. BV shaking his head. Me wondering what happened. Max annoyed. I'll just order another cab. They go back in to get a milkshake. I sit on the bench at the bus-stop outside. Order another cab from a different company. Thirty minutes. No worries. Sit. And. Wait. Sitting. Waiting. Patiently. Cold enough. Thank funk I brought my hoodie.

"Hold up, what's that commotion?"

Hear Police SIRENS.
Flurry of cars racing down the road.

"What's going on here?"

A police car WHIPS into the curb in front of me.

"Ehh?"

Three more police cars right behind.

"Oh dear Jesus.
What's this?
Who are they after?"

Look behind me. Everyone in McDonald's looking out. Turn back. Hands still in my pocket. Hood up. Freezing. Confused. Stand up. Cops JUMP out of the first police car. One fat white guy. One Hispanic female. Slight muffin-top. Both simultaneously yelling,

"YOU IN THE YELLOW HOOD!
Get your hands up!
Put your hands in the air!
NOW!!!"

"What?
Who?
Me?!"

As yet another flurry of blue and red lights come whipping around a corner from the opposite direction, my head instinctively turns right. More cars.
Sirens BLAZING.
Everyone YELLING.
Head SPINNING.

WHAT.
THE.
FUNK?!

Next minute I realise there's a light coming from above – no there's two. And they're shining down... On ME?! Look up. Two police helicopters overhead. What. What?! Scrunched up look of confusion and worry on my face. What did I do? Who have I done?! I'm sorry! Irate cops yelling at me from all angles,

> "HANDS OUT OF YOUR POCKETS!
> DOWN ON THE GROUND!
> DO IT –
> NOW!"

Six police cars, two police helicopters and a lot of crazy-looking uniformed stormtroopers are all shouting at me to put my hands up? Obviously my hands go up. My mind racing as to what I seriously might've done,

> "Oh Jesus. Why did I do it? How could I have been so stupid?!"

Hands in the air. Two cops in the first car barking out orders at me. Cops in the other cars stand around. All looking useless. Start questioning people nearby. By now Max and Barry are outside McDonald's in the car park. Look at me, ask,

> "What did you do?"

Shrug my scared shoulders,

> "I don't know?!"

Choppers hovering overhead. One cop shouts at me,

> "What's your name? Where are you coming from?"

Idiotically, I try to ease the tension by answering truthfully...,

> "Well, you'll never believe me buddy, I was on a savage yacht all day, some hoot on the boot..."

> "Shut up and put your hands back on your head! I don't want to hear a word from you!"

"OK. But you did just ask me two questions..."

Starts shouting again at me,

"SHUT UP!
Do you have I.D?"

"I do!"

Go to get my wallet out of my back pocket. Bad call.
Muffin-top goes straight for her GUN.
POINTS IT AT ME.

"OhdearsweetJesusGod.
I.
Am.
Goosed."

She starts screaming,

"HANDS OUT OF POCKETS.
PUT 'EM WERE I CAN SEE 'EM."

Fat-white slowly approaches me. Tells me,

"PUR YOUR HANDS BEHIND YOUR BACK."

I do as he says. Grabs my hands while I am. Shoves me forward up against the hood of his police car. To another cop,

"We have a hostile and potentially dangerous suspect."

"What?
No I'm not.
Ah cop on now. Lads, what are ye doing this for?"

At this point I realise these guys (and girls) are pretty clueless. But they do have guns. And one is being pointed at me. So they still trump me. For some reason fat-white's freaky side then comes out.

"Spread your legs."

And then in a low raspy voice...

"Bitch."

"Huh, pardon me?"

"SPREAD THEM!!!"

"OK OK. Why did you just call me a bitch though?"

"Bend over on the hood of the car, hands out."

I am bending over on the hood, the bonnet, whatever you call it.

"Should I be doing this another way?"

"Bend over, bitch!"

Continuously barking orders, then SCREAMING BITCH at me under his breath, sounding like a sexually perverted freak. At this point he starts patting me down. Searching for something. Assumed it would be just like an airport security type frisk. Brisk pat-down. Negative. I assumed wrong. WHACK! Punches me in the ass.

"What the funk was that for?! That's not just patting down my back pocket?"

WHACK. Punch in the other cheek.

"OWW. Stop please. You're punching me in the ass?! Sweet Jesus."

While he's punching me, I'm trying to turn my head around to see what he's doing.

"Don't look at me, bitch!"

"OK. Nutter Two."

Thing is, I had the hood of my yellow hoodie up before this happened. Cold night, and all. As I'm turning around to see why he's giving me a dead ass, I'm also blowing at the flock of hair that my hood is pushing into my eyes. Couldn't see a thing. Blowing my hair. Trying to knock my hood off with a flick of my head. All while my hands are handcuffed behind my back the whole time. Looked like a flapping fish on a pier. Obviously I had no joy getting the hood off my head. All I accomplished was making the fat cop-ape even more irate. Now I'm on the ground. Face in pavement. Listening to him go on and on...,

> "I said don't look at me bitch!"

Kept whispering the bitch part, I think so the other cops wouldn't hear him. Freak. Either way, between him calling me a bitch the whole time, handcuffing me for no reason, and then punching my buttocks, enough was enough. Time to subtly tell him he was a prick,

> "I'm not looking at you, (you prick), my hair is in my eyes."
>
> "What did you just say?!"
>
> "I said... Rick... My hair, is in, my eyes. Rick is your name, right?"

Punches me in my tailbone.

> "Don't talk to me. Look straight ahead you little bitch!"

I'm guessing he had issues. Finally he backs off. Pulls me back to my feet. Lays me face down on the hood of the car again. Takes my I.D out of my pocket. Goes off whispering into his radio. Stands. Waits. Listens. Leaves me to flop around trying to see what's going on. All I can do is just rest my cheek on the hood. Dirty hood, I might add. See him call over the Hispanic cop he arrived with. Mutters. Comes back to me. Takes off the handcuffs. Lifts me up off the bonnet. Hispanic cop - let's just call her Good Cop - tells me that I'm fine. Not the guy they were after actually,

> "Mistaken identity.
> Good to go.
> Have a good night, sir."
>
> "Excusemewhat?!
> Good to go?!
> That's it?!
> After all that?
> No apology, nothing?!"

"No, sir.
We're only doing our jobs."

"Cheers.
Ye are doing them well!"

So apparently there was some guy on the run who the police were looking for. Last time this guy was spotted, he was wearing a yellow hoodie. Well isn't that just mighty. Someone in McDonald's must've seen me outside. Reported a yellow hoodie. And this is where innocent Murk comes in. Good old yellow hoodie. Only wore it because of the hole in my leather jacket! Curses! While I'm busy looking perplexed and shaking my fist at the helicopters' lights shining down on me, the police cars all drive off. Helicopters follows suit. Light off. Flew off. Left me shaking my fist at the night's sky. BV and Max come over,

"What the funk?"

"I don't know. This place is nuts. Time to get out of here."

That was mental. Cab arrives. We jump in. Wave goodbye to the crowd looking out from inside McDonald's. Back to Hollywood we go. Time to go home. Call it a night. Well, not yet. Now I know this gibberish has been rambling on and I would like to tell you that that's the end of it. However, it wasn't. And I feel I should continue. Bear with me, please. So after those cop-apes, I could do with a booze. Max says he's up for coming with me. Night is not done yet. Get back to West Hollywood. Get in touch with India and Susie who were on the boat with us.

"Girls, are ye out?"

"We are. Come meet us at this club!"

"Cool cool.
Come on Max.
Funk those ape-cops.
Abuse!
Might make a good story in the future.
Maybe not.
For now, let's party on!"

Get into the club. Never been before. Absolutely horrendous. Weird music. We're the only white people. Just a strange buzz going on. India and Susie are in there with a friend over from England. They all also think it's horrendous. Ask me where else would be good?

> "Not sure, what is it a Monday?
> We could try Haute?
> I think the EC Twins are DJing there."

Up we go to Haute in Susie's car. Pull in. Text the twins. Tell me that it's already over. Private party for US Weekly. Finished early though. Try across the road maybe?

> "Eh, girls, up for the Abbey? Gay bar, but it's just here and a cool looking place. Let's go, night is getting late."

So in we go. After all that, we end up in a gay bar. Mighty. Even better, it's dead. Only one option: Booze on. So I'm sitting at the bar, talking to Susie. She goes to the bathroom. Her buddy is one seat over from me, talking to the barman. Overhear him telling the barman that he has a better body than the half-naked guy on the TV screen above us. Barman doesn't care,

> "I'm straight."

Susie's buddy gets annoyed.

> "Whatever."

Lifts up his top.
Shows the barman his body.

> "See!"

Susie comes back. I tell her I didn't realise her buddy was gay. She laughs,

> "He's not!"

> "Oh. I just thought...
> Doesn't matter."

She laughs. Her buddy overhears what I said. Gets annoyed. Asks me,

> "Do you not know who I am?"

"No.
Who?"

Turns out he's a well-known rugby player back in the UK.
Tells me,

"I'm not gay. What are you trying to say?"

"Well. I just assumed because of what you were saying, look, I got it wrong, my bad."

Now he's giving me dirty looks. Muttering stuff at me. Well isn't this fun?
(Never seem to get on with most rugby players. Not sure why. Soccer on!)
By now I realise I'm chasing an earlier high. Day peaked on the boat. Should just go home. Nay. Let's be dumb and keep chasing that high...,

"Maybe we could try the Chateau Marmont?
This place is crap.
What do ye think?
Up for it?"

They are. So we all get back into Susie's car. Susie and India in the front. Rugby buddy by one window. Max in the middle. Me by the other window. Driving along. All I hear from the other side of Max...,

"Were you calling me gay a minute ago?"

"No. Just that you were saying homosexual things."

"Have you an accent? Where are you from?"

"Ireland, calm down, shh."

"Oh, you're a Paddy, is it?"

"Oh. You're a prick, is it?
Dope."

Next minute I'm in a pushing match. He's reaching over pushing my face. I'm reaching back pushing the side of his shoulder/head. All with Max stuck in the middle. Susie sees us. SLAMS the brakes,

"STOP! STOP!"

"What are you doing?"

"Get out!"

I assume it's me she's talking to. Open the door. Jump out. Max follows along. So now we're on the side of the road, after been kicked out of a car. Again. Mighty. Look around. At least we're on Sunset. Just by the Andaz Hotel. In front of the Grafton Hotel. Next to the Sunset Tower Hotel. One over from the Standard Hotel. Looking at the Mondrian Hotel. Surrounded by hotels is basically what I'm trying to tell you. Car drives off. Leaving myself and Max standing on the footpath. Looking at each other. Confused. Perplexed. Bewildered. And then two girls come up to us,

"Do you guys know if there are any hotels around here?"

I laugh,

"Are ye joking?
I see about five just by twirling around."

"Well what's the best one?! Which is the cheapest?
Best value for money? What has the nicest pool?"

"Pardon?
Do I look like Google?"

Now maybe I was being curt. But a lot had happened. Still, I must admit, her response surprised me.

CLOCK!
Right into my cheekbone.
BANG!
My nose.
PUNCH!
Into the face!
Holy funk. Am I dreaming? Am I drunk? Is this death?
Wmmapfhh.
Lights. Out.
Knocked. Down.
Into a bush.
Goodnight, Eileen.

Chapter 42

Mhmm

"Murk!"

"Hm?"

"What happened to you last night? Did you get knocked out by a girl? Where did you go?"

"Hmm?"

"Are you still asleep?"

"Mhmm."

"Yesterday was a right laugh on the boot. When did you say your show is on at the Comedy Store – two or three weeks?"

"Mm."

"What are you doing until then?"

"Hmm..."

"Fancy coming to the Caribbean with us first?"

"Hm?"

"Go sail around on a yacht down there for a week or two?"

"Ehh..."

Duu?

THE END.

No of Course it's Not the Fecking End!

Trilogy. On!

ACKNOWLEDGMENTS

As always, Mum and Dad – Mucho gracias for everything!

To you, whoever you may be (no doubt you're amazing, by the by), thank you for reading until the very end. Mighty work, _____!

To everyone who read my first book RanDumb and then told all their friends and family and postman to go buy a copy AND THEN left a glowing review on Amazon as well, huge thanks for being such dancers! Feel free to do so again. Ahem. Thank you.

To Charles, the mighty editor of this fine book, thank you buckets for your wise words, spot-on suggestions and endless patience with my cantankerous ways.

To Kailand, mighty dancing with your keen eye and fine notes throughout the writing of this book. Ka. Kaw.

To Willie Moggs and Loopy Lou, fine work on numerous occasions that ye probably don't even remember.

To Korana, mighty cover design and patience with me. Gracias!

To Gustavo Bolster, good work boss. Also: L.A all the way.

To Rob (just in case you didn't understand my mumbled accent when I said it in person), amongst a bucket of other things, cheers for the mighty introduction. Dancing!

And last but by absolutely no means least in *any* way: Cheers to The Man! Gin. On!

About The Author

Mark Hayes is an Irish guy who now lives in L.A.

Chancer. Prancer. Midnight. Dancer.

Bestselling author of *RanDumb: The Adventures of an Irish Guy in L.A!* which has been rated #1 on Amazon Humor.

Mark currently runs dumb among West Hollywood. Writes books. Performs stand-up. DJigs. And chases his tail from one high to the other.

Top three talents are: Accent. Location. Ability to dodge.

Mark can be found sharing tales, slurring vlogs and rambling along on his blog 'Enough Talk, More Writing' http://trickaduu.com. You can also hunt him down tweeting at @trickaduu.

Mark is a big fan of people who leave nice reviews on Amazon.com.

Mark is the opposite of those folk who get out of bed to leave one star reviews.

Keep an eye out for Mark's next book. And also his... Romance novel. Duu.

www.ingramcontent.com/pod-product-compliance
Lightning Source LLC
Chambersburg PA
CBHW031948070426
42453CB00006BA/135
9780615570150